Studying for your Early Years Degree

Skills and knowledge for becoming an effective practitioner

EDITED BY JACKIE MUSGRAVE,
MAGGI SAVIN-BADEN & NICOLA STOBBS

**EARLY
YEARS**

First published in 2017 by Critical Publishing Ltd
Reprinted in 2017 and 2018

British Library Cataloguing in Publication Data
A CIP record for this book is available from the British Library

ISBN: 9781911106425

This book is also available in the following e-book formats:

MOBI: 9781911106432
EPUB: 9781911106449
Adobe e-book reader: 9781911106456

Text design by Greensplash Limited
Cover design by Out of House Limited
Project management by Out of House Publishing Solutions
Printed and bound in Great Britain by 4edge, Essex

Critical Publishing
3 Connaught Road
St Albans
AL3 5RX

www.criticalpublishing.com

Paper from responsible sources

Contents

Meet the editors

Jackie Musgrave is a senior lecturer and course leader for the BA in Early Childhood at the University of Worcester. She completed her doctoral research into the effects of chronic health conditions in young children on inclusion in their early education. Other research interests include issues relating to professionalism and problem-based learning. She contributed a chapter to *Well-being in the Early Years* and co-authored *Early Years Placements* with Niki Stobbs, both for Critical Publishing.

Maggi Savin-Baden is Professor of Education at the University of Worcester. She has researched and gained funding for the evaluation of staff and student experiences of learning for over 20 years. She has a strong publication record of over 40 research publications and 13 books, six in the field of problem-based learning. She is currently completing a book on researching education for a digital age. In her spare time she bakes, runs, rock climbs and is about to undertake her first Olympic-distance triathlon.

Nicola Stobbs was a mentor for many students on placement during her time as a setting manager. She is committed to providing excellent care for children and supporting students to become the excellent practitioners that children deserve. She now works at the University of Worcester supporting student practitioners. Niki is the co-author of another book for Critical Publishing entitled *Early Years Placements*.

Meet the authors

Karen Appleby is a principal lecturer within the Institute of Education (Centre for Early Childhood) at the University of Worcester. She teaches across a variety of early childhood programmes and modules. Her current responsibilities include leadership for learning, teaching and student experience. She has authored publications on reflective practice and takes a particular interest in the way reflective learning is positioned within undergraduate study.

Frances Brett is a lecturer at Shrewsbury College, leading the foundation degree Early Childhood and Education programmes, and the BA top-up (Education). She has taught theatre writing and fiction on the Birmingham University Cert. HE Creative Writing programme, and facilitated writing groups in a number of communities.

Derval Carey-Jenkins is a principal lecturer and course leader for PGCE Primary and Early Years School Direct at the University of Worcester. She teaches across a range of subjects including the Masters in Special and Inclusive Education, Early Years and English. Her research interests include values, leadership, policy and practice and curriculum development.

Stuart Gallagher teaches across undergraduate and postgraduate courses in the Centre for Early Childhood at the University of Worcester. His particular teaching interests include the development of critical higher education pedagogy that enables student practitioners to acquire the necessary know-how to safeguard children's holistic development.

Karen Hanson is a principal lecturer and Head of Centre for Early Childhood at the University of Worcester. Karen trained as a primary school teacher and has extensive knowledge and experience of working with young children and families. Her own learning experiences and her commitment to ensuring that learning is a lifelong transformational process have been the catalyst for her research interest in reflective practice.

Janet Harvell is course leader for the FdA EY FdL (Foundation Degree (Flexible and Distributed Learning)) and senior lecturer in Early Childhood at the University of Worcester. She has worked in the early years sector for the last 26 years with experience as a registered nursery inspector, childminder, pre-school supervisor and nursery manager. Her research interests are focused on international early childhood and student transitions.

Angela Hodgkins is the course leader of the BA (Hons) Integrated Working with Children and Families and senior lecturer in Early Childhood at the University of Worcester. She worked in a wide range of early years settings and schools for 20 years before becoming a lecturer in further education and higher education. She is also a qualified counsellor. Her research interests are children's identity, self-esteem and meeting the needs of students.

Michelle Malomo worked as a nursery manager for a number of years, and has taught in both higher and further education. This has included teaching both early years and play and playwork. Michelle has also worked as a youth worker within the voluntary sector. Her specialism is play and outdoor spaces for children and young people.

Alison Prowle is a senior lecturer at the University of Worcester. She has worked in schools, children's centres, the voluntary sector and local government. Her teaching and research interests include child poverty, integrated working, multiple adversity and learning and teaching in higher education early childhood courses.

Michael Reed is a senior lecturer at the Centre for Early Childhood, within the Institute of Education at the University of Worcester. He teaches on undergraduate and postgraduate courses exploring practice-based research and leadership. He has co-edited a number of books on early years education.

Michelle Rogers is course leader for the foundation degree in Early Years (flexible and distributed learning) at the University of Worcester. She has been involved with curriculum development and designing online learning environments, and is currently collaboratively designing an online top-up degree, and MA. Her current research interests revolve around teaching and learning, the student experience, online learning, curriculum development and communities of practice for children and adults.

Carla Solvason is a senior lecturer in the Centre for Early Childhood at the University of Worcester, but prior to this worked as a researcher, language and communication consultant for primary schools and as a primary teacher. Carla's most recent publications focus upon student research and ethical professionalism, but she has also published in the areas of school culture, educational equality and social justice, and the 'team around the student'.

Samantha Sutton-Tsang is a senior lecturer in early childhood studies within the Institute of Education, lecturing on the BA (Hons) Early Childhood Professional Practice, and the top-up degree Integrated Working with Children and Families at the University of Worcester. She is a qualified primary teacher.

Linda Tyler is a senior lecturer with responsibility for the co-ordination of practice-based learning within the Centre for Early Childhood at the University of Worcester. Lin's research interests focus on digital literacy.

Rosie Walker is a senior lecturer at the University of Worcester where she supports students in undergraduate and postgraduate courses. She is also partnership co-ordinator for the foundation degree in Early Years. Her career spans working within social care, the NSPCC, child protection training and, before joining the university, managing children's centres.

Nicola Watson is a senior lecturer in early childhood at the University of Worcester. In her career so far Nicola has worked as a family lawyer, a mediator and early years practitioner and as a primary school teacher. Her main area of interest is in children's development of social skills.

Introduction

JACKIE MUSGRAVE

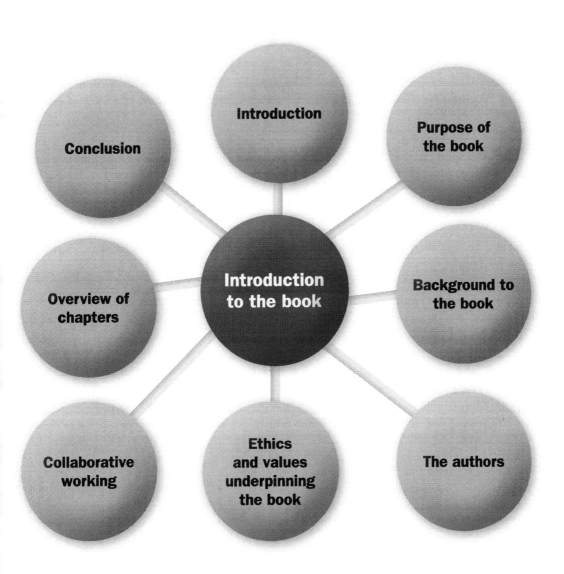

Educate every child as if he were your own.

Margaret McMillan, 1919, p 6

Wherever you are on your journey towards graduating with your early years degree, this book will be a valuable resource for you as a higher education (HE) student. We are aware that there are books that specifically address relevant issues relating to studying early childhood in HE and others available that address contemporary issues relating to HE and to early childhood education and care (ECEC). However, this book is different in two specific ways. Firstly, we have listened closely to students' perspectives, and as a result the content of the book is designed to help you to understand the complexities of developing the skills and knowledge that are essential to become an effective early years practitioner. Secondly, each chapter addresses an issue relevant for developing your academic skills, professional practice and professionalism.

Purpose of the book

The book is underpinned by our shared vision of our beliefs and values and what we consider are the foundations necessary for you to develop so that you are prepared to become effective educators of children in society. However, this book is not intended to be a platform for us to tell you what we think. We incorporated the voices of our students into the messages to help you relate more meaningfully with the content of the book, and hopefully you will find that these voices speak to you in a way that will be helpful as you navigate the path you have chosen to take.

When reflecting on the impact of having spent three years as an early years undergraduate one of our students, Anna Cook, wrote in her final summative assessment:

> *Since embarking on this course three years ago, my thinking has changed dramatically. I am not only a more professional practitioner, but a better version of myself, as many of the skills I have been taught can be used in my personal life. Embarking on this degree is just the start of shaping me into a professionally reflective leader within early childhood. As our political landscape is always changing, and new approaches are always on the horizon, continuing professional development is key. It is an ongoing process, I will never stop learning.*

Anna's reflections encapsulate what we hope all students will achieve. Her comments highlight her awareness that higher education does not simply extend your knowledge, but can help you to develop and enhance your personal qualities and capabilities. Anna is also aware that in an ever-changing world, there is always much to learn and therefore, learning is a lifelong endeavour.

We are aware of the need to acknowledge children's voices in their early education and care. However, this is an aim that is outside the scope of the book, but by developing this as part of your value base, combined with the necessary skills and acquired knowledge, you can learn to tune in to children's voices.

Background to the book

The idea for this book was born out of several discussions that I had with my colleagues over a period of a few days in the spring of 2015. At this point, I had been acting course leader for the BA in Early Childhood degree for several months and, as a consequence of taking on this role, I had been struck by three things. Firstly, it was clear that every member of the teaching team wanted students to succeed in their studies and achieve a good classification in their degree. Secondly, it was obvious that we were all united in concern for students' welfare. Thirdly, we wanted them to become equipped to be excellent early years educators.

Reflecting on these issues, I realised that, as the staff member responsible for the BA, I was well placed to lead the team in articulating these ideas about how we could try to achieve these aims. I thought that such discussions would help us to develop a shared understanding of the issues that sometimes got in the way of students' learning and prevented them from achieving their potential. Through these discussions, this book has enabled us as a team to develop a consistent approach to teaching and supporting our students. Therefore, I decided that the product of our discussions should be collected into one document that could be a reference point for staff and students. At this point, it occurred to me that there could be other staff and students across the globe also grappling with similar issues and who perhaps would welcome a book aimed at improving the experience of students studying for early childhood degrees.

The authors

This book is written by a team of authors who have worked in a range of different disciplines and roles with children and families before joining the Centre for Children and Families at the University of Worcester. Therefore, we have used our different professional knowledge gained from our work in education and health and social care to give different perspectives to the content of each chapter. This collaborative approach reflects the current beliefs about the importance of integrated working with children and families, with professionals coming together as a *team around the child and family* in order to support and achieve better outcomes. In a similar way, the content of this book reflects our belief that we work together as a *team around the student*, nurturing education and professional practice in order to help you to achieve good outcomes in your studies.

Ethics and values underpinning the book

The team has a strong value base that is underpinned by the foundations of research-based teaching. We aim to develop practitioners who are:

- ethical;
- reflective;
- inclusive;
- research-based teachers;
- leaders and agents of change;
- researchers;
- employable.

Collaborative working

Achieving success for students can only come about by working with students in a collaborative and consultative way. Karen Hanson's doctoral research findings (Hanson, 2012) revealed that there are some essential ingredients for success for early years HE students. Hanson illustrated her findings in her *bricolage* diagram. Bricolage is defined as *'the creation or construction of something from a range of diverse things'* (*Oxford English Dictionary*). Hanson's diagram (Figure 1.1) illustrates the building blocks of success and includes details of what makes up each of the blocks. The bricolage is sewn together using the theoretical views of some of the grand theorists who have built the foundations of our understanding of how humans, whatever their age, learn. Without these threads, or theories, the building blocks would not have a strong foundation. Some of these influential theorists are historic. For example, Dewey (1910) was a philosopher whose commitment to democracy revolutionised approaches to education. A contemporary theorist, Brookfield (1995), uses the analogy of lenses as a tool to develop our ability to consider a range of different perspectives. Wenger (1998) illustrates the benefit of working together collaboratively to enhance learning. More information about the influence of theorists and their educational theories is listed in the further reading section below.

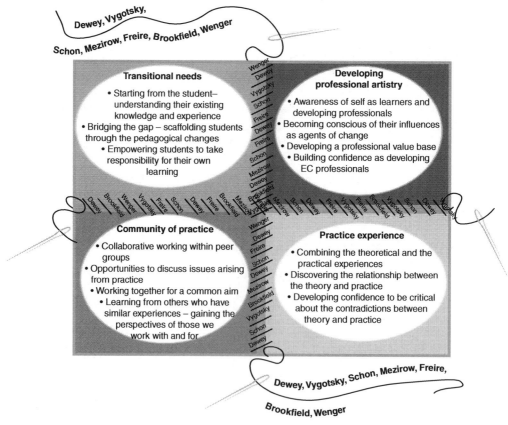

Figure 1.1 Bricolage diagram (Hanson, 2012)

Overview of chapters

The book is divided into two parts. Part A includes guidance for students about learning in HE, specifically in the context of ECEC. It includes national course requirements, academic skills and core knowledge. The chapters cover students' roles and responsibilities in relation to safeguarding, understanding policy, professionalism and ethical practice. Part B of the book looks explicitly at applying this knowledge and understanding in the workplace before tackling the final research project. Here is a summary of the chapters.

Part A: Learning in higher education

Chapter 1: Preparing for university and making effective use of induction

This chapter, written by Janet Harvell and Angela Hodgkins, provides advice and guidance on some of the questions you might have, and guides you to sources of help, underpinned by advice from students. It also explores the role and value of induction, its purpose and how to get the most from this. The role of the academic tutor is reviewed before considering your roles and responsibilities, as well as the benefits of making the most of opportunities to become active within the student community. There are explicit links about how developing these skills will be useful and essential for developing professionals working in ECEC.

Chapter 2: Learning to learn in the higher education context

In this chapter, Angela Hodgkins and Nicola Watson acknowledge the social and emotional demands of studying in HE and suggest that these demands are opportunities for personal development. They draw parallels between the theoretical framework and value base underpinning the current HE learning environment and that of ECEC pedagogy in the UK. The authors explore the dispositions, skills and attitudes that the learning environment of the early years undergraduate student is designed to engender. These qualities are linked with those of an outstanding practitioner in ECEC. The challenges you may face in both the social and emotional arenas are discussed and strategies enabling the optimisation of self-efficacy are suggested.

Chapter 3: Becoming a critically reflective thinker and learner

Here, Karen Appleby and Karen Hanson examine the concept of critical thinking and its role for learning in HE: academic learning and professional practice. Criticality is defined and the constituents are examined, such as: analysis, evaluation, reflection, creativity, problem-solving, decision-making, organisational skills, communication skills, understanding and using data. Critical thinking skills are introduced and examined and examples relevant to working in the early years are provided. These skills are based on models of critical thinking and reflective thinking. The difference between surface and deep approaches to learning (Marton and Säljo, 1984, pp 36–55) is examined through practical examples and activities. You are encouraged to examine your disposition to be curious and to learn through critical engagement, gaining knowledge and experience from different sources.

Chapter 4: Critical reading, writing and referencing

In this chapter, Janet Harvell discusses one of the most persistent problems that students comment on during their time at university, which is the challenge of referencing and avoiding plagiarism within academic writing. Similarly, teaching staff will often refer to the difficulty that students have in reading and writing critically. This chapter provides you with an understanding of the issues. The first section provides an introduction to reading and critical writing through a number of activities and exercises before moving on to referencing, including a range of practical activities and suggestions. The need to apply a critical approach to the selection of resources for referencing is explored.

Chapter 5: Assessment and feedback

In this chapter, Nicola Stobbs and Stuart Gallagher provide guidance about preparing and submitting work for peer and tutor assessment. It will enable you to understand the assessment process, different forms and types of assessment and how to use feedback effectively. The chapter demonstrates how you can prepare for assessment, reflect critically on how different types of assessment can offer new opportunities for academic and professional development, and indicates what needs to be done to submit quality assignments.

Chapter 6: Understanding and using policy and legislation

In this chapter, Rosie Walker, Mike Reed and Derval Carey-Jenkins explain why it is important that students understand global and national policy and legislation, as well as policies that affect settings. The purpose of policy and your roles and responsibilities are highlighted. The chapter explains the ways in which policy in the UK is influenced and forged (as in any other developed nation) by the OECD. The two tiers of policy formation, structural and process, are explained, and an explanation given of the impact of socio-political factors on policy formation. The national curriculum, the Early Years Foundation Stage, integrated working, inspection and accountability are addressed.

Chapter 7: Learning in a digital age

Michelle Rogers and Linda Tyler's chapter has two main emphases: digital learning for students and the impact of technology on young children (including digital safeguarding). The content explores the diverse range of technology that may be encountered during your HE journey. It introduces questions about the benefits and dilemmas of using technology in HE. It also explores the purpose and the extent of your digital footprints and the ethical and professional implications that need to be examined in light of these. By engaging with this chapter, you will begin to explore and challenge your own digital capabilities, and construct and track your digital identities through various online technologies.

Chapter 8: Exploring creativity

In this chapter, Alison Prowle and Frances Brett explore the role of creativity within early childhood courses in HE. They argue that academic life provides multiple opportunities for creative responses, and that creativity can provide a powerful tool for learning, development and practice. However, without explicit permission to be creative, students may feel constrained by perceptions that this is not something academia values. Hence, creativity needs to be enabled and encouraged by tutors. Using a case study and examples of creative responses in academic work, the authors tease out the benefits of creativity, relating this to problem-solving, criticality, communication and practice-based learning.

Chapter 9: Working with others at university

Linda Tyler and Michelle Rogers consider the implications of collaborative working with peers, tutors and others within the university environment. Group work can be challenging and group dynamics can seem counterproductive to learning. In this chapter you will examine your skill sets by completing self-assessment tasks. Recognition and exploration of communities of practice (Wenger, 1998) and digital tethering (Savin-Baden, 2015) are explored. This chapter will help you to recognise the skills that promote good communication when working within groups, both face-to-face and online. You are encouraged to reflect on the different types of collaborative work and how to get the most from the collaborative experience.

Part B: Applying learning to the workplace

Chapter 10: Learning in the workplace

In this chapter, Nicola Stobbs and Jackie Musgrave introduce the skills required of you as a student practitioner and your role in early years settings. It outlines your responsibilities as an emerging professional practitioner, and provides suggestions of how to make the most of the learning opportunities available to you. The chapter also offers advice about how to develop communication skills, such as the ability to negotiate with staff in order to achieve your learning goals in placement. It also discusses the importance of ethical issues relating to confidentiality, courtesy and understanding of your place in the setting, and the importance of applying theory to practice. The final section of the chapter includes responses to students' frequently asked questions about placement.

Chapter 11: Becoming a reflective practitioner

Karen Hanson and Karen Appleby explore the process of becoming a reflective practitioner within the context of integrated working. The content draws on previous research by Hanson and Appleby and develops the concept of the reflective activist within the context of students studying early years with professional practice. The professional qualities which support this role, such as emotional intelligence and creativity, are examined and examples provided. The significance of engaging with academic learning experience, practice-based learning and the development of a theory for and in practice are also explored.

Chapter 12: Safeguarding: understanding your responsibilities

Stuart Gallagher and Samantha Sutton-Tsang explain that learning how to safeguard the conditions of children's development is a vital aspect of early childhood professional development in HE. This is because of children's vulnerability to being harmed and the need for you to understand and act upon statutory duties to protect them from maltreatment. As a student, it is also important that you understand how to safeguard the relationship with the host setting and the university. This chapter presents safeguarding responsibilities as encompassing multi-dimensional relationships, with children and families, with settings and colleagues, with the university and peers, and students' academic and professional development. It presents and explores serious case reviews and statutory guidance designed to safeguard and protect children's well-being. A model is provided that can be used to prepare for each placement.

Chapter 13: Learning to be an ethical practitioner

In this chapter, Carla Solvason considers the ethical obligation of those choosing to work in the field of Early Childhood Education and Care. It considers what ethical practice might 'look like' and the types of dilemmas that you as a developing early childhood practitioner might face, both in practice and in your studies. It suggests the need to develop a lexicon of ethical processes and practices in order to create a shared understanding of concepts and expectations with peers. Finally, it explores the importance of making time and space to make reasoned ethical responses within a culture that functions at speed.

Chapter 14: Doing your research project

Maggi Savin-Baden explains the importance of planning and organising research, enabling you to consider the importance of research to practice. It begins by explaining the importance of the planning stage as a vital phase of the research process. The chapter explores the different methodologies, suggests research methods and provides guidance on writing up. This chapter also explores planning in partnership with the research community (supervisor, setting and professional staff), to enhance future research impact. The final section of the chapter provides a list of students' frequently asked questions about the research process.

Chapter 15: What next?

In this chapter, Michelle Malomo and Samantha Sutton-Tsang encourage you to think about the path that you will take after graduation. It examines the importance of continuing to develop both your practice and your academic progression routes. It will also help you to continue the process of 'becoming' an early years practitioner. The chapter includes case studies, reflection points and practical tasks to support you in your next steps, and in the creation of a professional development plan for the future.

Conclusion

We hope you enjoy reading this book and that you find it useful for maximising your chances of being successful in your early years degree. Bear in mind what Anna said at the start of this chapter, that your learning as an HE student is not just about the knowledge you gain, but that through engaging with critical thinking, the impact of this can improve other areas of your life.

Further reading

For more information about theorists and philosophers who have influenced education see:

Gray, C and MacBlain, S (2015) *Learning Theories in Childhood*. London: Sage.

Nutbrown, C, Clough, P and Selbie, P (2008) *Early Childhood Education: History, Philosophy and Experience*. London: Sage.

References

Brookfield, S (1995) *Becoming a Critically Reflective Teacher*. San Francisco: Jossey-Bass.

Dewey, J (1910) *How We Think*. New York: D. C. Heath.

Hanson, K (2012) *How Can I Support Early Childhood Studies Undergraduate Students to Develop Reflective Dispositions?* EdD thesis, Exeter University.

Marton, F and Säljö, R (1984) Approaches to learning, in F Marton, D Hounsell and N J Entwistle (eds) The Experience of Learning. Edinburgh: Scottish Academic Press.

McMillan, M (1919) The Nursery School. New York: Dent and Sons.

Savin-Baden, M (2015) Rethinking Learning in an Age of Digital Fluency: Is Being Digitally Tethered a New Learning Nexus? London: Routledge.

Wenger, E (1998) An introduction to communities of practice. [online] Available at: http://wenger-trayner.com/introduction-to-communities-of-practice/ (accessed November 2016).

Part A
Learning in higher education

1 Preparing for university and making effective use of induction

JANET HARVELL AND ANGELA HODGKINS

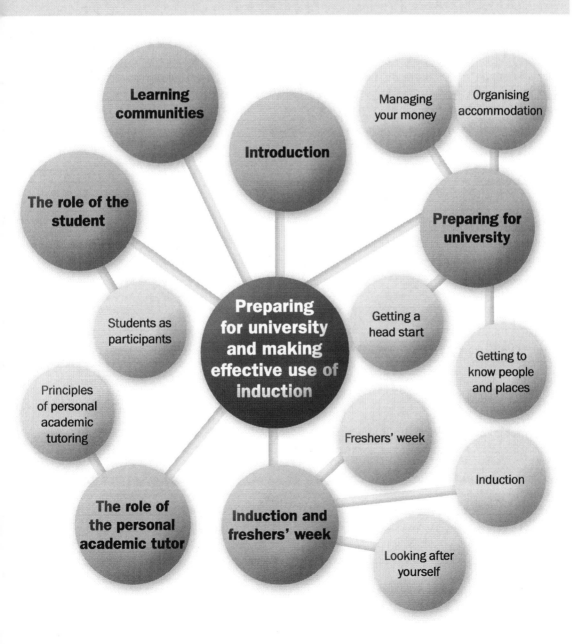

Education is the most powerful weapon which you can use to change the world.

Nelson Mandela, 2003

Introduction

Going to university is an exciting experience as you start this new stage of your life. As well as feeling excited, you will probably also be nervous about what lies ahead, with a number of questions but not sure who to ask. From the moment you are offered a place on your early years course, and when you start at university, you will have to find ways of processing the vast amounts of information that will come your way and decide what is worth following up or putting aside. This chapter provides advice and guidance on some of the questions you might have, and signposts you to sources of help, underpinned by advice from current students. It also explores the purpose and value of induction, and how to get the most from it. The role of the personal academic tutor is also reviewed before considering your roles and responsibilities as a student, including the opportunities to become an active member of the student community. The chapter ends with an introduction to the different learning communities that you might join, the role of group work and the importance of peer support/learning. It will be useful for you to make notes of the important information that you will want to keep close at hand. For example, this will include key names and contact details of people and services at university such as the finance department, personal tutor, course leader, student services and your new doctor.

Preparing for university

Congratulations on receiving your offer of a place at university. Your first feelings will be of excitement as you look forward to the new experiences ahead of you. At the same time you will start to think about what this means for you, including things like accommodation options, learning to cater for yourself, managing your money or grant effectively, meeting new people and making friends. You are not alone!

Managing your money

On starting university, you will have to manage your own finances and learn to budget. You should have already applied for loans to cover university fees and your living allowance from the government's student finance website (www.gov.uk/student-finance). It will be important for you to learn if there are loans and grants available to you and for you to gain a realistic understanding of how much university will cost you so that you can set a personal budget.

If you do not already have a personal bank account, it is important to get this in place. The number of banks and different services they provide can be overwhelming, but it is important to research a range of bank websites, and compare the different offers that they have for student accounts. For example, what overdraft arrangements do they offer, and what charges will they make if you go over the agreed limit? The website www.moneysavingexpert.com is very helpful and, under its *student bank accounts* pages, identifies a number of key questions.

If you have no experience of managing a budget, it is also important that you start to identify a weekly/monthly budget that you will be able to stick to while at university. The UCAS website (www.ucas.com) has a useful budget calculator to help you in managing your budget.

TOP TIP

Sign up to money-saving sites online, such as www.groupon.co.uk, www.vouchercodes.co.uk and www.myunidays.com, for access to a range of money-off vouchers for restaurants and clothing shops to name but a few. Remember to sign up to local supermarket loyalty cards as they also provide regular offers and money-off vouchers.

Critical question

» *Spend a few minutes thinking about how you will manage your money while studying at university. Use a budget planner like the one below to complete a realistic budget that you will be able to stick to.*

(a) Income	£	(b) Expenditure	£
Student loan		Food	
Work (part/full time)		Drink	
Grants		Transport	
Bank loans		Entertainment	
Other income		Telephone	
		Bills	
		Other expenses	
TOTAL INCOME (A)		TOTAL EXPENDITURE (B)	
		BALANCE (A–B)	£

Organising accommodation

- Accommodation is another key matter that needs to be addressed early on, as university accommodation tends to get taken quickly! If this is your first time living away from home, university accommodation is a good option as the rent tends to cover most bills, and payment dates tend to coincide with loan instalments.

- When deciding where you will live it is important to consider what is important to you as there are a number of decisions that you will need to make. For example, will you be happy to share a room with another student, or is it important for you to have your own room? What about bathroom facilities? Would you be happy to share or is an en-suite bathroom a key requirement? When choosing which hall of residence to select, review how close this is to the main campus and lecture rooms/theatres that you will need to get to. Remember that these choices will have an implication on the rent that you are charged. Take advantage of open days to view the student accommodation that will be on show.

- There will normally be internet access although this could come at an extra cost; and don't forget you will need a TV licence if you intend to watch live television programmes. If your family has a Sky television package then it might also be possible to access this via your own computer while living away from home. It is important to remember to get contents insurance cover for your personal items, such as your laptop/computer and mobile telephone at a minimum. When you have organised your accommodation, the next step will be identifying what you need to bring with you. There are a number of websites that provide checklists of what to take, including:

  - www.click2campus.com;

  - www.thestudentroom.co.uk;

  - www.savethestudent.org.

Getting a head start

Many universities will provide you with a pre-course reading list. This may be sent with your initial early years course information, or be accessed online. If you do not receive this, contact the course leader and ask if there is a pre-course reading list available. You should also find individual module reading lists within the early years course handbook, generally at the end of each module.

Additionally, you can be proactive and become familiar with a number of freely accessible documents that will have informed the programme content for many early years courses. Some of these, available on the internet, are included below. As you read them, you may find it useful to complete an annotated bibliography, which is explored in more detail in Chapter 4.

- Graham Allen's (2011) report: *Early Intervention: Smart Investment, Massive Savings*.

- Frank Field's (2010) report: *The Foundation Years: Preventing Poor Children Becoming Poor Adults*.

- *The Munro Review of Child Protection: Final Report – A Child-Centred System* (DfE, 2011).

- Cathy Nutbrown's (2012) report: *Foundations for Quality: The Independent Review of Early Education and Childcare Qualifications. Final Report*.

- June O'Sullivan and Sue Chambers' (2014) report: *The Twoness of Twos.*
- *Statutory Framework for the Early Years Foundation Stage* (EYFS) (DfE, 2014).
- Kathy Sylva et al's (2004) report: *The Effective Provision of Pre-School Education (EPPE) Project.*
- Tickell Review (2011): *The Early Years: Foundations for Life, Health and Learning. An Independent Report on the Early Years Foundation Stage to Her Majesty's Government.*

Getting to know people and places

Many universities set up social media pages, such as Facebook and Twitter, to enable new students to get to know other students prior to induction. This can be a good way to connect with other students, even if they are not on the same course, and arrange to meet up on your first day. It would also be useful to spend some time researching the local environment of your new base. Use the internet to explore the location and find out what else there is to do and to see. You can also search for your favourite coffee shops, bars and eating places so that you can visit a familiar place when you are getting used to your new home.

Critical questions

» *How far is the campus from local shops, towns, transport links?*

» *What are the accommodation options for first-year students?*

» *Will your maintenance loan cover the full cost of your rental?*

» *How easy would it be for you to travel to any early years placements that you may have to attend as part of your course?*

Induction and freshers' week

Induction and, in particular, freshers' week, are events that many new students look forward to, considering them a 'rite of passage' into university life. Induction relates to the academic aspects of your degree. Freshers' week is designed to introduce you to the social aspects of university life.

Induction

During induction you will have the opportunity to attend a number of presentations that will introduce you to your early years course, the faculty and give you an overview of the academic support services to which you will have access. Most importantly, this is an opportunity to get to know your fellow students, and meet the different staff who will be teaching on your modules.

You will also get a feel for the different teaching methods that you will encounter at university. For example, you may attend lectures with larger numbers of students than you are used to – many lecture theatres will accommodate 200 or more people. Seminars tend to be smaller groups of students and provide opportunities for you to discuss different topics in more depth. Undergraduate study is different from previous courses you will have experienced.

Rather than *giving* you knowledge it is about the co-construction of knowledge between you and your lecturer, developing knowledge together.

Your early years course handbook is your best friend and the answers to many questions that you have are likely to be found there, so spend some time reading this important document.

A-level study is transitional; higher education (HE) transformational – social constructivist – co-constructed between lecturer and students; about developing knowledge together, not giving knowledge.

Most universities also use a Virtual Learning Environment (VLE), such as Blackboard, Moodle or WebCT, where additional information on support services and course-specific learning resources are located. It is likely that you will be able to access general information on study skills and lecture presentations that have been uploaded or use this to access online library services. Many of the books and articles from your reading lists will also be accessible online. It is important to spend time finding your way around the VLE as this will be invaluable for you as your studies progress.

Critical questions

» *Does your university use a VLE? If so, find out how this is used – for example, is it just used to post lecture notes or is it used for group work and assignment submissions?*

» *Are you expected to make contributions to the VLE and, if so, how is this monitored and what impact will this have on module outcomes?*

During induction there will be a number of talks and practical opportunities to become familiar with the study skills that will support you to become a successful student. Key to effective study is time management, and induction is an ideal time to start. Take advantage of the year planners that are available to make a note of key dates in the year, especially assignment deadlines. Unlike your previous experience, you will find that universities are not flexible with deadlines and will expect you to manage your time effectively. At the same time, they do realise that in exceptional circumstances there may be genuine reasons that students have been unable to complete assessments by the deadlines. Find out what your university's procedures are for such circumstances, which may be referred to as *extenuating* or *mitigating circumstances*, and do not be reluctant to apply for this if you have valid reasons for doing so.

Critical question

» *Where can you find information on your institute's policy and procedure related to 'extenuating and mitigating circumstances'?*

Freshers' week

Freshers' week is organised by the Students' Union, who will be there to welcome you and will plan a number of social events to show what the university has to offer. This also provides an effective opportunity for you to meet other students and make new friends from across the university. The social events will most likely include daytime activities and evening events run by the different clubs and societies that you will have the opportunity of joining. It is also worthwhile to join the National Union of Students (www.nus.org.uk), not least for the wide range of discounts that membership gives you.

You will probably be overwhelmed during the first few weeks, but remember that this is natural and you will soon develop your own routine as you become more settled.

Looking after yourself

Leaving home for the first time, and becoming independent, can be exciting and with that independence comes the responsibility of looking after yourself. This includes making sure that you are up to date with your immunisations, ensuring that you eat regularly and healthily, and also that you drink responsibly.

Ensuring you are up to date with immunisations

Before leaving for university, it is important to ensure that you are up to date with all immunisations. Most children are now routinely vaccinated against mumps, measles and rubella (MMR), and meningitis vaccinations have recently been introduced. Now that you have your place at university, check your vaccination record and make an appointment with your doctor to get inoculated for any that you have not had. The NHS provides free immunisations for meningitis and septicaemia for all young people up to 24 years of age, and for MMR at any time. The NHS has produced a useful document on this: *Starting University? Protect Yourself Against Meningitis and Septicaemia* (NHS, 2014)

Eating well

Starting university may also be the first time that you have had to cater for yourself. In the beginning you may find it easier to purchase meals from the range of university eating places, but this will soon become boring and expensive. At some time you will need to start cooking for yourself. Many students in shared accommodation decide to set up a shared kitty for basic food items and will often prepare group meals. There are also a number of internet sites that are specifically aimed at supporting students in cooking inexpensive and nutritious meals. Some of these include www.bbcgoodfood.com and www.foodnetwork.co.uk. Before leaving for university, spend some time experimenting with a range of simple meals that you will be able to reproduce when you are away from home.

Drinking safely

The social life that you will experience at university is one aspect of university life that many students look forward to. It is important that you are familiar with the recommended alcohol limits and the NHS website Change4Life (www.nhs.uk/change4life) recommends a maximum of two to three units of alcohol a day for women, and three to four units a day for men. You should have at least two alcohol-free days a week. The same website has a fun, interactive *drinks checker* app that you can download to your smart phone to help you to keep track of how many units you have drunk. There is also guidance on swapping your regular drink for a healthier option. Make sure that you drink plenty of water when out drinking, and a good habit to get into is drinking a glass of water for each alcoholic drink that you consume. It is a good idea to take it in turns to nominate a member of the group to remain alcohol free when out socialising. They can then take care of anyone who may become ill, and also take on the role of designated driver.

Managing homesickness

Remember, it is natural to miss home at the very beginning. Identifying a date for your first trip home will give you something to look forward to if homesickness sets in; and remember that others will be feeling just the same as you. Occasionally you may need more specialist support, so remember that the university has a range of support services to meet individual student needs. During the induction week you will be made aware of these – for example, accommodation, counselling, finance, learning support, mental health adviser, doctor and academic support services – so ensure that you make a note of how to access them in case the need arises. Do not forget that you will need to register with a local doctor's surgery.

The role of the personal academic tutor

In all universities, there is some sort of academic or personal tutoring system. Although there are variations in different establishments, there are basic principles which will apply to them all. When you join your early years course, you will be given the name of someone who will be your first point of contact. This named person may be called an academic tutor, a personal tutor or a personal coach. They may not always be someone who teaches you, but it will be someone who has a good understanding of the early years programme that you are studying.

Principles of personal academic tutoring

It is important that you make the most of the support that is offered by your personal tutor. The following is a list of some of the support processes that will be in place and how to make best use of these.

- **Regular meetings**. It is important that you build a good relationship with your tutor, as this will be a good source of support and constancy throughout your time at university. Building a rapport by getting to know each other will be mutually beneficial. As an HE student, it will be your responsibility to make sure that you arrange regular meetings with your tutor.

- **Monitoring progress and attendance**. Your tutor will be the person responsible for having an overview of your progress and attendance. Module lecturers will often liaise with personal tutors if they have any concerns about a student's attendance or progress. Concerns about attendance are taken seriously, as staff have a commitment to ensure that you are safe and well and that you are engaging with the course. On an early years course, your attendance on placement is as important as your attendance in class. After all, this is the career that you are training for and so it is important to behave in a professional manner at all times, which includes regular attendance, punctuality and informing your placement if you are unable to attend.

- **Academic support**. Your personal tutor can help with your academic skills. If you find that you are struggling, or that your grades are falling below expectations, then you can see your tutor for advice. They will also be able to signpost you to more specialist support that is available. For example, many universities have specialist 'drop in' sessions to support students with assignment writing.

- **Personal reference**. Your tutor is usually the person who will provide you with a reference when you leave your early years course. The more you see your tutor and the better you get to know them, the more accurate your reference is likely to be. Your tutor will also liaise with your placement and will include placement feedback in your reference.

- **Emotional support**. By building a good relationship with your tutor, you will hopefully find that you have a person that you can go to with any worries or concerns that you might have. Sometimes, an informal chat with someone can make you feel supported and cared for, which can be particularly important when you are living away from home for the first time.

- **Signposting**. If your tutor cannot help you directly, then they will be able to signpost you to other services that are available to you.

- **Individual learning needs**. It is important that you inform both your personal academic tutor and module tutors of any individual needs that you might have and how these can be supported. This is important as, in some instances, this may mean that you are eligible for extra time in examinations or when completing assignments. You will need to ensure that you have completed the Disabled Student Allowance forms (www.gov.uk/disabled-students-allowances-dsas) to be eligible for specific support such as additional time.

The role of the student

Learning at university is very different from learning at school. In an HE setting, students are not seen as recipients of knowledge, with the teacher being the person who imparts knowledge. Instead, lecturers are facilitators who will guide you and enable you to learn. So, rather than sitting passively in a classroom and being given information, you are more likely to be engaging in discussions and problem-based learning in order to develop your own skills. This is much more of an equal role and, as a student, you should feel that you are an active participant in the learning process. Students in HE are participants, partners and often representatives and ambassadors.

Students as participants

You are more likely to get the most out of your learning if you participate fully in the process.

RESEARCH FOCUS

Findings from O'Connor (2013) suggest that students in active learning situations support the benefits of participatory engagement (O'Connor, 2013). Examples of active learning include:

- class participation – questions and answers;
- presentations;
- group work;
- reading and discussion outside the class.

It is important to be fully involved and to participate actively in all learning activities, both in class and outside lesson times. *'Optimal learning comes from active engagement with the material being taught'* (Prince, 2004, p 340, cited in O'Connor, 2013); therefore, the more you get involved, the more you will get out of it. Additionally, you will find that classes where you are actively involved will be more enjoyable (Levy and Peters, 2010, cited in O'Connor, 2013). If you enjoy your classes, you are likely to be more motivated and to achieve well.

An essential aspect of an early years degree is that of sharing experiences and learning from others. Your examples of practice with children will be great learning experiences for your peers on the course.

Students as partners

In many universities there are opportunities to work in partnership with academic staff. Students should ideally be involved in the processes of the department and this involvement leads to greater understanding. For example, if teaching staff and students work together in constructing assignment support, then students are likely to understand the assignment much more than if they were simply given it. Some universities have schemes which encourage students and academic staff to write and research together and these schemes can be mutually beneficial, giving students the opportunity to engage in academic research and giving staff an insight into the world and viewpoints of the students.

STUDENT VOICE

The whole process has been enjoyable and has enriched my knowledge. I have gained many skills along the way which has given me confidence in working in collaboration with others and I have developed skills to be able to present the findings at a conference. I have enjoyed being a part of the team.

Abbie Phillips, Students as Partners project, 2015

Student representatives

In your first few weeks as a student, it is likely that staff will ask for volunteers for student representatives. Student reps are students who represent their group or class and who are responsible for attending meetings with staff in order to give feedback on students' views. They are then responsible for feeding responses back to the students. To be a student rep you need to be someone who is a good communicator and who is confident at expressing the views of the group. Being a student rep can be a great way of making a difference to students in your group or future students, as suggestions are taken seriously and will be used when planning for future cohorts of students. Because students have access to experiences and information that teaching staff do not have, this can be very valuable and can improve quality and inform decision-making (Lizzio and Wilson, 2009). Being a student rep can be very worthwhile and it will help to develop transferable skills which may be a useful addition to your CV.

Student ambassadors

A student ambassador is a student who takes on additional responsibilities, often as a paid member of university staff. Duties may include working at open days and university events and visiting schools and colleges to talk to prospective students. This leadership role can be very advantageous to students and can significantly improve your academic success and your personal development (Cress, 2001, cited in Lizzio and Wilson, 2009).

STUDENT VOICE

In my time as a student at the university, I was given a great opportunity, working as a student ambassador within the Centre for Early Childhood. I took part in open days, conferences, applicant days and visits to local colleges, talking to prospective students about the university through the eyes of a student. Through this role, I have been able to share something I am passionate about with students and tutors. This has enabled me to grow in confidence and believe in myself and my abilities. Before I started university, I lacked confidence, but now I truly believe that you can do anything you put your mind to. I would urge future students to really take advantage of any opportunities that become available to you along your own personal and academic learning journey.

Stacey Hodgkins, Student Ambassador, 2014–2015

Critical question

» *What are the advantages and disadvantages of becoming more involved in university life at an academic level?*

Learning communities

As an HE student, you are an important part of a learning community. Teaching and learning should not be a one-way process; rather, it is a relationship between lecturer and students and between students and each other.

Learning as a community, as a whole group, encourages transformative learning which challenges your thinking and leads to growth and development.

> *Students are seriously challenged to assess their value system and world view and are subsequently changed by the experience.*
>
> (Quinnan, 1997, cited in Mezirow and Taylor, 2009, p 4)

This involves communicating, identifying problems, critically assessing assumptions, and working together to solve problems. Learning is then at a deep level and it becomes a part of who you are and it transforms you as a person and as a professional.

Wenger (1998, p 8) suggests that learning is social and is generated from our experiences of participating in daily life, so learning takes place through participation and interaction with others. Students often say in module evaluations that they have learned a lot from others and if you are lucky enough to find yourself learning in a group of diverse professionals, then you have a wealth of experience and knowledge to benefit from and to contribute to.

Critical questions

» *What are some of the challenges that you might face when working within groups?*

» *What can you do to overcome these challenges?*

Chapter reflections

Starting university is likely to involve lots of different emotions. At times, it will feel like a really exciting stage of your life, at other times it will feel stressful and you may feel overwhelmed.

The keys to success at the beginning of this process are to find out as much information as you can and to get to know the people and organisations that can help you.

Be mindful of how much you are taking on, but try to get involved in the life of the university. Being as prepared as you can be will remove unnecessary worry and help you to enjoy your first year, and become fully involved in all that HE has to offer you.

The next three years will change you in ways that you won't expect. There will be the obvious changes in your knowledge and understanding of topics you will study, but there are also the softer skills that you will gain as you prepare for work within the early years. These include experience of working in groups, gaining confidence at doing presentations and managing deadlines, to mention just a few. At the top of the list is the development in self-confidence and the impact this has on life and work opportunities.

Your early years degree will provide you with the skills to work in a range of roles that support children and their families.

Further training and experience may be required but some of these long-term opportunities include: educational psychologist, family support worker/manager, children's centre manager, teaching, occupational therapy, speech therapy, play worker, registered nursery inspector, Special Educational Needs Co-ordinator.

Finally, as you start to pack your bags, practise new recipes and say goodbye to family and friends, watch the animated version of the Dr Seuss book 'Oh the places you'll go' (2003), and look forward to starting your early years course.

Further reading

King, T (2016) How to Survive University: An Essential Pocket Guide. Chichester: Summersdale.

Tobin, L (2015) A Guide to Uni Life: The One Stop Guide to What University is REALLY Like. Bath: Trotman.

University of Worcester Study Skills. [online] Available from www.worcester.ac.uk/studyskills/ (accessed February 2017).

References

Allen, G (2011) *Early Intervention: Smart Investment, Massive Savings*. [online] Available at: www.gov.uk/government/uploads/system/uploads/attachment_data/file/61012/earlyintervention-smartinvestment.pdf (accessed November 2016).

Department for Education (DfE) (2011) *Munro Review of Child Protection: Final Report – A Child-Centred System*. [online] Available at: www.gov.uk/government/publications/munro-review-of-child-protection-final-report-a-child-centred-system (accessed November 2016).

Department for Education (DfE) (2014) *Statutory Framework for the Early Years Foundation Stage (EYFS)*. [online] Available at: www.gov.uk/government/publications/early-years-foundation-stage-framework-2 (accessed November 2016).

Field, F (2010) *The Foundation Years: Preventing Poor Children Becoming Poor Adults*. [online] Available at: http://webarchive.nationalarchives.gov.uk/20110120090128/http:/povertyreview.independent.gov.uk/media/20254/poverty-report.pdf (accessed November 2016).

Lizzio, A and Wilson, K (2009) Student Participation in University Governance: The Role Conceptions and Sense of Efficacy of Student Representatives on Departmental Committees. *Studies in Higher Education*, 34(1): 69–84.

Mandela, N (2003) 'Lighting your way to a better future' address at the launch of Mindset Network, Johannesburg. [online] Available at: www.mandela.gov.za/mandela_speeches/2003/030716_mindset.htm (accessed February 2017).

Mezirow, J and Taylor, E (2009) *Transformative Learning in Practice*. San Francisco, CA: Wiley.

National Health Service (NHS) (2014) *Starting University? Protect Yourself against Meningitis and Septicaemia*. [online] Available at: www.gov.uk/government/uploads/system/uploads/attachment_data/file/301103/Meningitis_C_leaflet_for_university_students.pdf (accessed November 2016).

Nutbrown, C (2012) *Foundations for Quality: The Independent Review of Early Education and Childcare Qualifications. Final Report*. [online] Available at: www.gov.uk/government/uploads/system/uploads/attachment_data/file/175463/Nutbrown-Review.pdf (accessed November 2016).

O'Connor, K (2013) Class Participation: Promoting In-Class Student Engagement. *Education*, 133(3): 340–44.

O'Sullivan, J and Chambers, S (2014) *The Twoness of Twos*. [online] Available at: www.leyf.org.uk/blog/wp-content/uploads/2014/02/The-Twoness-of-Twos-Final.pdf (accessed November 2016).

Dr Seuss (2003) Oh, the places you'll go. [online] Available at: www.youtube.com/watch?v=oxdVOFdtx7I (accessed November 2016).

Sylva, K, Melhuish, E, Sammons, P, Siraj-Blatchford, I and Taggart, B (2004) *The Effective Provision of Pre-School Education (EPPE) Project: Final Report. A Longitudinal Study Funded by the DfES 1997–2004*. [online] Available at: http://eprints.ioe.ac.uk/5309/1/sylva2004EPPEfinal.pdf (accessed November 2016).

Tickell Review (2011) *The Early Years: Foundations for Life, Health and Learning. An Independent Report on the Early Years Foundation Stage to Her Majesty's Government.* [online] Available at: www.gov.uk/government/uploads/system/uploads/attachment_data/file/180919/DFE-00177-2011.pdf (accessed November 2016).

Wenger, E (1998) *Communities of Practice: Learning, Meaning and Identity.* Cambridge: Cambridge University Press.

Useful websites referred to in this chapter

(all accessed November 2016)

Abe Books www.abebooks.co.uk

Amazon www.amazon.co.uk

BBC Good Food www.bbcgoodfood.com

Change4life www.nhs.uk/change4life/

Click2Campus www.click2campus.com/store/checklist.pdf

Food Network www.foodnetwork.co.uk

Disabled Students' Allowances www.gov.uk/disabled-students-allowances-dsas/overview

Gov.uk www.gov.uk/apply-online-for-student-finance

Groupon www.groupon.co.uk

Money Saving Expert www.moneysavingexpert.com

Unidays www.myunidays.com

NUS www.nus.org.uk

Save the Student www.savethestudent.org/accommodation/what-to-take-to-university.html

The Student Room www.thestudentroom.co.uk/content.php?r=15855-what-to-take-to-university-checklist

UCAS www.ucas.com/ucas/undergraduate/finance-and-support/budget-calculator

Unilist www.unilist.co.uk

Voucher Codes www.vouchercodes.co.uk

2 Learning to learn in the higher education context

ANGELA HODGKINS AND NICOLA WATSON

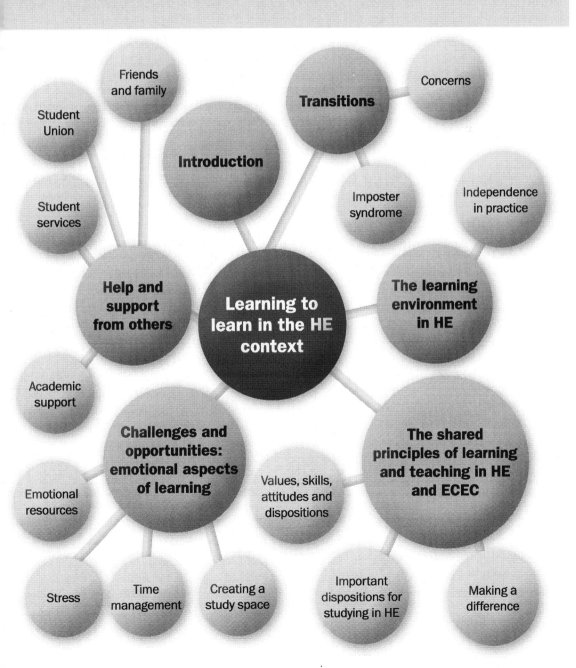

A journey of a thousand miles must begin with a single step.

Lao Tzu

Introduction

Learning does not take place in isolation but with those around us. None of us will achieve perfection but each of us is capable of building on what we can do already and of enhancing the value of our own lives and the lives of those around us. We all have to learn to learn. This chapter aims to help you understand your transition to university, the nature of the learning experience and how that prepares you to become an outstanding early years practitioner. It offers insights and guidance into managing your life at university and maintaining your well-being.

Critical questions

Think of a situation which was once new but became completely familiar to you. It might be your first day in a new job, or your first day at secondary school.

» *How would you feel if presented with the same scenario now?*

» *How can you use that experience and apply it to your emotions on being a new student at university?*

Transitions

Throughout our lives we are constantly changing. None of us is born fully equipped and capable of coping with the challenges and opportunities life presents. We each have to learn the knowledge, skills and attitudes which enable us to function effectively as members of communities. You are unique. To some degree you are aware of your own strengths and achievements, weaknesses and imperfections. As a student, new to university, your self-awareness will be heightened. Research suggests that for many this means experiencing feelings of doubt, fear and insecurity (Morgan, 2015). You may feel anxious as to whether you will cope with the challenges ahead. You may experience some discomfort in the transition to university simply because of the newness of so much around you. Getting to know tutors and fellow students, perhaps in completely new surroundings, can be challenging. On top of that you will be coping with the demands of your course, which will require you to draw upon and develop skills of independence in your thinking, organisation and ideas. This can feel uncomfortable and you may feel frustrated that you are not simply told by your tutors what you need to know so that you can get on and learn. Starting university can be an exciting, even thrilling, time but it can also be stressful. Just as a child starting school on their first day experiences a whole range of emotions, so too do adults embarking on a new stage of their lives.

Since the publication of the Dearing Report (National Committee of Inquiry into Higher Education, 1997), social policy has sought to ensure 'widening participation' in higher education, so that people from previously underrepresented groups, such as those of lower socio-economic status, ethnic minorities, people with disabilities and older people, would have greater access to higher education. As a consequence, there is much more participation in higher education of people from diverse backgrounds than traditionally was the case. Such diversity means that every individual's experience is unique, 'there is no one student experience' (Kandiko and Mawer, 2013, p 11). Your own experience is unique to you but individual features will be common to many others. For many the transition to university can prove an intensely emotional experience (Christie, 2009). Researchers have identified many aspects which add up to cause particular concern to new students, some of which may apply to you. You may:

- be the first person in your family to go to university;
- be a mature student;
- be a male in a female-dominated environment;
- have not been in education for a long time or feel that your previous professional or education experience is of little relevance;
- have work and family responsibilities to juggle as well as your studying;
- be worried about the level of your technology skills or academic writing skills.

(Ashton and Elliott, 2007; Christie, 2009; Leese, 2010; Morgan, 2015)

CASE STUDY

Helen's story

Helen had been a police officer for 19 years when she decided to follow her ambition of working with children. She enrolled as a mature student on a foundation degree studying early childhood. Helen now works in an early years setting. She explains:

The prospect of returning to study after such a long time was a daunting prospect but I had the self-confidence and self-belief in my ability to achieve and applied to undertake the foundation degree course. Having been successful in my application, I turned up on the first day and quickly realised that I was the oldest in the room by 15 years, and older than some of my peers' parents!! This age difference was not evident as a problem and as a cohort, we gelled as supportive peers. I certainly forgot the age difference between us all. As a group, the cohort was there to support each other and I made new friends, whom I am still in contact with having completed the BA Hons top-up degree. I found the tutors supportive and encouraging and had faith in my ability to achieve when I doubted my own capabilities. Some of my classmates, who were 18 years old, were fully up to date with theorists and theories but I could draw on personal life experiences based on my career as an officer but also as a parent of two young children, who were seven and nine at the time. The ability to work in a school environment with the continued support of staff and my personal tutor at university gave me the experience and confidence to achieve. I needed to be organised to ensure I was juggling a home/work/study balance and not missing deadlines. The bottom line is that I did survive and now at 45 have passed my BA and am looking forward to graduating at Worcester Cathedral in November 2015.

Helen O'Brien-Coleman

Critical question

»   *Take some time to think about what you are looking forward to and what, if anything, is worrying you.*

Imposter syndrome

Many students starting university experience a lack of confidence in their abilities or in their entitlement to be there. The word *university* has connotations of grandeur and academic excellence and you may experience feelings of '*not belonging*' or '*not being good enough*' (Morgan, 2015). This is a very common feeling, particularly among (although not restricted to) female students. Clance and Imes (1978, p 241) write about '*the imposter phenomenon*', involving women believing that they are not really intelligent and that they have fooled everyone into thinking that they are. This feeling of low self-worth is often associated with early family experiences and gender role stereotyping. Despite much evidence that they are capable and intelligent, some people still feel that one day they will be 'found out'.

Concerns

A key concern of students in their transition to HE identified by Kandiko and Mawer (2013, p 11) was of '*'feeling in the loop' with what was expected of them, balancing the various demands of higher education and developing independent learning approaches*'. The transition from school or college to university will involve you getting used to different ways of working. One of the differences between school and HE is that you will be studying more independently. This is a skill that you will need to develop, as there is an expectation that you will read and study in preparation for your classes. Therefore, preparation and reading is key. Many students are surprised at the amount from reading they need to do in order to be successful. Reading for study is different from reading for pleasure (although it can also be very pleasurable). When reading for study purposes, it is usual to write notes as you read and it is important that you note down all details of the book or journal in case you need to reference it later. See Chapter 4 for help in this area.

The learning environment in higher education

Rather than the mode of delivery you may be used to, the teaching approach in HE requires you to be much more active in your engagement with learning. Instead of passively receiving information, you are invited to question and reflect upon the topic being explored, consider issues from varying perspectives, form opinions and seek to justify those opinions through reading the works of other academics who have written and researched your area of study. Knowledge and ideas are shared and ideas are created *with* the tutor rather than *by* the tutor. As Tyler and Rogers identify in Chapter 9, learning is reciprocal rather than directed. The distinction between teaching and learning is much less defined since learning is constructed in collaboration. It is recognised that although the tutor has expertise and can use this to guide and support you, *you* have ideas, thoughts, questions and experiences that can make a valuable contribution to the issue under consideration. This is *constructivist* teaching and learning and is typical of the approach of HE courses in early childhood education and care (ECEC). Constructivism is a branch of philosophy based on the tenet that meaning is made or constructed by people rather than discovered. The psychologist Piaget (1896–1980) was a prominent advocate of constructivist theory. His work regarding how children *construct* their knowledge of the world by observing the effects of their actions on the environment greatly influenced educational theory and practice in the twentieth century. Another psychologist, Vygotsky (1896–1934), emphasised the social element which he advocated was essential to the construction of knowledge.

> *Each of us will build an idiosyncratic version of reality based partly on identical experiences but shaped by individual experience and, importantly, upon an individual's prior knowledge, understanding and experience.*
>
> (Pritchard and Woollard, 2010, p 5)

This approach challenges the notion of a *right answer* and of the expert whose job it is to impart knowledge to novice students with no prior learning. Instead, learning is regarded as an active, social process whereby knowledge is constructed in collaboration with others and is added to the existing knowledge and experience of each individual.

CASE STUDY

Amina's story

When I started at university I felt really unsettled at first and I thought that was because I wasn't getting enough guidance from my tutors. I was disappointed with my grades in the first semester; they weren't great even though I had worked hard. I had attended lectures, taken lots of notes and been really organised. Looking back now, I can see that my work showed what I had read but that was it. It didn't demonstrate what I had learned and how I had shifted in my thinking and my practice. I realise now that the discomfort I felt wasn't due to the tutors not bothering to help me. It was down to my lack of confidence in my own capabilities. I came to understand that my tutors value *my* thoughts and *my* position when it was backed up by what I had read. That's what I needed to show them.

Critical question

» *How will Amina's learning experience help her become an excellent early years practitioner?*

RESEARCH FOCUS

Research on teaching and learning suggests that methods which optimise independent learning reflect the way adults use knowledge in the modern world (Ashton and Elliott, 2007). In other words, your independent learning will help you not just acquire knowledge but also develop the skills and attitudes that will be most valuable to you as a practitioner, meaning that you will be encouraged and supported in becoming an increasingly independent learner as shown in Figure 2.1.

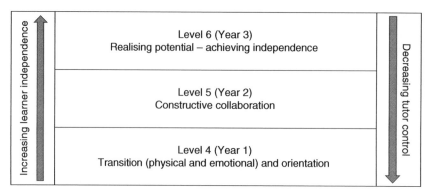

Figure 2.1 *The undergraduate journey to learner independence*

Critical question

» *Think of a list of questions to which there is a right answer. Now think of a list to which there are no right answers but a range of views. What makes some views more interesting and valuable than others?*

Independence in practice

As an ECEC practitioner you will need to be able to work effectively with a diverse range of people including children, parents, colleagues and other professionals. You will need to be adaptable, reflective, creative and ethical. Therefore, ECEC courses are designed to challenge not just your intellect but your personal and interpersonal skills and support you in recognising and developing those skills. Courses are designed to help you develop a critical and reflective approach to your work so that you are confident and secure enough in your professional role to make judgements, decisions and to be accountable in and for your practice. Chapter 4 explores the important area of what it means to be a critical reflective learner.

Developments in technology mean that a vast array of factual information is available at the touch of a button. However, what counts as knowledge at any one time may quickly become obsolete. Knowledge can be seen as provisional. In other words, as advancements in science, technology and politics are made, one set of truths are replaced by another. Reed and Canning (2010) note that relentless policy development and change in ECEC means that practitioners need the ability to respond to external forces which impact on personal experience of practice. Hanson and Appleby (2015, p 24) make the point that '*there are few textbook answers to most of the diverse and complex situations you will be asked to deal with when working with young children*'; another rationale for your tutors to help you develop independence in your learning.

The shared principles of learning and teaching in higher education and early childhood education and care

The *Statutory Framework for the Foundation Stage* 2014 (DfE, 2014) sets out the legal requirements for those working with children from birth to age five in England. It states the *'over-arching principles'* which govern the learning and development requirements for young children. These emphasise the potential for every individual to be resilient, capable and confident through building positive relationships working in partnership with those around them.

> *The learning and development requirements are informed by the best available evidence on how children learn and reflect the broad range of skills, knowledge and attitudes children need as foundations for good future progress.*
>
> (DfE, 2014, p 6)

The current approach to pedagogy in ECEC in England is mirrored by the learning framework in HE for students studying early childhood in that both have roots in social constructivist learning theory, as discussed above. As an ECEC practitioner, it will be your responsibility to ensure that all children are given opportunities to realise their potential by working in partnership in an atmosphere of mutual respect, providing them with support and guidance where needed and recognising areas of strength and achievement; just as your tutors aim to do for you.

Values, skills, attitudes and dispositions

Values: the measure of the worth or importance you attach to something; these are often reflected in the way we live our lives, eg *I value diversity.*

Skills: the ability to do something, eg football skills.

Attitudes: the way you express your values and beliefs through words and behaviour, eg *I love all babies because they are cute.*

Dispositions: *'a tendency to exhibit frequently, consciously and voluntarily a pattern of behaviour'* (Katz, 1985, cited in Katz, 1993, p 16), eg *I have a curious disposition.*

Important dispositions for studying in higher education

Dispositions are the predominant tendencies of a person's spirit; the natural mental and emotional outlook or mood; characteristic attitude – for example, *a girl with a pleasant disposition.* Dispositions are associated with personality but they can be developed. For example, a reflective disposition can be developed through experience of reflective practice.

A professional disposition

In most ECEC degree programmes, there will be strong links between theory and practice. Professional and personal development are closely linked, and so both professional and personal values and dispositions will be developed during your course. As you learn more about an aspect of early years practice, your confidence in that aspect increases and so will your ability to use your skills in the workplace. Therefore, your personal confidence will impact on your professional practice. This was evident in recent research conducted with foundation degree early years students at the University of Worcester in 2015, which concluded that:

> Findings revealed that 'impact' was perceived as an interrelationship between personal growth and professional influence and the course provided the basis to acquire knowledge, develop professional capability and reflect upon and influence practice.

The professional values that underpin learning in higher education mirror those values that support working with children, such as ethical practice, reflective practice, listening to the child's voice, respect and making a difference. As an early years HE student, you are an emerging practitioner and you will develop the ingredients of professionalism.

An ethical disposition

Ethics underpin every aspect of practice with young children and they are likely to be included in every aspect of early childhood study. Ethics involve much more than filling in an ethics form before carrying out research. They are an agreed set of values for professionals and integral to ECEC. BERA's guidelines for ethical research (2011) cover a range of aspects of ethical practice, such as confidentiality, anonymity and informed consent. In the HE environment, students are likely to discuss and to write about children and families that they work, or have worked, with, and this is an important aspect of learning together. However, it is as important that ethical guidelines are followed with other students. This means, for example, not using real names of children, families, staff or settings in your discussions. It also means that you should exercise care when talking about your studies outside university, as you never know who may be listening. Many students have got themselves into real trouble in this area, for example by discussing children with their friends on the bus, only to find that the person sitting behind them knows the family. See Chapter 13 for further discussion on becoming an ethical practitioner.

A reflective disposition

Developing a reflective disposition is important, as this will result in thoughtful and developmental practice. You will be encouraged to take a reflective stance within practice and within class too, and keeping a journal may be a good way to keep a record of these reflections, which you may be able to utilise later in assignment work. This aspect of practice is covered in detail in Chapter 11.

A respectful disposition

Respecting, valuing and listening to others are all important aspects of early years practice, as they are in any profession where you are working with people. You will find that ECEC practitioners are increasingly working in partnership with others. This increase in multi-agency working means that professionals need, more than ever, to develop effective but sensitive communication and listening skills. Respect for the views of others is essential. Working alongside others who have different knowledge and skills requires us to listen to different perspectives in order to best meet the needs of the children in our care. This is never more important than in a safeguarding situation, where the sharing of information can make a huge difference to a child in need. The professionals, parents and carers can all contribute to the holistic care of young children to ensure that all needs are met. This requires the ECEC professional to exercise skilful management and leadership to ensure that multi-agency working results in true partnership.

In a university classroom situation, it is equally important to value and respect the views of others. Your fellow students will be from a diverse range of backgrounds and experiences. It is vital that members of the group listen to and respect the views of others. It is possible to respect someone's view even if you disagree with them and this is an important personal and professional skill to develop.

Making a difference

Many people, when asked why they chose a career working with children, say that they *want to make a difference*. Indeed, this is one of the most common phrases used in applications for early years programmes. In most ECEC programmes, the concept of being an *agent of change* will be developed. Being an *agent of change* for children may involve making huge changes to policy and practice or doing something which makes a small but significant change for one child. Learning and sharing good practice will result in improvements in outcomes for children and families. You can also make a difference to your fellow students. Sharing your experiences and views enables others to construct their own understanding of the concepts being studied. There are further ways to be an *agent of change* such as volunteering to be a student representative. There is more about this in Chapter 1.

Critical question

» *What influenced your decision to study early childhood education and care? Think about the Values, Skills, Attitudes and Dispositions that you have which will help you to be effective in the role.*

Challenges and opportunities: emotional aspects of learning

Developing your ability to recognise opportunities will help to optimise your experience of HE. Self-awareness is key here, and involves having a clear understanding of your own personality, dispositions, strengths, weaknesses, and emotions. By understanding yourself, you can identify your needs. For example, if you know that you work best in silence, then you will be able to make sure that you find a suitable area with no distractions where you can work alone. If you know that you need your friends around you to *bounce ideas off*, then you can organise times to work with *study buddies*. Your potential challenges and opportunities will be personal to you. Remember that these challenges and opportunities may be professional and/ or personal. Learning involves struggle, excitement, frustration and pride. '*Learning itself is an intrinsically emotional business*' (Claxton, 1999, p 15). It is important to reflect on your motivation for learning. Why are you doing this? Is it for your own benefit and self-fulfilment? To make someone else proud of you? To further your career? Again, self-awareness is key, as having a good understanding of your motivation will keep you going through the tougher times. For some people, picturing themselves at graduation wearing a cap and gown is very motivating. For others, it is having letters after their name. These motivating images can be very powerful and can give us the momentum to keep going through the tough times.

Creating a study space

When beginning your learning adventure, preparation is important; being well prepared and well informed will help to make the transition go smoothly. Before you start university, make sure that you identify a place of your own in which to study and read as much as you can about the course, so that you feel prepared. In your first weeks, make sure that you know where you are going, what you need to take and what you will be doing; this will help to keep any anxiety manageable. You can do this by making sure that you read information provided for you and finding out all you can about what you will be doing.

Time management

Managing your time and responsibilities is key to success in creating a work/life balance. Set aside time to study and to read, but ensure that you make time for yourself, and for your family and friends. If you have other responsibilities, such as children or work, then it is important to acknowledge this and decide how to organise these responsibilities. Using a model, such as Covey's time management grid (see Figure 2.2), will help you to identify your priorities. Identifying specific dates to carry out tasks can also help you to organise your time successfully. Some students find that drawing up a plan of their week and identifying *available time* can be a real eye-opener. You may find that there is time in your week that you could use more effectively.

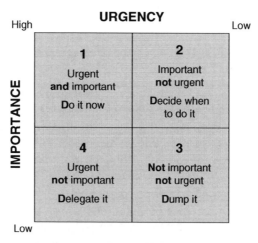

Figure 2.2 *Covey's time management grid (Covey, 1999)*

Stress

It is likely that, at some point in your learning journey, you will experience some sort of stress. Stress is your body's way of coping with too much mental or emotional pressure. People have different ways of reacting to and coping with stress, and so what may be motivating for one person may be extremely stressful to another (NHS, 2014).

Common effects of stress:

- problems with sleeping;
- lack of appetite;
- difficulty concentrating;
- irritability;
- anxiety/worry;
- headaches;
- muscle tension.

Stress is not an illness, but it can cause illness if it is not managed. This is another instance where being self-aware is a good thing, being able to recognise that the stress is getting too much for you to handle.

Emotional resources

There are several things that you can do in order to look after yourself emotionally and protect your mental health, thereby avoiding some of the effects of stress. Developing your own *mental toolkit* will help at these times and can include:

- talking to others about your feelings – sharing experiences and feelings with your peers can make you feel less isolated;
- eating well – foods can have both immediate and long-lasting effects on your mental health;
- keeping in touch with friends and family – this will help to keep you feeling grounded;
- taking breaks – a short break or a change of scene can help to de-stress you;
- accepting who you are – we are all different and we all have our own strengths and it is important to acknowledge what you bring to the group;
- keeping active – this boosts self-esteem and helps your concentration;
- drinking sensibly – drinking alcohol is a popular method of dealing with stress, but its effect is temporary and so caution should be used;
- doing things you love – work/life balance is important so take the time to dance, shop, laugh, swim, whatever makes you feel good;
- caring for each other – mutual care for each other will help you all to succeed.

Be aware of your own needs and do consider contacting a counsellor if you feel that you are not coping and need more help. Every university has trained counsellors and they can usually be accessed through your personal academic tutor.

Help and support from others

To get the most from your time in HE you will need to engage deeply with your studies. There will be times when life gets in the way and events and circumstances prevent you from giving your undivided attention to your work. This is inevitable and the key to getting through those times unscathed is to draw upon people who will give you the right kind of support. In their review of the literature on student engagement in HE, Wimpenny and Savin-Baden (2013, p 6) identified themes which characterised student engagement. These included having '*a wide set of relationships including student to tutor, student to student, student to family, and student to career... a shift from unfamiliarity and self-consciousness to self-sufficiency in learning... and emotional resilience*'. Learning independently does not mean working alone. Quite the opposite. Learning is a social process (Moore et al, 2010). Engagement with others will help you to maximise the development of your disposition and skills as well as increase your knowledge base.

Academic support

It is common for students to feel unsure of what is expected of them and not sure of where to go for assistance (Kandiko and Mawer, 2013). When problems arise, there are sources of help available and your university will have mechanisms in place to help you access the help you need. For example, you will be given an academic tutor who will be available to you one-to-one or in small group sessions to assist you at the start of your course and throughout your course to help with study issues and to provide you with a consistent and enduring point of contact throughout your studies. Study skills guides and workshops are often available to provide advice and support with diverse aspects relating to coursework and assessment from coping with induction, time management and essay writing to revision referencing and using technology. If you struggle with academic writing or lack confidence about your IT skills, you will not be the first. There will be resources in place to help you. Just ask.

Student services

The structure of support will be different in each university but there will be provision for students who have particular needs such as overseas students or students who have a disability. There will also be support available for general problems such as financial worries or personal problems. Have a look at your chosen university's website to see what's available.

Student Union

When you become a student you automatically become a member of the Student Union. Your union can provide free, confidential and impartial advice on a diverse range of issues including academic issues, health and well-being, housing and finance.

Friends and family

Your relationships with others will impact heavily on your level of engagement with your studies. If you have the support of others who understand the demands of this challenging time in your professional life, then you are fortunate. However, they may have their limitations, however well-meaning they are.

Chapter reflections

» *You are worthy of being on your chosen course.*

» *Support is available for you on your journey to becoming an independent learner.*

» *You will benefit from social constructivist learning and teaching as it will help you develop holistically, building on your thinking skills, your presentation skills, your ability to work collaboratively and your ability to reflect critically.*

» *Although you are a unique person, the challenges and problems you may encounter will not be unique to you. There is a raft of support and resources available to you to help you manage problems and ensure you stay afloat. Make sure you know where to find them when you need them!*

Further reading

Ashton, J and Elliott, R (2007) Juggling the Balls – Study, Work, Family and Play: Student Perspectives on Flexible and Blended Heutagogy. *European Early Childhood Education Research Journal*, 15(2).

Moore, S, Neville, C, Murphy, M and Connelly, C (2010) *The Ultimate Study Skills Handbook*. Maidenhead, Berkshire: Open University Press.

References

Ashton, J and Elliott, R (2007) Juggling the Balls – Study, Work, Family and Play: Student Perspectives on Flexible and Blended Heutagogy. *European Early Childhood Education Research Journal*, 15(2).

BERA (2011) *Ethical Guidelines for Educational Research*. [online] Available at: www.bera.ac.uk (accessed November 2016).

Christie, H (2009) Emotional Journeys: Young People and Transitions to University. *British Journal of Sociology of Education*, 30(2): 123–36. doi:10.1080/01425690802700123 (accessed November 2016).

Clance, P R and Imes, S A (1978) The Imposter Phenomenon in High Achieving Women: Dynamics and Therapeutic Interventions. *Theory Research and Practice*, 15: 241–47.

Claxton, G (1999) *Learning to Learn: A Key Goal in a 21st Century Curriculum*. QCA. [online] Available at: www.qca.org.uk/futures/ (accessed November 2016).

Covey, S R (1999) *The 7 Habits of Highly Successful People*. New York: Simon & Schuster.

Department for Education (DfE) (2014) *Statutory Framework for the Early Years Foundation Stage*. London: DfE.

Hanson, K and Appleby, K (2015) *Reflective Practice*, in Reed, M and Walker, R (eds) *Early Childhood Studies: A Critical Reader*. London: Sage.

Higher Education Statistics Agency (2015) Headline statistics. [online] Available at: www.hesa.ac.uk/ (accessed November 2016).

Kandiko, C B and Mawer, M (2013) *Student Expectations and Perceptions of Higher Education: Executive Summary*. London: King's Learning Institute. [online] Available at: www.kcl.ac.uk/study/learningteaching/kli/research/student-experience/QAASummary.pdf (accessed November 2016).

Katz, L (1993) *Dispositions: Definitions and Implications for Early Childhood Practices*. Washington, DC: ERIC Clearinghouse on Elementary and Early Childhood Education.

Leese, M (2010) Bridging the Gap: Supporting Student Transitions into Higher Education. *Journal of Further and Higher Education*, 34(2): 239–51. doi:10.1080/03098771003695494 (accessed November 2016).

Moore, S, Neville, C, Murphy, M and Connelly, C (2010) *The Ultimate Study Skills Handbook*. Maidenhead, Berkshire: Open University Press.

Morgan, J (2015) Foundation Degree to Honours Degree: The Transition Experiences of Students on an Early Years Programme. *Journal of Further and Higher Education*, 39(1): 108–26. doi: 10.1080/0309877X.2013.817005 (accessed November 2016).

National Committee of Inquiry into Higher Education (1997) *Higher Education in the Learning Society. The Dearing Report*. Norwich: HMSO. [online] Available at: www.educationengland.org.uk/documents/dearing1997/dearing1997.html (accessed November 2016).

Nutbrown, C (2012) *Foundations for Quality: The Independent Review of Early Education and Childcare Qualifications. The Nutbrown Review*, DfE. [online] Available at: www.education.gov.uk/nutbrownreview (accessed November 2016).

Osgood, J (2006) Deconstructing Professionalism in Early Childhood Education: Resisting the Regulatory Gaze. *Contemporary Issues in Early Childhood*, 7(1): 5–15.

Pritchard, A and Woollard, J (2010) *Psychology for the Classroom: Constructivism and Social Learning*. Taylor and Francis e-library (accessed November 2016).

Reed, M and Canning, N (2010) *Reflective Practice in the Early Years*. London: Sage.

Tzu, Lao (date unknown) *Tao Te Ching*.

Wimpenny, K and Savin-Baden, M (2013) Alienation, Agency and Authenticity: A Synthesis of Practice and Effects in Student Engagement. *Teaching in Higher Education*, 18(3): 311–26.

3 Becoming a critically reflective thinker and learner

KAREN APPLEBY AND KAREN HANSON

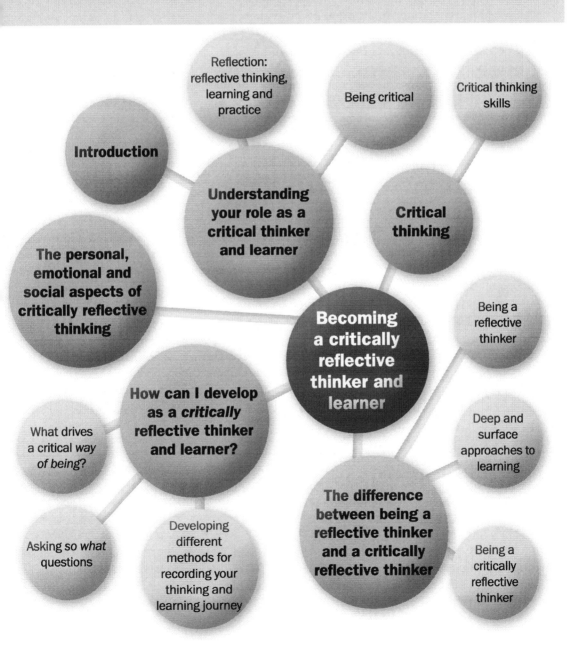

It is the mark of an educated mind to be able to entertain a thought without accepting it.

Aristotle

Introduction

This chapter examines critically reflective thinking and its relevance to you as a learner and developing professional practitioner in higher education. It is a complex but interesting area of study which requires you to examine and explain yourself as a thinker and learner using a range of theory. In a case study on 'Gemma', diagrams and critical questions are used to help you apply theory to your own practice, to develop a deeper understanding of your approach and how to develop it in ways which will support your success in higher education. The role of critical thinking within reflective practice is explained in preparation for a deeper examination of *criticality* and ways of describing key thinking skills such as analysis, evaluation and creativity. Building on this foundation, the significance and role of being a critically reflective thinker and learner is examined with consideration of how this supports, and is supported by, your ability to process and understand information and data from different sources, organise, problem-solve, make decisions and communicate with others.

Being a critically reflective thinker and the learning that this stimulates are essential to your success in your academic work but will also support the development of your practice and future employability. This is because what distinguishes an effective graduate early years practitioner from other practitioners is the ability to learn from a process of thinking deeply about children's needs and their experiences. Knowledge from valid, relevant and trusted sources is necessary for critical thinking (Moon, 2008); it is the 'stuff' we think about and consequently learn from. However, it is also essential to question knowledge from different sources to create new knowledge; knowledge that is specific to the wide range of individual professional contexts and the children, families and professionals involved. As an emerging practitioner, it is essential that you are able to recognise, examine and learn from knowledge as *seen* and experienced in practice, supported by engagement with theoretical subject knowledge. Thinking critically about knowledge from different sources, including your own perspective, will nurture a deeper understanding of children, childhood and practice which can then be used in your role as a reflective practitioner (see Chapter 11) in developing high-quality provision. Therefore, developing your role and identity as a *learner practitioner* who develops a deep rather than surface approach to thinking and learning, is a significant theme in this chapter.

Understanding your role as a critical thinker and learner

Understanding and developing your role and identity as a thinker and learner provides you with a powerful tool for owning and taking responsibility for your development and achievement. The significance of this is supported by Marton and Säljo's (1984) research which found that students' understanding of their learning process enabled them to adopt a *deep* rather than *surface* approach to their learning.

The ability to describe how you think and learn using language which is understood by you, other students and tutors is empowering. It facilitates effective communication with peers and tutors. You can better understand expectations of you as a learner. It enables you to understand guidance on learning activities in taught sessions and personal academic tutor meetings. It will enable you to interpret written information such as learning outcomes, study/assessment tasks and feedback, and wider academic sources. You will be able to identify areas of strength and areas for development, with the potential of improving the quality and impact of your academic reading and writing.

Reflection: reflective thinking, learning and practice

As learners within higher education, you will be asked to *reflect* on your existing and new knowledge and experience. For many students, being asked to think in this way is a new and often confusing experience with many questioning what it is they are being asked to do. Unfortunately, there are many definitions of reflection, which can be very confusing. This chapter provides a straightforward introduction to some key ideas and approaches to get you started.

As your course of study includes both academic study and professional practice, it is helpful to understand the difference and relationship between reflection, reflective learning and reflective practice. As shown in Figure 3.1, reflection on academic sources and evidence from practice such as observations of children's learning will support the development of knowledge which is relevant to both your academic study and professional practice. The learning from this process stimulates the development of knowledge which will help you to develop and explain your theory for practice (what you plan to do and why) and theory in practice (what you actually do and why). (Read Chapter 11 for further insights into reflective practice and reflective activism.)

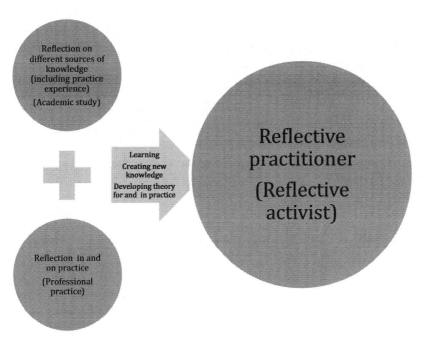

Figure 3.1 Becoming a reflective practitioner

Being critical

At some point in your studies you will be asked to think critically or to introduce more critical-ity into discussions and writing. However, it can be difficult to understand what is expected. As Moon (2008) identifies, critical thinking is very difficult to define. For many of us *being crit-ical* can be associated with being negative or judgemental and involve criticising something or someone. Within this chapter, we define and examine critical reflection in a more positive way as a '*disposition and ability to learn through the interrogation of different sources of knowledge and experience*'. Critically reflective thinking is therefore seen as necessary to learning. However, having the ability to think and learn in a particular way is not enough; you also need to focus on how you engage with thinking and learning opportunities and how this has developed your knowledge, understanding, values and beliefs. Significantly, in higher education learners are assessed on their ability to demonstrate both the 'act' of *critical thinking* and the outcome, *critical thought* (Barnett, 1994); what and how you have learned rather than producing a predetermined *right answer*.

Developing a disposition to think and learn in this way will be supported by what you bring to your university experience, including your interests, motivation, skills and knowledge. Learning experiences will be designed to stimulate, use and further develop your learning resources but it is your responsibility to actively participate and use these opportunities to support your achievement. The ultimate aim of higher education is to support the develop-ment of autonomous and effective thinkers and learners.

Your ability to learn through the interrogation of different sources of knowledge and experi-ence will be supported by the development of study skills, including a range of different criti-cal thinking and communication skills. These will enable you to access and use knowledge effectively. Further guidance on how to learn through critical reading and writing can be found in Chapter 4.

Critical thinking

Critical thinking skills

It is helpful to understand the language used to describe different thinking skills as you will come across these terms in directed study activities, learning outcomes, assessment tasks and feedback. Understanding how you are being asked to think will support your learning process. Read the following case study and consider how you might describe Gemma's think-ing processes.

CASE STUDY

Gemma's account of her learning from practice

A deeper understanding of the role of the adult in communicating with children has informed my practice development. During my second placement, I was particularly focused on being able to communicate confidently with the children in the setting. I felt this was an area for me to work on, as previously I held back during my first placement because of nerves, and I was not really sure how to approach and talk to young children. However, this time around I found it much easier to start up a conversation and engage with the children. For example, I would ask the child what they liked and would build a conversation around that specific topic. The room leader commented on my evaluation form, saying that 'Gemma uses short, simple sentences, words and phrases during her communication with the children. She will always be sat with them and talks to them at their level'. The significance of communicating with children is highlighted by the Early Years Foundation Stage (EYFS) guidance (DfE, 2014, p 8), which identifies the importance of 'giving children opportunities to experience a rich language environment; to develop their confidence and skills in expressing themselves; and to speak and listen in a range of situations'. This suggests that children should and do have the right to express themselves through language and that talking to the children enables them to gain new skills. This may include understanding emotions and body language.

Communicating with the children enabled me to see things from their perspective, and allowed the child's voice to be expressed. For example, a group of two year olds came up to me and said that they didn't like eating bananas. I then approached a practitioner and explained what they had told me, and the practitioner wrote down the names of the children who did not like bananas. By the children having the confidence and trust to be able to confide in me, it meant that I was able to support the improvement of their experience at the setting. However, at times I did find it difficult to communicate with the babies because there was not always a clear or verbal response, so I had to focus more on their body language and facial expressions, in order to see how they responded. During placement, it became much easier to recognise the responses of the babies, and I found it much easier to communicate with them. I changed my tone of voice and the language I was using, so it would be easier for them to understand me. I also accentuated my facial expressions when with the babies.

Many people have written about thinking skills and the process of critical thinking, including Bloom (1956). In a revision of Bloom's work developed by Anderson and Krathwohl (2001, cited in Wilson, 2013), different levels of knowledge and ways of engaging with knowledge are explained. The guidance supports *'thinking about one's thinking in a purposeful way so that one knows about cognition and also knows how to regulate one's cognition'* (Owen Wilson, 2013, np). In Table 3.1 key terms are explained and then used to identify different thinking skills demonstrated in Gemma's writing.

Table 3.1 *Different thinking skills demonstrated in Gemma's writing (adapted from Anderson and Krathwohl, 2001)*

Term	Explanation	Case study (Gemma)
Remembering	Remembering or repeating information	Gemma remembers and describes examples such as '*I would ask the child what they liked and would build a conversation around that specific topic*'.
Understanding	Explaining ideas, theories or behaviours	The significance of Gemma's practice is explained in relation to the EYFS guidance.
Applying	Using information in a different situation	Knowledge from reading the EYFS guidance is applied to experience in practice.
Analysing	Extracting different themes, ideas or patterns within information	Gemma has analysed her experience in practice, focusing on her communication with babies and children. From this she has further analysed and identified her communication skills.
Evaluating	Identifying/ justifying validity or quality	Gemma has evaluated her practice, identifying initial weaknesses and how these have been improved. She has used the application of knowledge from the description of practice, practitioner feedback and wider reading to make a judgement on how the quality of her practice has improved.
Creating	Creating a new interpretation or theory or product	Gemma has developed a new interpretation of her competence in communicating with children and babies. She has created a thinking and learning journey.

The difference between being a reflective thinker and a critically reflective thinker

Being a reflective thinker

Dewey (1910, p 34) proposed that '*there are three natural resources in the creation of a reflective thinker; curiosity, suggestion and depth*'. It is now possible to consider whether Gemma (Case study) is a reflective thinker. She has demonstrated curiosity about her competence in practice and the impact this has on children and babies. She has been open to *suggestion* from the practitioner and from the EYFS guidance. The evidence of applying a range of thinking skills demonstrates a shift from a surface level of thinking and learning. The development of some depth is demonstrated by her shift from describing practice to the application of different perspectives on her practice, her ability to explain and justify the relevance of her practice for children and babies and the creation of a new interpretation of her practice. At this point it is useful to consider further what we mean by deep and surface approaches to learning.

Deep and surface approaches to learning

Research by Marton and Säljo (1984) identified that a deep rather than surface approach to learning requires you to be intrinsically motivated and to feel an 'absence of anxiety'. This suggests that your motivation should be nurtured by your curiosity as suggested by Dewey (1910) and genuine interest in a topic rather than a focus on grades. This approach will encourage you to own your thinking and learning process and to make sense of new sources of knowledge and to thereby create your own interpretation. This is relevant to your academic studies but also in practice where this approach can support innovation, decision-making and problem-solving. For example, Gemma may use her learning to inform her interaction with children and babies in the future.

Critical question

» How do you see learning and how is this demonstrated in the way you approach thinking and learning? Complete Table 3.2 below to help capture your ideas.

Table 3.2 Your approach to thinking and learning (adapted from Marton and Säljo, 1984)

	I see learning as:	My approach is to:
1	Increasing my knowledge	
2	Memorising facts	
3	Acquiring facts to be applied when needed	
4	Making sense of knowledge and experience	
5	Interpretation with the purpose of understanding and learning from situations, issues, problems etc...	

Understanding and developing your approach to thinking and learning

Gemma (Case study) is supported in deepening her reflection on knowledge gained from reading and experience in practice. This is achieved through researching useful publications applicable to her practice – reflective practice does require some relevant knowledge or experience to reflect on or think about. Gemma also records knowledge that has made her think, and her responses: she then engages in discussion and dialogue with her peers, tutors and practitioners to support her in the process of making sense of her knowledge and experience.

She now needs to develop the depth of her thinking and learning through revisiting her previous learning. Her confidence will grow further as she discusses her developing thinking and learning within peer group and class situations. Once her confidence has grown, she should be able to challenge pre-existing assumptions about what is *known* by her and others. This will be further developed through reflection on wider reading and other learning opportunities. Gemma will then be in a position to evaluate the impact of her thinking and learning for developing new knowledge and her professional practice. From this foundation *critically* reflective thinking and learning can be developed.

Being a critically reflective thinker

Brookfield (1995, p 28) describes becoming critically reflective as '*a process of learning and change*'. To support this development, your role as a learner involves *actively* engaging with a wide range of relevant evidence, for example academic texts, experiences in practice and the perspectives of others. You should adopt the role of a meaning maker, engaging in an ongoing process of creating *new* knowledge, as represented by numbers 4 and 5 in Table 3.2. This is in contrast to numbers 1, 2 and 3, which reflect a *passive* acceptance that what you are told, read and observe is *the truth*. Adopting a questioning approach when you engage with your own and others' knowledge as seen in practice and presented in policy and publications, including research, is an essential habit to cultivate. It is therefore important that you continuously review the validity of your own and others' knowledge, recognising that there is no *right* answer. This may differ significantly from your previous experience of learning and may require you to make a significant change in your approach to learning. It might feel daunting initially, but is a key part of your journey towards becoming critically reflective.

RESEARCH FOCUS

Brookfield (1995) suggests the use of different *lenses* to stimulate critical reflection within the context of professional practice, including autobiographical, students', theoretical and colleagues' lenses. He argues that it involves searching below the surface of our '*taken for granted beliefs about the world*'; a process of '*hunting assumptions*' (Brookfield, 1995, p 2). See Chapter 11 for further information on this perspective and Hanson's fifth *socio-cultural lens*.

Critical question

»   *Which of Brookfield's lenses does Gemma use in the case study?*

How can I develop as a *critically* reflective thinker and learner?

What drives a critical *way of being*?

Most of us are born with an innate disposition to be curious, to explore and inquire (Dewey, 1910). This is most evident when observing children as they play and explore their world. Just as they are driven by their interests, so are we as adults. We too are going to be more motivated to research and think about knowledge and experiences that interest us. Sometimes, however, we may be asked to engage with knowledge which has been deemed by others as relevant but does not at first stimulate our curiosity. Some subjects are less clearly related to working with young children and consequently it can be harder to find a reason to develop an interest in the subject and the motivation required to critically examine different sources of knowledge. This then requires an element of trust in 'experts' and their wider knowledge of what is relevant or even essential. It involves questioning our assumptions (Brookfield, 1995) about what is relevant and being '*open to suggestion*' (Dewey, 1910) from other perspectives. It requires intrinsic motivation (Marton and Säljo, 1984) from within your own resources, commitment to researching new sources of knowledge and to exercising your brain to make it work effectively (just as you would exercise your body to improve your physical fitness). When your motivation is flagging, you need to be resilient. Identifying the purpose for your thinking and learning activity can make the difference. Many students find that applying academic knowledge to practice not only motivates them to find out more, it also helps them to make sense of the content and to achieve a deeper level of understanding. The *ah-ha* moment in your learning, when you 'see' something differently from before, can be an emotional and potentially addictive experience.

Critical questions

» *Have you had an experience of an 'ah-ha' moment in your learning?*

» *What was it that helped you to 'see things differently'?*

RESEARCH FOCUS

Mezirow (2006) later identified the development of positive '*habits of mind*' as being significant to professional learning. Mezirow (2000) also explores professional learning as a process of '*perspective transformation*' supported by reflection which includes:

- being critically aware of our assumptions;

- identifying how these affect how we see ourselves and relationships with others;

- learning from this to permit a clearer interpretation of experience.

Critical question

»   *Can you identify any examples of learning in this way?*

Asking *so what* questions

Figure 3.2 represents how asking questions about different sources of knowledge (as discussed previously) can stimulate critical reflection and reflective learning, which then informs reflective practice. Developing and asking *so what* questions is a straightforward approach which has worked well for those new to reflection. Sometimes you may start with a relatively open question such as '**So what** *is the relevance of this knowledge for my understanding of how children develop?*' You may develop (or be given) a more specific focus for your questions. For example, Gemma (Case Study) focused on her ability to communicate with babies and young children. This approach can support you in evaluating and selecting the sources of knowledge which have had the most significant impact on your thinking and learning. Gemma identified a specific section within the EYFS guidance (DfE, 2014) that made her think and helped her to develop a deeper understanding of her practice. As she develops, she will identify more sources of knowledge and will develop the ability to compare different perspectives and to evaluate which have more value and impact than others on her learning. As she progresses through the course, she will be encouraged to examine and develop her knowledge in relation to wider socio-cultural, historical and political perspectives. She will need to consider her position and that of others within a dynamic and changing world. For example, this may include reflection on the significance of enabling communication with children living in refugee camps and how you work with cultural and linguistic diversity.

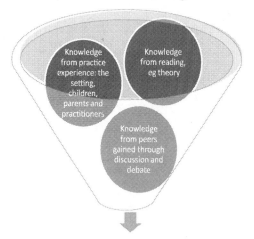

Critically reflective thinking and learning: asking 'so what' questions about 'knowledge'

Knowledge from practice experience: the setting, children, parents and practitioners

Knowledge from reading, eg theory

Knowledge from peers gained through discussion and debate

Your reflection on this knowledge – asking 'so what' questions

Questioning the significance of your own existing assumptions, knowledge, understanding, emotional responses, values, beliefs etc

YOU CREATE **REFLECTIVE LEARNING**

INFORMS REFLECTIVE PRACTICE (REFLECTIVE ACTIVISM)

Figure 3.2 Critically reflective thinking and learning

As emerging practitioners, developing the *habit* of questioning personal assumptions and how these affect your *openness* to and interpretation of different perspectives is significant. For example, we could ask whether Gemma (Case Study) considered whether her previous knowledge, values or beliefs affected or were affected by her learning experience. Brookfield (1995) refers to this as the *autobiographical lens*.

Critical question

»   *Where do Brookfield's (1995) lenses fit into the content of Figure 3.2?*

Developing different methods for recording your thinking and learning journey

Developing your skills in recording your learning journey provides you with a valuable resource for deeper critical thinking and learning. As discussed by Bolton (2010), writing can be a valuable tool for articulating and revisiting knowledge, thoughts and assumptions. You may start with notes which record knowledge gained from reading or lectures, narrative observations and descriptive accounts of experiences in practice. To achieve a deeper level of thinking and learning, it is important to also revisit and record your response to what you have read, heard and experienced. A reflective journal can provide you with a record of information and any responses, including your thoughts and insights; a resource which can be revisited and reviewed. You will be able to see how your thinking has changed.

There are other tools you can use. For example, you may develop a simple grid to support reflection on knowledge, as shown in Table 3.3.

Table 3.3 *Reflection on sources of knowledge*

Source of knowledge	Key point	How has this made me think?	So what have I learned?
Reference if appropriate			

You may develop the grid further to support your ability to compare different sources of knowledge, as shown in Table 3.4.

Table 3.4 *Comparing different sources of knowledge*

Source of knowledge	Key point	How has this made me think?	How does this knowledge link to other sources?	So what have I learned?
Reference if appropriate				

Other approaches can include making notes (annotations) on narrative observations from practice to help you analyse (extract) key information. For example, you can note key ways in which children are communicating with others. You can then evaluate the significance of these behaviours through the application of relevant theory. You can then reflect on what you have learned about how children communicate and how this might be supported in practice (asking *so what* questions). You may also develop diagrams or other visual representations to help you think more deeply about complex issues. We use diagrams in this chapter to communicate complicated ideas in a different way; a way which may be easier to understand for some learners.

The personal, emotional and social aspects of critically reflective thinking

Although the main focus of this chapter is on thinking and learning (the cognitive dimension), there has also been a strong emphasis on personal responsibility, dispositions, attitudes and other qualities such as motivation and resilience. Your approach is clearly located within your role and identity as a learner but also in your emerging role as a practitioner. Your tutors will scaffold learning experiences and introduce knowledge to inform and provoke your thinking but how you use these learning opportunities is in your hands; it is your responsibility.

It is also important to recognise the emotional dimension. As Dewey (1910) reminds us:

> *reflective thinking is always more or less troublesome because it involves overcoming the inertia that inclines one to accept suggestions at their face value; it involves willingness to endure a condition of mental unrest and disturbance.*

As discussed previously, being a critically reflective thinker and learner involves being challenged, constantly questioning and recreating your knowledge and position on everything you thought you knew and believed. Regardless of your experience, this can be an emotionally challenging experience.

Critical question

»   *Where are you on your journey of being comfortable 'not knowing'?*

Fortunately, we do not need to face these challenges alone. The social dimension plays a significant role in supporting our critical thinking and learning experience. This includes the knowledge gained from others, their experience and research as well as the more dynamic learning opportunities involving social interaction with others. Significantly, Barnett (1994) argues that the *act* of critical thinking can be supported by interaction with others while the outcome, critical thought, requires collaboration with others. For Gemma the personal and social dimensions are intertwined.

> *Reflection involves taking a step back and trying to look at things from a different perspective... it is something personal but sometimes it takes someone else to help you to discuss things, think them through and see it differently.*
>
> (Appleby, 2010, p 19)

The role of dialogue, debate and other relevant learning processes is significant for both academic and professional learning. Tutors will facilitate opportunities for discussing, questioning and challenging the relevance of different sources of knowledge, including their own and yours. This will not involve telling you what to think but will support you in developing how to think. Peer group learning is a particularly powerful context for critically reflective thinking when supported by a shared and high level of commitment.

Chapter reflections

» *The academic and professional aspects of critically reflective thinking need to work together.*

» *Working with children and families from diverse social and cultural backgrounds requires a flexibility of thinking to understand their sometimes complex needs.*

» *A 'one-size-fits-all' mentality is inappropriate and can be harmful when handling situations that can be sensitive and impact upon people's lives.*

» *Situations or issues outside of your personal knowledge and experience clearly require research from other sources to inform understanding and next steps. It can be even more challenging when the experience or situation is familiar or comfortable. Even with situations that appear familiar, we do not 'know' everything and will need to seek knowledge from other sources.*

» *We can never know the complex nature of individual families' lives. However, a disposition and ability to think about and learn from a range of perspectives can support understanding of specific needs and how best to respond. By developing this approach, you are on the journey to becoming a reflective activist (Hanson and Appleby, 2015).*

Further reading

Bolton, G (2014) *Reflective Practice: Writing and Professional Development*. 4th ed. London: Sage Publications.

Hanson, K and Appleby, K (2015) Reflective Practice, in Reed, M and Walker, R (eds) *Early Childhood Studies: A Critical Reader*. London: Sage, pp 7–13.

References

Anderson, L W and Krathwohl, D R, et al (eds) (2001) *A Taxonomy for Learning, Teaching, and Assessing: A Revision of Bloom's Taxonomy of Educational Objectives*. Boston, MA: Allyn & Bacon.

Appleby, K (2010) Reflective Thinking, Reflective Practice, in *Reflective Practice in the Early Years*. London: Sage, pp 7–23.

Barnett, R (1994) *The Limits of Competence*. Buckingham: Open University Press/SRHE.

Bloom, B (1956) *A Taxonomy of Educational Objectives*. New York: Longmans Green.

Bolton, G (2010) *Reflective Practice: Writing and Professional Development*. 3rd ed. London: Sage.

Brookfield, S (1995) *Becoming a Critically Reflective Teacher*. San Francisco: Jossey-Bass.

Department for Education (DfE) (2014) *Statutory Framework for the Early Years Foundation Stage*. London: DfE.

Dewey, J (1910) *How We Think*. Boston/New York/Chicago: D.C. Heath & Co.

Hanson, K and Appleby, K (2015) Reflective Practice, in Reed, M and Walker, R (eds) *Early Childhood Studies: A Critical Reader*. London: Sage, pp 7–13.

Marton, F and Säljo, J (1984) Approaches to Learning, in Marton, F, Hounsall, D and Entwhistle, N (eds) *The Experience of Learning*. Edinburgh: Scottish Academic Press, pp 36–55.

Mezirow, J (2000) *Learning as Transformation*. San Francisco: Jossey-Bass.

Mezirow, J (2006) An Overview of Transformative Learning, in Sutherland, P and Crowther, J (eds) *Lifelong Learning: Concepts and Contexts*. Abingdon, Oxford: Routledge.

Moon, J (2008) *Critical Thinking: An Exploration of Theory and Practice*. London: Routledge.

Owen Wilson, L (2013) Anderson and Krathwohl – Understanding the new version of Bloom's taxonomy. [online] Available at: http://thesecondprinciple.com/teaching-essentials/beyond-bloom-cognitive-taxonomy-revised/ (accessed November 2016).

4 Critical reading, writing and referencing

JANET HARVELL

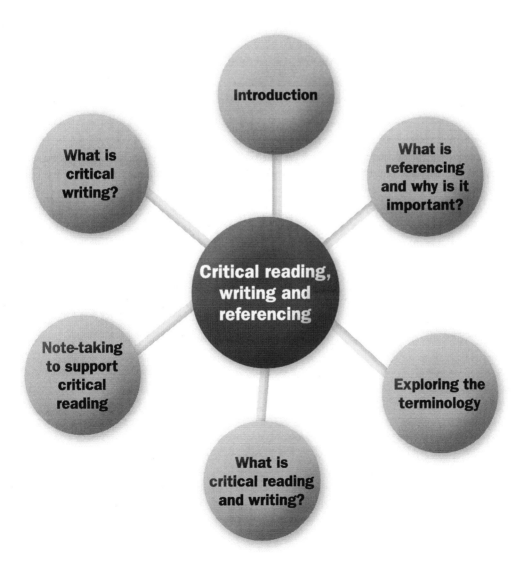

- Introduction
- What is critical writing?
- What is referencing and why is it important?
- Note-taking to support critical reading
- Critical reading, writing and referencing
- Exploring the terminology
- What is critical reading and writing?

He that loves reading has everything within his reach.

William Godwin

Introduction

One of the most challenging issues that students comment on during their time at university is the challenge of referencing, and understanding how to avoid plagiarism within their academic work. Similarly, teaching staff will often refer to the difficulty that students have in reading critically and transferring this to their writing. This chapter will guide you in your understanding of both topics. The first section will provide an introduction to referencing through a number of activities and exercises and you will be encouraged to produce your own *aide-memoire*, the Reference Dice, which can be printed off for ease of referencing when completing course and assignment work. This is seen as a *starter kit* to referencing, to give students confidence when tackling written work in their first year. We will then move on to reading critically, exploring what is meant by this and reinforcing critical reading through a range of practical activities. You will be encouraged to explore the strengths and weaknesses of different arguments and to form a set of *beginner* questions to develop skills in critical reading and writing, in addition to being supported in effective note-taking during the critical reading process.

What is referencing and why is it important?

Referencing is where you formally recognise another author's work, in order to acknowledge the work and indicate where further information can be found. If you do not include any references, you are implying that all of the ideas that you have written about are your own. Ultimately this is dishonest and is referred to as *plagiarism*, which is a serious offence and could result in accusations of cheating. Referencing ensures that you give credit to the appropriate author(s) for the ideas that are being discussed. In addition, it moves your writing from personal opinion to a valid argument, showing how this is supported by evidence from a range of sources. In addition to the vast range of books and journal articles that you will be encouraged to read, it is important to become familiar with some of the key websites, Twitter feeds and bloggers linked to your area of research, and sign up for regular updates. In this way you will ensure that you are aware of new research that is going on and can become aware of some of the current discussions and debates within your area of study.

> Take a moment to access your university's academic site and familiarise yourself with its referencing guidelines and policy on plagiarism.

Defining plagiarism

Plagiarism is where you do not give credit to another person's work in your writing or presentations. This means that either intentionally or unintentionally you are giving the impression that the content of your work and the ideas that you have written about are your own. You also need to be aware of self-plagiarism, which occurs when you submit the same assignment for different courses, or use substantial chunks of text from previous assignments in your work without acknowledging this.

Many universities will have access to different software programs that allow lecturers, and students, to evaluate the originality of their work by comparing this against a wide-ranging database of authors' work. Turnitin (turnitin.com) is an example of a common software program that your university or college might use.

There are a number of useful online quizzes that can help you to better understand the complexity of plagiarism. Test your knowledge and understanding using the following sites:

Cornell University: Recognizing and avoiding plagiarism. https://plagiarism.arts.cornell. edu/tutorial/exercises.cfm

Aiming for integrity: How well do you know plagiarism?

http://turnitin.com/assets/en_us/media/plagiarism-quiz

In addition to acknowledging the source of your material, this is also an opportunity to demonstrate to the reader the validity and strength of the information that you are writing about. I am sure that you will be encouraged to use more *academic sources*, and referencing will demonstrate whether the sources you are using are sufficiently academic; ie that the evidence is reliable and valid and written from an authoritative and objective point of view. For example, lecturers will encourage you to refer to articles from *peer-reviewed* journals because of the validation process that each article goes through before being published. This means that experts in that discipline check for objectivity and personal bias and consider the strength of the evidence provided before accepting the paper for publication. It gives the reader confidence in the reliability of the information that is being provided. Massey University (owll.massey.ac.nz) provides a useful explanation of what defines a source as being academic.

Critical question

» *What are the advantages and disadvantages of reading from a wide range of sources?*

Exploring the terminology

What is the difference between citing, quoting, referencing and a bibliography?

Very often when used in conversation these terms are interchanged and used incorrectly. Some common terms include:

* Citing/citations: when referring to someone else's work in your own writing, you will show this by including names and date of publication in brackets.

* Quote and quotation: this is when you use the exact words, phrases or text that has been taken from a different source. These will be identified by quotation marks, and the page number(s) that this quotation can be accessed from.

- Paraphrasing: if you put what someone else has written and/or said into your own words.

- Reference list: at the end of your assignment you will provide a list of all the different sources that you have *referred to* in your assignment.

- Bibliography: the bibliography will include the same information that will be found in the reference list, but it will also contain the details of all of the resources that you used/accessed and that have informed your writing, although you did not refer to them.

Both your reference list and bibliography will identify these sources in alphabetical order, beginning with the first letter of the alphabet. Refer to Table 4.1, and the reference section at the end of each chapter, for practical examples.

Again, it is important that you refer to your own institution's referencing guidelines to make sure that you are following the correct format.

Refer to Table 4.1 later in the chapter, which reinforces the points discussed above.

Critical question

» *What is the difference between referencing and citing and why do you think it is important to understand this?*

Annotated bibliography

Developing an annotated bibliography is a useful method for noting essential and key points of the article, book or chapter that you are reading. A few notes will be very helpful in reminding you of the content of the source materials. These notes should not be over-detailed, but act as a prompt. For example:

- How valid is the source and/or author?

- Who has the item been written for, ie which audience – academics, general public?

- How might this link to your module(s) and how might you use it in your work?

- What other sources have been referred to that support or disagree with what has been written?

- What are the strengths and/or limitations of the work?

There are a number of different templates that can be used. The following is an example of an entry from the author's annotated bibliography.

Hanson, K and Appleby, K (2015) Reflective Practice, in Reed, M and Walker, R (eds) *A Critical Companion to Early Childhood Studies*. London: Sage, pp 24–35.

This chapter is written for early childhood students and examines and redefines our existing understanding of reflective practice. The authors explore the implications of reflection for practice and introduce the concept of 'reflective activism' which was developed as a result of this. Underpinning the discussions are references to key reflective models including Kolb, Dewey and Brookfield. Suggestions are then made for developing individual identities as reflective practitioners, and the importance of making links between theory and practice. Underpinning this is the introduction of a 'fifth' socio-cultural lens to Brookfield's (1995) original four lenses.

Critical question

» *What are the advantages and disadvantages of completing an annotated bibliography?*

Referencing different sources

The previous section looked at citing and referencing evidence taken from a book. Unfortunately, it is not always as simple as this! When you are researching, you are likely to come across many different types of evidence and each of these will be referenced slightly differently. For example, you might make reference to a journal article, a website, an ebook, video clips, a newspaper article … the list goes on. To list the different types of referencing would be a book in itself, and your own institution is likely to have its own guidelines. An example of such a handbook is the one produced by the University of Worcester, a link for which can be found in the reference list at the end of this chapter.

I recommend to new students that they become familiar with the referencing format for those sources that they are likely to use most often, and then they can always refer to individual course handbooks for the more irregular sources that might be used. For example, many students are likely to refer to books, both online and in hard copy. It would also be expected that you would make reference to peer-reviewed articles, and many assignments will make reference to statutory documents and government publications and papers. You are also likely to reference individual chapters in edited books and to reference online videos.

The following table provides examples of different citations and references from a range of sources. Now produce a similar chart using resources from your own course reading and research, making sure that you follow the referencing guidelines for your own institute.

Table 4.1 illustrates how these more familiar resources will be cited (referred to in your work) and referenced (listed within the reference list). If you are a visual and practical learner, you might want to transfer this information to the reference die template (Figure 4.1) that is illustrated below. Each face of the die can be used to write the reference layout for a different source. You can then cut out the template and fold this into a die, which you can keep on your desk as a handy reference tool.

Table 4.1 Citing and referencing: putting it into practice

Source	Citing within your work	How this would appear in a reference list
Book	*Reed and Walker (2015) suggest that...* Where direct quotes are used then these would be inside quotation marks and the page number would appear in the brackets, eg (2015: xx).	Reed, M and Walker, S (2015) *A Critical Companion to Early Childhood Studies.* London: Sage
Peer-reviewed journal article	*Solvason and Elliott (2013) write about...* Where direct quotes are used then these would be inside quotation marks and the page number would appear in the brackets, eg (2013: xx).	Solvason, C and Elliott, G (2013) Why is Research Still Invisible in Further Education? *Journal of Learning Development in Higher Education,* 6: 1–17. [online] Available at: www.aldinhe.ac.uk/ojs/index.php?journal=jldhe&page=article&op=view&path%5B%5D=206&path%5B%5D=139 (accessed 1 November 2015).
Website	*The Foundation Years (www.foundationyears.org.uk) is a useful site for accessing up-to-date information and support specific to early years care and education.*	Foundation Years (2015) [online] Available at: www.foundationyears.org.uk (accessed 1 November 2015).
Statutory document	*The Early Years Foundation Stage (EYFS) Statutory Framework (DfE, 2014) identifies the legal requirements that all early years settings need to meet when considering the care and education of children from birth to five years of age.* Where direct quotes are used then these would be inside quotation marks and the page number would appear in the brackets, eg (DfE, 2014: xx).	Department for Education (DfE) (2014) *Statutory Framework for the Early Years Foundation Stage.* [online] Available at: www.gov.uk/government/uploads/system/uploads/attachment_data/file/335504/EYFS_framework_from_1_September_2014_with_clarification_note.pdf (accessed 2 November 2015).
Newspaper article	*Hanson (2012) argues that...* Where direct quotes are used then these would be inside quotation marks and the page number would appear in the brackets, eg (2012: xx).	Hanson, K (2012) Early years professionals deserve more recognition. *The Guardian,* 18 September. [online] Available at: www.theguardian.com/teacher-network/2012/sep/18/early-years-professionals-deserve-more-recognition (accessed 1 November 2015).
Video	*Krista Kiuru (2014), the Minister of Education in Finland, explores the crucial role of early childhood education and care in promoting children's well-being and equality.*	Kiuru, K (2014) Learning by playing in Finnish early childhood education and care. [online] Available at: www.youtube.com/watch?v=2G0DvLZuW60 (accessed 1 November 2015).

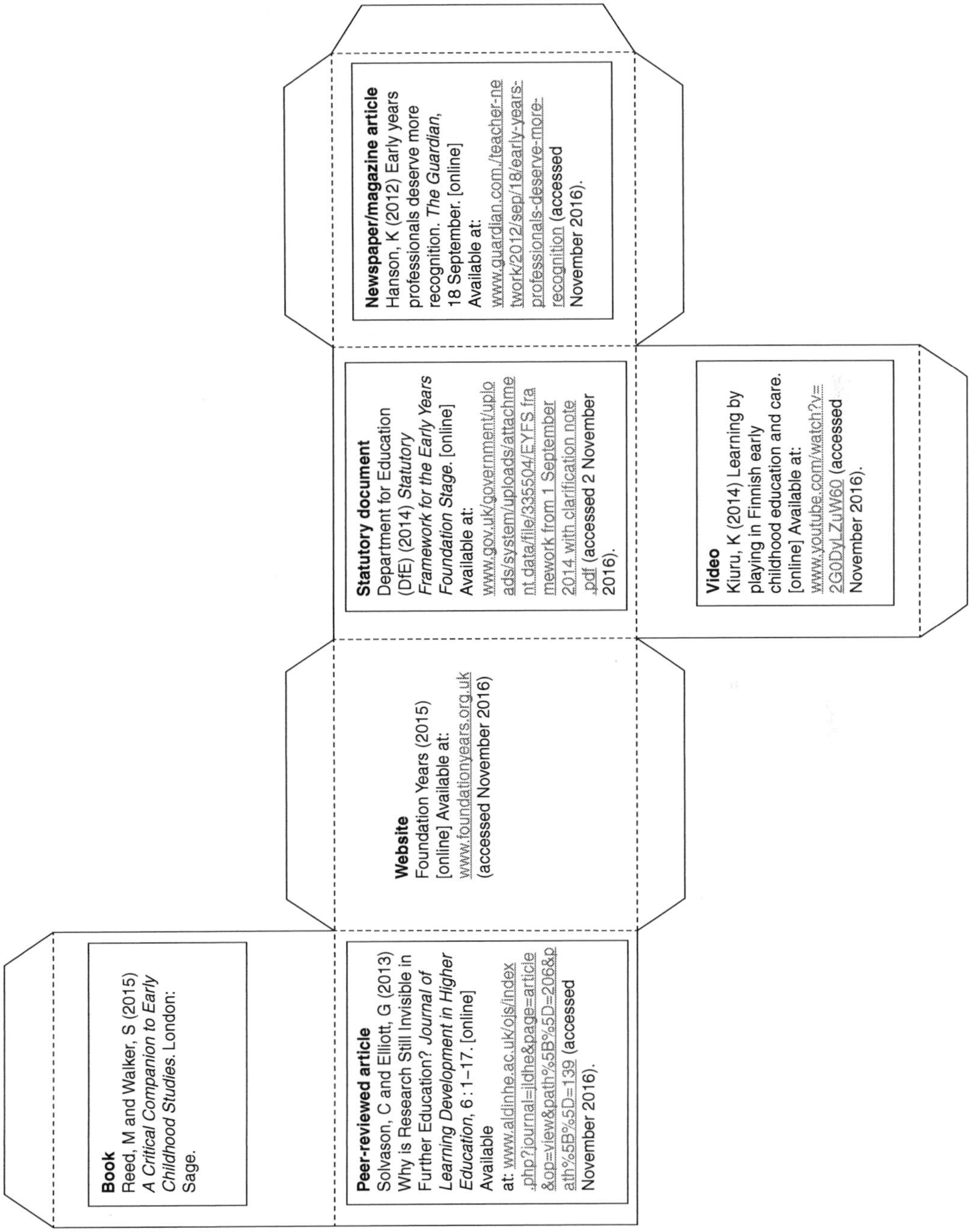

Book
Reed, M and Walker, S (2015) *A Critical Companion to Early Childhood Studies*. London: Sage.

Peer-reviewed article
Solvason, C and Elliott, G (2013) Why is Research Still Invisible in Further Education? *Journal of Learning Development in Higher Education*, 6:1–17. [online] Available at: www.aldinhe.ac.uk/ojs/index .php?journal=jldhe&page=article &op=view&path%5B%5D=206&p ath%5B%5D=139 (accessed November 2016).

Website
Foundation Years (2015) [online] Available at: www.foundationyears.org.uk (accessed November 2016)

Statutory document
Department for Education (DfE) (2014) *Statutory Framework for the Early Years Foundation Stage*. [online] Available at: www.gov.uk/government/uplo ads/system/uploads/attachme nt data/file/335504/EYFS fra mework from 1 September 2014 with clarification note .pdf (accessed 2 November 2016).

Video
Kiuru, K (2014) Learning by playing in Finnish early childhood education and care. [online] Available at: www.youtube.com/watch?v= 2G0DyLZUW60 (accessed November 2016).

Newspaper/magazine article
Hanson, K (2012) Early years professionals deserve more recognition. *The Guardian*, 18 September. [online] Available at: www.guardian.com/teacher-ne twork/2012/sep/18/early-years- professionals-deserve-more- recognition (accessed November 2016).

Figure 4.1 Reference die

Critical question

» *Using the format of Table 4.1, copy and complete the table using sources from your own course of study and making reference to your own institute's referencing guide. Add to this if appropriate, for example how would you reference a chapter in a book? What are the advantages and disadvantages to doing this?*

What is critical reading and writing?

What is meant by critical reading *and what is the difference between critical and non-critical reading?*

A familiar phrase that is regularly used in feedback is the need to read (or write) *more critically*. This is often misinterpreted as the need to criticise what is being read. Instead, when you read critically you examine the reading from a range of different viewpoints, identifying the strengths and weaknesses in the arguments being put forward. You will also make links to how the writing agrees, or disagrees, with the current understanding of the topic being discussed; making reference to other books and articles on the topic. Non-critical reading tends to focus on providing facts with limited evidence of discussion or argument. For instance, if you read an article that simply describes the early years curriculum and the Early Learning Goals, this would be a non-critical example. In contrast, if the article also explored the strengths and weaknesses of the early years curriculum and supported this with evidence from wider, academic reading and research this would suggest a more critical piece of work. Wilson et al (2004) suggest that the ability to read critically is one of the essential generic skills that students should gain during their time at university.

Critical questions

» *Why is it important to understand the differences between critical and non-critical reading?*

» *Read a current article, chapter or blog entry and identify whether they have written in a predominantly critical or non-critical style. What is the impact of this?*

Why is critical reading so important?

Critical reading ensures that you gain an informed view of the topic that you are researching. It means that you have read the views of a number of authors who are knowledgeable about the subject, and that you have used this information to come to an informed viewpoint. Consider that you have been asked to put forward a proposal for the purchase of an expensive piece of equipment for an early years setting, such as a computer. You will most likely research the different computers that are available, then get feedback on the appropriateness of these for the age and stage of the children that will be using it. You will also look at the programs that come with it, the cost of additional programs, the after service, independent reviews and the cost. At the end of this research you will take into account all of the information that you have gathered and then put forward a rationale for the computer that you will be recommending that the setting purchases. If you did not go through this critical process, you would be unlikely to choose the best piece of equipment to meet the needs of your setting and children, and could end up making an expensive mistake. At one level, taking a critical approach ensures that you become an active consumer of information as you consider a range of views on a given topic, and make reference to these, when putting forward your own position about a given topic.

Becoming an academic reader: how to read critically

It is hoped that the introduction has demonstrated that reading critically is about asking lots of questions, and searching for answers, from a range of valid, reliable and academic sources. It is likely that your university lectures will introduce a topic and make reference to a number of different viewpoints. These are signposting you to independent research that should be followed up after each lecture. Similarly, during seminar sessions, small groups of peers are likely to explore a range of themes in more depth, sharing their own research and introducing differing ideas on a subject that you might wish to explore for yourself. Simply put, 'University study is principally concerned with what is not known and not agreed on: ie why something happened, why it is important, what should be done and why it should be done' (Edge Hill University, nd, pp 2–3). The University of Plymouth (2006) has produced a handy leaflet which suggests a number of questions that can be used to support more critical thinking, using what, where, who, when, why, how, what if, so what and what next? These questions could be useful prompts during your critical reading and writing.

Note-taking to support critical reading

A key feature of effective reading is the quality of notes that are made throughout the process. Use the prompting questions, identified in the previous section, to highlight key statements that would answer these questions. Make annotations in the margins of paper documents, use the notes facility on pdf documents or the comments box on Word documents to record your observations. This information could be used to inform the annotated bibliography referred to previously. Be careful that your notes do not 'overwhelm' the piece of writing that is being examined, just focus on the key issues. Some useful examples can be found in the Oxford Brookes University guide *Be More Critical!* (2009, pp 10–11).

The following activity will give you the chance to read in a more critical way. The articles and papers identified in the box below are all accessible online, and have a common theme centred on the controversial issue of school readiness.

ANNOTATED READING ACTIVITY

School readiness: who's right?

Choose at least three of these references, with the intention of gaining an understanding of the issue from a range of perspectives. As you read, annotate the reading sources, using some of the strategies identified in the previous section, and answer the questions posed in the section on *How to read critically*. Are there any other references that have been identified and that would be useful to follow up in order to provide a more secure argument?

- Brown, C P and Pickard, H (2014) Balancing the School Readiness Equation in Early Learning Environments. *Childhood Education*, 90(6): 418–26.

- O'Connor, D and Angus, J (2012) Give Them Time – An Analysis of School Readiness in Ireland's Early Education System: A Steiner Waldorf Perspective. *Education 3–13: International Journal of Primary, Elementary and Early Years Education*, 1(10). [online] Available at: www.ecswe.org/wren/documents/Give-them-time-school-readiness-20120913.pdf (accessed November 2016).

- Ofsted (2014) *Are You Ready? Good Practice in School Readiness Campaign*. [online] Available at: www.gov.uk/government/publications/are-you-ready-good-practice-in-school-readiness (accessed November 2016).

- Paton, G (2013) Start schooling later than age five, say experts. *The Telegraph*, 11 September. [online] Available at: www.telegraph.co.uk/education/educationnews/10302249/Start-schooling-later-than-age-five-say-experts.html (accessed November 2016).

- Rhode Island Kids Count (2005) *Getting Ready. Findings from the National School Readiness Indicators Initiative A 17 State Partnership*. [online] Available at: www.doe.k12.de.us/cms/lib09/DE01922744/Centricity/Domain/146/gettingready.pdf?_sm_au_=iVV6P5RRRDvMrfHr (accessed November 2016).

- Too much too soon campaign (nd). [online] Available at: www.toomuchtoosoon.org/school-readiness.html (accessed November 2016).

- UNICEF (2012) *School Readiness A Conceptual Framework*. [online] Available at: www.unicef.org/education/files/Chil2Child_ConceptualFramework_FINAL(1).pdf (accessed November 2016).

Critical question

» *Reflect upon your own opinion about the topic. How will you ensure that this does not unfairly influence your judgement?*

Making a judgement: exploring the strengths and weaknesses of an argument

Having completed the above activity, it is now time to pull together the different strands of the discussion in order to provide a cohesive overview.

Critical question

» *Use your annotated notes to synthesise the range of arguments that have been presented, and the evidence that has been provided, in order to formulate an answer to the title 'School readiness: who's right?'*

You might find it useful to use a template with a basic set of questions to support a critical discussion. An example can be found in Table 4.2 and can be populated with your own focus questions, or you could select appropriate questions from those listed below.

Table 4.2 *Synthesising information: comparing notes*

Critical question prompts	Article 1	Article 2	Article 3
What did the article say? What key points/ideas were identified?			
How relevant was the article to the topic of study?			

- After completing the above activity, do you feel that the evidence you have collected from the different sources reflects the differing opinions on the subject?

- Do you feel that this is sufficient evidence to make a reliable and informed judgement?

The following, additional questions may allow you to explore the strengths and weaknesses of an argument in greater depth and help you to reach a more secure conclusion.

- What did the different articles say? What key points/ideas were identified?

- How relevant was the article to the topic of study?

- Is the information reliable? Where was it published, ie in a magazine, peer-reviewed journal, textbook? How current is the article, when was it written?

- What are the limitations, weaknesses and shortcomings of the source?

- What evidence have the author(s) put forward? Is this descriptive or analytical?

- Who is the author? Do they demonstrate any bias, or hidden assumptions?

- Does the evidence provided support the author's assertions?

- Has the author referred to contrasting views?

- Do you agree/disagree with the author – why?

Having completed the initial reading, did this signpost you to any other sources that would help you to make a more secure decision? What do you know about the topic – are you able to make any links to what you have observed in practice? Now analyse the different arguments and then provide your opinion based upon the facts that you have considered, and ensure that you are aware of any personal biases that could impact upon your final decision. As you begin to draw together your final thoughts, the University of Manchester (2015) has produced a useful phrasebank to support academic writing, with specific *sentence starters* that can be used in relation to *critical writing*. It would be worthwhile spending some time exploring this site and considering how you could use this in your writing.

What is critical writing?

Students will often report that lecturers describe their work as *too descriptive* or *not critical enough*. Critical writing does not mean that you have to be critical of something. It is about ensuring that you have researched any topic in depth, and making sure that you provide a balanced discussion which considers the evidence you have found. But it is not just about *describing* what you have researched. It is about considering the strength of the differing viewpoints and arguments that you have read, evaluating their strengths, weaknesses and relevance to the argument. In this sense *criticality* means that you have considered all of the options and made a judgement based on this evidence. The activities that you have completed earlier in this chapter are the key stages to be completed in order to produce an effective piece of critical writing. You will have the opportunity to explore this topic more fully in later chapters.

Critical questions

» *What is the difference between 'critical writing' and 'descriptive writing'? Review your notes on 'school readiness' and consider how 'descriptive' or 'critical' they are. How might you ensure that your work is more critical?*

» *Why is so much emphasis placed on writing critically?*

Chapter reflections

During the course of your degree, you will spend a significant amount of time engaged in reading to support a deep understanding of the subjects being studied. There is no shortcut to this. Without extensive reading from a wide range of sources, you will not gain a real understanding of, or be aware of, the differing perceptions and biases that are attached to the topics being discussed.

The significance of accurate referencing has been examined and you have been encouraged to practise referencing a range of sources, ensuring that you follow your own institution's guidelines.

In addition to reading, the importance of effective note-taking is key to focusing on the key messages within a text and the ability to record these effectively. A range of strategies have been introduced to support you in this, and like the best advice it is there to be reflected upon and developed to suit your own learning styles.

Rather than reading passively, this chapter has outlined the importance of active reading that explores a range of perspectives while being aware of the impact of bias on these.

Further reading

Cottrell, S (2011) *Critical Thinking Skills: Developing Effective Analysis and Argument.* 2nd ed. London: Palgrave MacMillan.

Eales-Reynolds, L-J, Judge, B, McCreery, E and Jones, P (2013) *Critical Thinking Skills for Education Students.* 2nd ed. London: Learning Matters/Sage.

References

Brown, C P and Pickard, H (2014) Balancing the School Readiness Equation in Early Learning Environments. *Childhood Education*, 90(6): 418–26.

Edge Hill University (nd) *Critical Analysis Explained.* [online] Available at: www.eshare.edgehill.ac.uk/1958/1/AW_Guide_CA_explained.pdf (accessed November 2016).

Massey University (2012) Identifying academic sources. [online] Available at: owll.massey.ac.nz/academic-writing/identifying-academic-sources.php (accessed November 2016).

O'Connor, D and Angus, J (2012) Give Them Time – An Analysis of School Readiness in Ireland's Early Education System: A Steiner Waldorf Perspective. *Education 3–13: International Journal of Primary, Elementary and Early Years Education*, 1(10): [online] Available at: www.ecswe.org/wren/documents/Give-them-time-school-readiness-20120913.pdf (accessed November 2016).

Ofsted (2014) *Are You Ready? Good Practice in School Readiness Campaign.* [online] Available at: www.gov.uk/government/publications/are-you-ready-good-practice-in-school-readiness (accessed November 2016).

Oxford Brookes University (2009) '*Be More Critical!' A Practical Guide for Health and Social Care Students.* [online] Available at: www.brookes.ac.uk/library/health/Be%20More%20Critical%20Guide%202011_web.pdf?fDocumentId=2622 (accessed November 2016).

Rhode Island Kids Count (2005) *Getting Ready: Findings from the National School Readiness Indicators Initiative A 17 State Partnership.* [online] Available at: www.doe.k12.de.us/cms/lib09/DE01922744/Centricity/Domain/146/gettingready.pdf?_sm_au_=iVV6P5RRRDvMrfHr (accessed November 2016).

The State of Queensland (Queensland Studies Authority) (2006) *Annotated Bibliography: Early Years Curriculum Materials. Research on Curriculum and Pedagogy for the Early Years.* [online] Available at: www.qcaa.qld.edu.au/downloads/p_10/ey_annotated_bibliography.pdf (accessed November 2016).

Too much too soon campaign (nd). [online] Available at: www.toomuchtoosoon.org/school-readiness.html (accessed November 2016).

Turnitin (nd). [online] Available at: http://turnitin.com/en_us/turnitin-for-higher-education (accessed November 2016).

UNICEF (2012) *School Readiness: A Conceptual Framework.* [online] Available at: www.unicef.org/education/files/Chil2Child_ConceptualFramework_FINAL(1).pdf (accessed November 2016).

University of Manchester (2015) Academic phrasebank: Being critical. [online] Available at: www.phrasebank.manchester.ac.uk/being-critical/ (accessed November 2016).

University of Plymouth (2006) *Model to Generate Critical Thinking.* [online] Available at: www.nottingham.ac.uk/student-services/documents/criticalthinkingmodelflyerhandoutfromlearnhigher.pdf (accessed November 2016).

University of Worcester (2012) *Study Skills Advice Sheet: Plagiarism and Referencing.* [online] Available at: www.worcester.ac.uk/studyskills/documents/Plagiarism_and_Referencing_2012.pdf (accessed November 2016).

University of Worcester (2015) *Harvard Referencing Guide: How to Cite & Reference in University of Worcester Harvard Style.* 5th ed. 2015/16. [online] Available at: https://drive.google.com/file/d/0B2wGAyiHm0nAdWlwSTNxOEZhRzA/view (accessed November 2016).

Wilson, K, Devereaus, L, Macken-Horarik, M and Trimingham-Jack, C (2004) *Reading Readings: How Students Learn to (Dis)engage with Critical Reading.* [online] Available at: citeseerx.ist.psu.edu/viewdoc/download?doi=10.1.1.476.7752&rep=rep1&type=pdf (accessed November 2016).

5 Assessment and feedback

NICOLA STOBBS AND STUART GALLAGHER

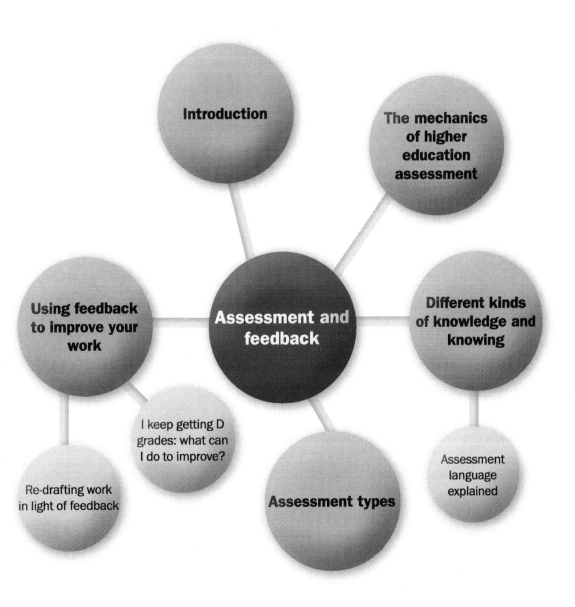

- Introduction
- The mechanics of higher education assessment
- Using feedback to improve your work
- **Assessment and feedback**
- Different kinds of knowledge and knowing
- I keep getting D grades: what can I do to improve?
- Re-drafting work in light of feedback
- Assessment types
- Assessment language explained

The focus of individual programmes varies, but... the subject is based on the principle of developing independent, critical students who are insightful advocates of children.

QAA (2014, p 1)

Introduction

Assessment is an inevitable and crucial aspect of your engagement with learning and your development. This chapter aims to demystify much of what makes academic assessment off-putting and enable you to see it as providing an invitation to demonstrate your increasingly central role in making a difference to children's care and education. It will help you prepare for successful assessment in a range of formative and summative tasks. It focuses on *knowing what* is being assessed and then moving on to *learning how* to organise relevant material in writing *to persuade* an assessor *why* your response meets the task requirements.

This chapter encourages you to view your preparation for assignments in a framework of feedback and *feed-forward*. It shows the difference in expectation at each level and gives examples of how assignments will develop as your experience and thinking evolve.

Finally, in order to address the issue of improving assessment outcomes (*'I keep getting Ds! How can I improve my work?'*), the chapter guides you through generic strategies for improvement.

The mechanics of higher education assessment

Assessment in higher education is a process that makes different demands on you, presenting more difficult challenges as you progress through your course. In recent years, assessment has shifted from Assessment *of* Learning (showing that you know lots), to Assessment *for* Learning. This means that the emphasis is on your growing awareness of what is involved in being a successful early years practitioner. You are encouraged to reflect where you are on this journey currently and how preparing for the assignment has supported your progression.

Regardless of the institution you are studying at, your early childhood studies course will be designed in relation to the *Framework for Higher Education Qualifications in England, Wales and Northern Ireland* (QAA, 2008). This means that each assessment you undertake will have been designed to enable you to demonstrate consistent aspects of academic development. We list them here, moving from Level 4 (your first year on a full-time course) through to Level 6 (the third and final year of a full-time bachelor's degree).

Assessment in the first year requires you to demonstrate your *'sound knowledge of the basic concepts'* of early childhood in theory and in practice, as well as *'how to take different approaches to solving problems'* (QAA, 2008, p 16, para 33). Assessors will value your ability *'to communicate accurately'* and to show how, in practice, you took advantage of opportunities to *'exercise [...] some personal responsibility'* (QAA, 2008, p 16, para 33).

Expectations shift at Level 5. Here, your assessor looks for evidence that you have learned, *throughout* your Level 5 studies, not only the principles of early childhood theory and practice, but how '*to apply those principles more widely*' (QAA, 2008, p 18, para 35). The emphasis here is to show you can '*evaluate the appropriateness of different approaches to solving problems*' (QAA, 2008, p 18, para 35).

The framework also requires focus on the quality of your decision-making and whether or not you '*perform effectively*' in the field of early childhood. The shift is from the *know-what + know-how* of Level 4 to the *know-how + know-why* of Level 5.

At Level 6 the terms shift from decision-making and personal reflection to your ability to get to grips with '*a complex body of knowledge*', including research and practice at the forefront of early childhood care and education. Your final year's work will be characterised by the '*analytical techniques and problem-solving skills*' that you will have developed, plus the ability to '*evaluate evidence, arguments and assumptions, to reach sound judgements and to communicate them effectively*' (QAA, 2008, p 19, para 36). Success requires you to produce *new knowledge* and insights. You will be expected to defend your position in relation to evidence. There is little chance of being able to do this well by cramming the night before deadlines.

Different kinds of knowledge and knowing

This ascending classification from *lower-order thinking* to *higher-order thinking* was presented by Benjamin Bloom and his colleagues over half a century ago (Bloom et al, 1956). What became known as *Bloom's taxonomy* originally organised thinking from *knowledge* upwards through to *evaluation*. A more recent revision of the taxonomy (Anderson et al, 2001) offers the following organisation of the kinds of thinking you are expected to demonstrate through the course of your academic journey:

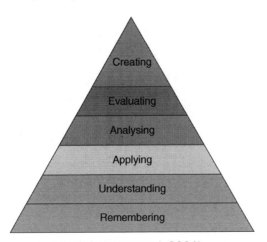

Figure 5.1 *Bloom's taxonomy revised (Anderson et al, 2001)*

Figure 5.1 shows that your assessors will expect you to move away from simply remembering points made in lectures or gleaned from key texts and repeating these in assignments. Instead, you will be expected to demonstrate understanding, and then apply your knowledge, analyse consequences and evaluate the merits of particular approaches before, as we have seen at Level 6, creating new knowledge to contribute to the field of early childhood studies. Once you can apply theory to a practice problem, draw evidence together (and integrate knowledge with experience) to create (synthesise) a new insight, idea or argument, you will see your grades improve.

Assessment language explained

The language of assessment will be found in your modules' intended learning outcomes. It is there that assessment expectations at each level of study will be made clear to you and you must address all of them to pass an assignment. Below is a brief explanation of words that you may encounter when undertaking assessments. The explanations are intended to be indicative rather than universal interpretations of specific assignment tasks.

When required *to evaluate*, consider the extent to which some aspect of theory, practice or knowledge has value based on the evidence you present. Conclude by showing the significant factors that informed your decision.

When asked to assess, present a thorough examination of evidence for and against a particular aspect of practice or theory, coming to an informed conclusion. *Appraising* similarly explores the merits or otherwise of an issue, concept or idea, especially in terms of its contribution to the wider field of early childhood.

Reviewing requires you to return to key texts or experiences to draw out their value to either your own development or the progress of a particular dimension of early childhood practice or studies. You are likely to look at a particular text or experience in depth, or a broad range of texts organised around a particular theme.

When *interpreting*, offer an explanation of the issue or concept, experience or even data and what it means from your own perspective. Explain any patterns or themes that you draw from your evidence.

When *analysing*, break subjects down into their component parts – distinguishing them and showing how they relate to one another. *Critical analysis* adds a range of further evidence that may concur or disagree with your perspective, demonstrating that the issue is not clear-cut.

Synthesising requires you to integrate sources to create a new, coherent perspective. This may mean bringing together what, superficially, would appear to be opposing views to reveal deeper insight.

Critical questions

» *To what extent are the terms above the same or different?*

» *Why is it important to understand these terms?*

» *How do they link to Bloom's (revised) higher-order thinking skills?*

CASE STUDIES

Here are some concrete examples using a case study of undergraduate academic writing to illustrate the expectations of essay content at the three different levels (4–6). The assignment is to *reflect upon the ethics of observation*.

Level 4

As early years practitioners, we have a statutory duty to observe children (DfE, 2014). Informed consent for observing children is normally sought from parents on their child's entry to the setting and is essential to ensure that children are not exploited (Nuremberg Code, 1947). I assumed that by following this process my responsibility to act ethically was fulfilled. However, as I have progressed throughout my first year, I have become aware of the importance of the child's voice and I now consider it imperative not only to gain the consent of parents, but consent and assent from the child themselves. This, however, brings difficulties; I have found that the act of asking children's permission to watch them play impacts on their behaviour and I am uncertain that what I am recording is truly representative of their interests and abilities. While research has confirmed that this is a common issue, referred to as the Observer or Hawthorne Effect (cited in Papatheodorou et al, 2011), research has been limited regarding the way to overcome this.

Level 5

Palaiologou (2012, p 42) defines observation as '*a systematic method of studying human behaviour or phenomena within a specific context and should always have a precise purpose*'. On first reading, I considered this quote from a pedantic perspective. In my experience of observing children, very often observations undertaken were not to provide evidence of a child's assessed knowledge, but instead to provide insight into the child's world; in this regard it could be suggested that they had no precise purpose. However, as I have reflected further I realise that I was using the terms *outcome* and *purpose* synonymously. While narrative observations may not have an initial intended outcome in terms of Assessment of Knowledge, they should always have a precise purpose.

As researchers we have a responsibility not only to do no harm but to do good (Nuremberg Code, 1947) and it could be argued that the continual observation of children where there is not a precise purpose amounts to surveillance. I have seen observations written by practitioners which give very little (if any) new information, suggesting that observations are not being analysed. This has implications from a child development perspective as children may not be supported in their next steps. On a deeper level it could be suggested that observation robs children of the freedom to construct their own culture, described by Sutton-Smith (1997) as a '*play culture*'; '*children always seek to have their own play culture, and within that, resistance against adult power and conventions is a hidden transcript of childhood*' (cited in Wood, 2013, p 11). Robbing children of their culture is clearly not acting in a way that 'does good'. In terms of my own practice I have realised that while watching children to ensure they are safe is a must, justification for continually observing them without respect for their right to privacy is increasingly difficult to assert.

Level 6

As I reflect on my developing understanding of the ethics of child observation, I realise what a value-laden practice it is; I compare it to peeling the layers of an onion. The first layer could be said to represent the subjectivity of the observer and the importance of observer bias awareness (Papatheodorou et al, 2011).

The next layer involves the recognition of childhood as a socially constructed phenomenon (McDowell Clark, 2013; Smidt, 2013) and there are different perspectives on how society's construction of childhood benefits the child. On the one hand, regulations protect children from viewing unsuitable films (for example) and against unrealistic developmental expectations (Kilderry, 2015). However, the compromise is that childhood becomes regulated by the adult world and children's enjoyment of their environment is restricted, leaving '*a trade-off between protection and participation, with loss of power to the child*' (Qvortrup, 2000, p 97). I have been aware of this as an adult observing children in practice and have endeavoured to ensure that my observations have been respectful of children's '*play culture*' (Sutton-Smith, 1997, cited in Wood, 2013, p 11). However, to continue the onion analogy, when peeling away the social-construction layer, I have become increasingly disquieted regarding the way the observation discourse can frame children.

One perspective is that the developmental model as advocated by the EYFS (DfE, 2014) and *Development Matters* (Early Education, 2012) frames adults as all-knowing and powerful, aiming to produce future citizens to replace the retiring generation in the economic market and children as passive recipients of their knowledge (Rix and Parry, 2014). The position of children as passive is well illustrated by Cannella and Viruru (2004, p 110) who note that adults frequently claim that observations '*give children a voice*' as if children are '*allowed*' to speak by benevolent, paternalistic superiors. They cite Said's (1996) juxtaposition of children and the colonial view of orientalism – once viewed through an '*exotic*' lens of European invention; similarly, children have been constructed as '*exotic*', evidenced in dominant discourse by their '*innocence, weakness, immaturity, lack of responsibility and cuteness*' (Cannella and Viruru, 2004, p 110). In critiquing this perspective, the authors propose that this discourse of the static, passive child ready to be moulded by adults enforces the power not only of others over those who are younger, but of us all.

This represents the final layer of the observation onion analogy. When considering whether observations in practice genuinely inform planning for the holistic '*needs and interests of each child*' (DfE, 2014, p 5) or whether the child's voice is subsumed by adults' pre-occupation with outcomes (Katz, 2014), I realise that the practice of observation to discover children's interests is often little more than '*window dressing*' (McDowell Clark, 2013, p 115) resulting in the perpetuation of conformity and the status quo. Upon deeper reflection, I realised that there is no opportunity for practitioners to challenge this and I too am in danger of sleepwalking into maintaining the power hierarchies of establishment systems.

The examples above illustrate how learning throughout your degree will inform the reflective process. In particular, the Level 6 writing demonstrates how reading, reflection and practice experience draw on and extend reading and reflection from Levels 4 and 5. In each case, the writing goes through a process of description of context, analysis of how the part to be examined fits within the whole and then evaluates the limitations of certain perspectives.

As was outlined in Chapter 4, critical writing means ensuring that you include some descriptive elements to introduce context (*what* and *when* types of information), quickly moving on to *Why, how* and *what if?* elements, before finishing with *So what?* and *What now?* questions. In organising your materials, you could divide a piece of paper into sections moving from description through to analysis and on to evaluation. In each section you could add bullet points of content, reflections on/links to practice and references to substantiate your points. This initial organising of materials will help you to keep the thread of your argument going throughout your assignment. Not every paragraph will necessarily include all the sections, but think carefully before dismissing them; how a researcher carried out their data collection, for example, may provide the interesting detail that enables you to spot flaws in their conclusions.

Table 5.1 *Organising your material: using an assessment grid*

What?	When?	Why?	How?	What if?	So what?	What now?

Critical questions

» *What aspects of the Levels 4–6 examples indicate the movement from know-what through to new knowledge?*

» *Complete the assessment grid in Table 5.1 for each of the case study examples at each level. Is there anything missing that you would add to develop each essay?*

» *Using the language of the assessment grid, what learning outcomes would you expect to see for the case study examples?*

Assessment types

There are several different assessment types you may be expected to engage with and each has its own particular requirements. Here we briefly explain the characteristics of each type.

After introducing a main point, *essays* proceed with the main body of argument, divided into paragraphs; each paragraph contains a sub-point that relates clearly to the broader point being made and supports it. A conclusion should summarise the main and sub-points and may make further links to other, related contexts. Essays should be written as continuous prose with no headings.

Reports are likely to include a title page, terms of reference (audience, purpose and methods used), an abstract, a table of contents, an introduction, methods, results, discussion, a conclusion, references and appendices. (Your tutors will detail their own specific requirements.)

Should you be asked to make an *oral presentation*, you will be told which specific presentation skills are being assessed, for example clarity of expression, tone of voice, body language, use of audio-visuals/initiative in gathering sources, effectiveness of the argument, ability to answer questions and interact with an audience, and so on.

You may instead be asked to submit a *podcast* that will demonstrate your ability to speak for a specified amount of time in relation to your own organisation of material and argument. You will need to learn how to record your presentation and how to save it securely so that you can submit your final recording for assessment.

A *portfolio* is your bank or store of evidence, often involving examples from practice, such as reports on your performance, planning documents and reflections linking theory to practice. It should indicate your progression over time, demonstrating the breadth and depth of your ability to apply knowledge and theory to practice situations.

An *annotated bibliography* requires you to review various sources (usually articles in academic journals) to assess the relevance of each to your studies, as well as to evaluate the accuracy and validity of the evidence they present. You should consider each author's background, the article's intended audience and how each compares to other sources you have cited. You will likely also need to explain how each item in your bibliography contributes to your knowledge and learning. Each annotation would normally be about 150 words long.

Using feedback to improve your work

Feedback takes many different forms and can be divided into two types: *summative feedback* sums up your achievement, usually at the end of your module or course, and *formative feedback* informs your understanding of your progress in order for you to improve or maintain the standard of your work. Formative feedback is sometimes referred to as *feed-forward* as it is intended to direct you to what you need to do next (Race, 2014). It may take the form of verbal feedback (when you respond to a question or make a point in sessions or in a tutorial) or it may be written or online feedback (eg via your online journal). For feedback to have the most impact it must be timely; however, it is impossible for tutors to give detailed feedback to up to 60 students within a few days of submission. It is therefore likely that you will be asked to bring some writing to a lecture to gain peer feedback.

Research indicates that students are initially reluctant to engage in this, considering it a the lecturer's responsibility (Biggs, 2003). The research also shows that, even when kept anonymous, students experience anxiety and avoid engaging with this exercise. However, consider the arguments for participating in peer feedback by relating it to the Characteristics of Effective Learning as outlined in the EYFS guidance (DfE, 2014).

One of the Characteristics of Effective Learning is *'playing and exploring – have a go'* (DfE, 2014, p 9). This implies that we should encourage children to take physical risks – which, of course, we should. However, we should also encourage them to take cognitive risks; risking being wrong. It is unfair to expect children to do this if we are unwilling to take a cognitive risk ourselves. As well as the moral case for being willing to 'have a go' and take a risk by allowing your peers to assess your work formatively, subsequently reflecting on the experience in your assignment will elevate your writing to a higher grade. You would now be engaging in what is known as *meta-cognition* – thinking about *how* you are learning as well as *what* you are learning.

Another *Characteristic of Effective Learning* is: '*active learning – children concentrate and keep on trying if they encounter difficulties...*' (DfE, 2014, p 9). While we may accept that children need to be active in their learning, you may feel that this does not apply to you. However, you are more likely to achieve high grades when you engage with the assessment criteria. Your tutor may attempt to transmit this to you in a passive way but it is not going to be as effective as you being actively involved, knowing not just what the criteria are but how to apply them to your own work (Nicol, 2010).

Re-drafting work in light of feedback

When your graded work is returned to you, you are likely to experience an emotional response and you may focus on the grade. However, taking the time to use all your feedback and feed-forward to redraft your work is time well spent.

Below is an example of a student's work, some feedback from the tutor and the subsequent redraft in light of the feedback.

First draft

Piaget (1952) believed in four distinct learning phases regarding his cognitive theory that children go through – sensorimotor, preoperational, concrete operations and formal operations.

Sensorimotor is usually from birth to 2 years, focusing on object permanence; preoperational from 2–7 years, focusing on egocentrism; concrete operations 7–11 years on conservation and finally formal operations from age 11 onwards, manipulating ideas in their heads, such as abstract reasoning (MacBlain, 2014).

Tutor feedback

- Use academic language.

- Avoid description.

- Add analysis and evaluation.

- Make links to practice to illustrate your understanding.

Second draft

Piaget (1952) proposed that children develop cognitively by advancing through distinct phases; sensorimotor (age 0–2), preoperational (age 2–7), concrete operations (age

7–11) and formal operations (age 11 onwards). While Piaget is still respected for his contribution to our understanding of child development, scrutiny by other theorists (eg Donaldson, 1978, Vygotsky, 1978) has highlighted that Piaget drew his conclusions mainly after observing his own children, who lived in an affluent, predominantly white, European country. It could therefore be suggested that it is impossible to make generalisations that apply to all children.

In practice I played a game of *higher or lower* using a pack of cards with a four-year-old child. He could predict that if the card shown was less than 7 there was a greater probability that the next card would be higher, and vice versa, yet according to Piaget this should not happen until the concrete operational stage. If practitioners regarded the stages as anything more than a guide, children may be pigeon-holed in a way that does consider individual and cultural factors.

I keep getting D grades: what can I do to improve?

It can be very disappointing to be awarded low grades, particularly if you have spent a great deal of time on an assignment. Some common reasons for low grades are given below with suggestions for improvement.

'*Your work is descriptive*': take a more analytical approach to your work. Break concepts into small parts – consider using mindmaps to help you discern these parts.

'*You have presented…*': Consider the subject from a wider range of perspectives. Perhaps choose a model of reflective practice to help you make meaning from the evidence you present (see, for example, Brookfield's lenses, Hanson's reflective activism or Johari's Window).

'*You have not addressed all the learning outcomes*': you have overlooked the specific language of the task's intended learning outcomes. Highlight the verbs underpinning each learning outcome – for example, *evaluate, discuss, identify* – and keep a definition close by. Periodically check your writing to ensure that this is what you are actually doing.

'*You have not gone into sufficient depth*': Firstly, check that you have met the word limit. Then, re-read the question and make sure you grasp the wider issues and implications of the assignment. Decide what to delete from your writing in the event you need to provide room for new depth. This will require you to make good choices and accept reasonable trade-offs.

'*Some parts were interesting but not relevant*': Focus on answering the assessment question *only*. Avoid digressions. Write the task on a sticky note and stick it somewhere you will see it often. At the end of each paragraph, check that writing relates clearly and consistently to that task.

'*Your work is poorly structured*': You need paragraphs that follow one another logically. Organise your main points before writing and decide which points follow others. Start by writing the points on sticky notes and then shuffle them around until there is a clear progression between them.

'*You have made grammatical, punctuation and spelling errors*': Read your work aloud using Google Translate, then listen to your work for errors as it is read back to you. Ask a friend to proofread your writing before re-drafting it for submission.

'*Use your own words*': Reflect on and summarise the main point from the source, make a reference to it, then articulate this point from your own perspective. Do not merely change one or two words – if you cannot explain something without looking at your source, consider excluding it.

'*You have not substantiated your argument*': Include supporting evidence. Gather, interpret and evaluate evidence for and against your argument from valid sources, including examples from practice.

'*You are over-reliant on sources*': Aim for quality in your insights and interpretations rather than sheer quantity of listed references. Use sources to support your argument – do not assume that a quotation or reference relieves you of the responsibility to demonstrate your own thinking.

Critical questions

» *In your own words, reflect on the difference between feed-forward and feedback. Can you list opportunities to elicit feedback other than written feedback on your summative assessment?*

» *Write a sample paragraph that could form part of your assignment. Swap it with a friend and apply the suggestions for improvement, asking them to do the same for you. How useful is this?*

Chapter reflections

» *National benchmarks underpin all degree courses, including your early childhood degree.*

» *At each level of your course, expectations of assessment requirements will increase. Examples have been provided for you to consider.*

» *Feedback is best used as feed-forward, to inform and increase your attainment level.*

» *Some generic solutions can be applied to prevent low grades.*

Further reading

Greasley, P (2011) *Doing Essays and Assignments: Essential Tips for Students*. London. Sage.

Moore, S, Neville, C, Murphy, M and Connolly, C (2010) *The Ultimate Study Skills Handbook*. Maidenhead: Open University Press.

Redman, P (2006) *Good Essay Writing*. 3rd ed. London: Sage.

References

Anderson, L W, Krathwoh, D R, Airasian, P W, Cruikshank, K A, Mayer, R E, Pintrich, P R, Raths, J and Witlrock, M C (2001) *A Taxonomy for Learning, Teaching, and Assessing: A Revision of Bloom's Taxonomy of Educational Objectives.* London: Pearson Education.

Biggs, J (2003) *Teaching for Quality Learning at University.* 2nd ed. Maidenhead: Open University Press.

Bloom, B, Englehart, M, Furst, E, Hill, W and Krathwohl, D (1956) *Taxonomy of Educational Objectives. Vol 1: Cognitive Domain.* New York and Toronto: Longmans Green.

Cannella, G S and Viruru, R (2004) *Childhood and Postcolonization: Power, Education, and Contemporary Practice (Changing Images of Early Childhood).* London: Routledge Falmer.

Department for Education (DfE) (2014) *Statutory Framework for the Early Years Foundation Stage. Setting the Standards for Learning, Development and Care for Children from Birth to Five.* [online] Available at: www.gov. uk/government/uploads/system/uploads/attachment_data/file/335504/EYFS_framework_from_1_September_ 2014__with_clarification_note.pdf (accessed November 2016).

Donaldson, M (1978) *Children's Minds.* London: Fontana Press.

Early Education (2012) Development Matters. [online] Available at: www.gov.gg/CHttpHandler.ashx?id=104249&p=0 (accessed January 2017).

Katz, L (2014) International Perspectives on the Early Years Foundation Stage, in Moyles, J, Palmer, J and Georgeson, J (eds) *Early Years Foundations: Critical Issues.* Maidenhead: Open University Press, pp 215–23.

Kilderry, A (2015) Re-positioning Developmentalism, in Reed, M and Walker, R (eds) *A Critical Companion to Early Childhood.* London: Sage, pp 116–26.

MacBlain, S (2014) *How Children Learn.* London: Sage.

McDowell Clark, R (2013) *Childhood in Society.* London: Sage.

Nicol, D (2010) From Monologue to Dialogue: Improving Written Feedback Processes in Mass Higher Education. *Assessment & Evaluation in Higher Education,* 35(5): 501–17.

Palaiologou, I (2012). *Child Observation for the Early Years.* 2nd ed. London: Learning Matters.

Papatheodorou, T, Luff, P and Gill, J (2011) *Child Observation for Learning and Research.* Abingdon, Oxford: Routledge.

Piaget, J (1952) *The Origins of Intelligence in Children.* London: Routledge & Kegan Paul.

Quality Assurance Agency for Higher Education (QAA) (2008) *The Framework for Higher Education Qualifications in England, Wales and Northern Ireland.* Mansfield: QAA.

Quality Assurance Agency for Higher Education (QAA) (2014) *Subject Benchmark Statement: Early Childhood Studies. UK Quality Code for Higher Education Part A: Setting and Maintaining Academic Standards.* [online] Available at: www. qaa.ac.uk/en/Publications/Documents/SBS-early-childhood-studies-14.pdf (accessed November 2016).

Qvortrup, J (2000) Microanalysis of Childhood, in Christensen, P and James, A (eds) *Research with Children: Perspectives and Practices.* London: Falmer Press, pp 66–86.

Race, P (2014) *Making Learning Happen: A Guide for Post-Compulsory Education.* London: Sage.

Rix, J and Parry, J (2014) Without Foundation: The EYFS Framework and its Creation of Needs, in Moyles, J, Palmer, J and Georgeson, J (eds) *Early Years Foundations: Critical Issues.* Maidenhead: Open University Press, pp 203–14.

Smidt, S (2013) *The Developing Child in the 21st Century.* Abingdon, Oxford: Routledge.

Trials of War Criminals before the Nuremberg Military Tribunals under Control Council Law No. 10, Vol. 2 (1949). Washington, DC: US Government Printing Office, pp 181–82. [online] Available at: https://history.nih.gov/research/ downloads/nuremberg.pdf (accessed November 2016).

Vygotsky, L S (1978) *Mind in Society.* Cambridge, MA: Harvard University Press.

Wood, E (2013) *Play, Learning and the Early Childhood Curriculum.* 3rd ed. London: Sage.

6 Understanding and using policy and legislation

**ROSIE WALKER, MIKE REED AND
DERVAL CAREY-JENKINS**

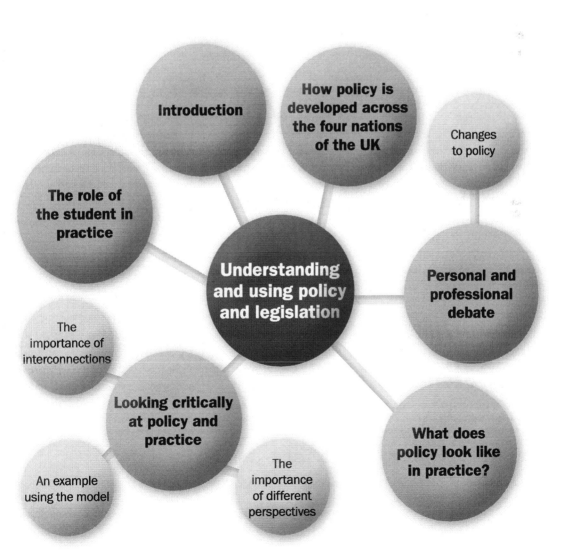

Changes and progress very rarely are gifts from above. They come out of struggles from below.

Noam Chomsky

Introduction

This chapter provides an introduction to the way national early education policy is formed by governments, parliaments and assemblies and translated into action. Policies are an important part of professional life for an early educator because they often determine what the early educator has to do in the workplace. It is therefore vital to consider carefully which factors have influenced the content and design of a policy, in particular, social and political influences. Policies are intended to be a positive and responsive way of developing quality provision and to deliver the best outcomes for children and families. This chapter will explain the ways in which policy in the UK is influenced and forged and the two tiers of policy formation, structural and process, will be explained. The educational policy of the four nations of the UK including national curriculum, the Early Years Foundation Stage (EYFS) (DfE, 2014), integrated working, inspection and accountability will be considered along with examples of local policy concerns. The chapter will provide a mechanism for the ongoing critical investigation of policy which allows those studying early education to recognise the complex range of factors this involves and to consider what this means for children and families.

In the UK (England, Northern Ireland, Wales and Scotland), there is a general agreement that early childhood education and care (ECEC) is seen as important and should be part of education and social policy. Before looking at how policy is formed and how it influences practice, it is helpful to understand what policy is. In general terms, policy is a framework or a guideline for behaviour. Sometimes this can take the form of legislation, sometimes guidance which gives us the opportunity as practitioners to really think about what we are doing in relation to achieving the best outcomes for children and families. Baldock et al (2013) identify four ways in which policy is used: as a stated intention; an action taken by those with responsibility; an organisational or administrative practice; or the indication of a formal adoption of a course of action. Policy is formed through a variety of forms including a statutory (legal) framework as well as direction through government departments.

This implies that a policy will formally belong to a body of people such as a government or indeed a setting, there will be commitment to taking a course of action and it will outline ways in which issues need to be managed. The purpose of policy is either to enhance quality through addressing social issues such as early intervention to support disadvantaged families, or developing opportunities for families such as by encouraging employment by having high-quality childcare for them to access. In other words, policy relates to quality and an understanding of what makes for quality provision.

How policy is developed across the four nations of the UK

Within the four nations of the UK, a process of devolution has meant that since 1999 government has been decentralised to give more powers to the three nations which together with England make up the UK. This resulted in the creation of the Scottish Parliament, the National Assembly for Wales and the Northern Ireland Assembly. In terms of early childhood and primary school education, this has meant that each of the four nations has a different curriculum for its children. In England, for example, this is EYFS and national curriculum. These policies and practices have been shaped over time and are inevitably subjected to review and change. Having been introduced in 2006, the EYFS was revised in 2012 and most recently in 2014. It is therefore wise to keep up to date with the policies of each nation and importantly the reviews and changes that take place. Take time to look at the web links at the end of the chapter and you will find quite significant similarities and differences in terms of national priorities, curriculum content (what young children should know and do at a particular time in their lives), and economic and political influences.

However, each nation will have in place:

- early education goals – long and short term;

- national standards for care and welfare;

- inspection and accountability processes;

- an early education curriculum that includes the importance of working with parents and carers;

- regulations about qualifications for practitioners and ways to safeguard the welfare of children.

Differences and distinctions emerge with regard to the way each government, parliament or assembly designs its curriculum and prioritises the finance it provides for early education. These are structural features of policy. There are also very significant but less visible influences upon policy which are called process features. This is how policy is actually enacted on the ground, which means the day-to-day interactions between professionals in the setting and what children and families actually experience as a result of a policy decision. This relies on the actions of people who actually implement policy and are therefore effectively translating the views of government into practice. To a parent and child this represents the very real face of policy and practice. What they experience may well be guided by regulations or curriculum design but it will also be about warmth, kindness, concern for others, professional behaviour and the quality of planned learning opportunities, which include teaching and learning. In essence, these are the features of policy which they can 'see' and which have a direct impact on children's development and well-being.

Educational policies emerge when governments put in place strategies to educate, care for and protect the welfare of young children. Policies are influenced by interconnected factors such as:

- research evidence which suggests the best way to educate and care for young children and protect their welfare;

- the political leanings of government and how the government wishes to steer policy so that it meets its objectives;

- the economic cost of implementing a policy;

- the social and cultural factors which may influence policy;

- what needs to be put in place to make this happen, such as training or buildings or other resources.

Within each nation, there will be regulatory and inspection processes in place to determine how a setting is meeting national standards set by a government organisation; for example, in England the Office for Standards in Education, Children's Services and Skills (Ofsted) will undertake this role and report back to policy makers on the effectiveness of the services offered. Their policy 'position' cannot be ignored as these inspection services offer a determinant of quality which emanates from regulation and inspection processes (Ofsted, 2015).

Critical questions

When you are next visiting an early education setting (or looking online at inspection reports), consider the way the provision:

» *follows early childhood quality curriculum goals and aims;*

» *promotes qualifications to develop a quality workforce;*

» *knows what works through research and promotes family and community engagement;*

» *follows regulations and strategies such as adult to child ratios, curriculum content and inspection and monitoring requirements;*

» *demonstrates positive interactions between practitioners and children that show warmth, care and consideration, which are aimed at allowing children to have a positive learning experience.*

You can then think about when these features are interconnected, for example a policy that promotes a well-designed curriculum implemented by caring well-trained, well-qualified, capable staff who are able to work in an integrated way with other professionals working with children; the result is likely to be effective learning and quality practice. It is therefore highly important for those who work directly with children to have a clear understanding of the influence of policy and to continuously question how and why they are required to implement policy in practice.

Personal and professional debate

Policies are important because they shape the educational world of the child and directly influence the professional world of the early education practitioner. All governments argue how their particular policy has the same aim: to build a solid and lasting framework for the development of quality early education. However, there are many different perspectives about what this actually means and how it can be applied and managed. Consequently, there are a variety of opinions about any policy and there is always questioning and debate.

- Who are the opinion formers (politicians, media and educationalists) who are proposing a particular policy or change to an existing policy?

- Where did their evidence for a policy or any change to policy come from?

- Does the policy (or any changes to existing policy) have a clear aim and purpose?

- What resources are necessary to make it work?

- How will it be implemented? By whom and over what timescale?

- What are the costs, both socially and financially, and what will the early education profession need to do in order to implement the policy?

It is what Apple (2003, p 1) sees as part of a never-ending professional and personal debate: he argues that the educational system will constantly be in the middle of crucial struggles over definitions of what is the right way to do things and who should benefit the most from government policies and practices.

Changes to policy

A national election may bring a change in government policy, as will an economic problem or changing government priorities. Policy change may also occur as a result of a government review of the curriculum or an existing policy. Policy can change as the result of an incident that has threatened the welfare of children and consequently requires a change in regulation or policy. Politicians and policy makers are therefore always shaping an existing policy or introducing new structures. These are called the drivers of policy formation.

When it comes to a significant change of policy – for example, after a general election – the policy makers will be asking questions such as:

- Why is this aspect of early education a real priority?

- Is there political and public support to make changes?

- Is it practical?

- What will it cost?

- What are the benefits?

- How long will it take to implement?

Early education policy will also be shaped by other forces. For example:

- A policy which has at its core improving educational outcomes for all children, especially the most disadvantaged.

- A policy that prioritises learning aims for young children. The intention is to better prepare them for entry into school.

- There may be other social and economic priorities. For example, seeing childcare not only as a way of providing a secure base for children's learning but as a way of putting in place day care provision that will promote access to employment – especially for mothers and female carers.

- The way national policies have to reach all early education provision – for example, large nurseries, children's centres, childminders and the voluntary sector.

- The way a policy can be monitored and subjected to regulation, which means inspection and monitoring.

- The capability of the workforce to implement the policy.

These forces move policy much wider than a measure to enhance effective learning and there are inevitably tensions between some of these objectives which widens the debate about the nature of early education.

Critical questions

Think of the settings you have worked in so far and consider the different ways that national policy has been implemented.

» *Were there similarities in the ways national policy was implemented?*

» *What were the factors that may have influenced the ways that national policy was implemented in your different settings? For example, do children's ages and stages of development impact on policy implantation? If you think they do, give examples.*

What does policy look like in practice?

Below is a snapshot of an imaginary national policy: *partnership working with parents and carers*. This aspect is chosen because it is a local concern found within all the policy structures in the four nations of the UK.

The aim is to describe the policy and show what this looks like in practice. We hope this shows how policy implementation is not a simple task and requires considerable energy, commitment and professional skill.

Table 6.1 Policy in practice

An example of one policy	In practice this can mean...
The EYFS Framework (2014) requires that parents be provided with a written summary of their child's progress in the prime areas of learning at age two (www.foundationyears.org.uk/files/2012/03/A-Know-How-Guide.pdf). This is an example of a national policy. However, it can be interpreted flexibly locally as it does not require the check to be completed in a prescribed or standard format. This policy prioritises the value of partnership working between practitioners and parents/carers. The policy is then translated into regulations which are monitored by inspection.	*Finding ways for parents to contribute to the organisation and management of the provision.* *Meeting with parents on a regular basis – for example, to keep parents informed about the ways children learn in the setting.* *Newsletter for parents – online information for parents.* *Recording examples of the way children and parents feel secure when they start at the setting and equally secure when they are ready to transfer to the next stage in their learning.*

Table 6.1 (cont.)

An example of one policy	In practice this can mean...
The policy sees relationships with parents as central in supporting the well-being and development of the child.	*Developing ways to assist parents in helping their children to learn.*
	Using parental questionnaires or asking questions at parent meetings to find out what parents think about the provision and how it can be improved.
	All staff and volunteers should be professionally aware of their responsibilities surrounding the protection of children from harm and what to do and how to approach parents if there are concerns. This should include knowing which agencies to contact and what to do if there are concerns about a child's welfare.

Looking critically at policy and practice

We hope you are now becoming aware of how policy is formed and have an understanding of some of the issues surrounding its implementation.

The intention of this chapter is to enable you to critically examine policy through a number of standpoints in order to gain a deeper understanding of how it is forged and how national policy may be implemented locally. The idea is not to define what a particular policy should contain or the way children should be educated. Instead, the aim is to concentrate on the way the policy is forged and influenced by a multiplicity of features – some are easily visible such as specific goals or targets, others are less visible features such as political ideas, personal values and beliefs. Therefore, there is a need to view policy in the round by considering the views of all involved in the learning process, including the perspective of parents and the child.

To do this, we suggest using a process based on the work of Carey-Jenkins (2015), as we see this as a way of providing a close examination of educational issues. Her work has therefore been adapted for this chapter as a way of shedding light on the components of policy, and focusing thinking in order to consider what are called multiple perspectives (Merriam et al, 2007):

> *This means seeing things through different viewpoints and the aim is to reflect and develop a deeper understanding of how political and educational theory can be aligned with practice.*

The process starts by looking at early education policy from six different viewpoints. Figure 6.1 indicates what each of these are and briefly summarises their particular focus.

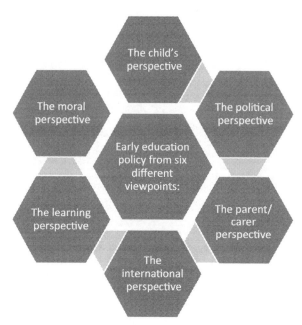

Figure 6.1 *Policy from six different viewpoints*

The different viewpoints can be summarised as:

- **The moral perspective.** How will educational beliefs relate to an examination of the underlying values of a policy?

- **The child's perspective.** Does the child have an entitlement to quality early education? Does the policy support this view? How will the child experience a particular policy?

- **The political perspective.** How will the policy be translated into legislation and regulation? What is its impact on society and is a policy sustainable?

- **The parent/carer perspective.** How will policy look through the eyes of a parent?

- **The learning perspective.** Is the policy rooted in a learning process which is based on research and has educational integrity?

- **The international perspective.** Is it useful to examine wider views and approaches which may accept or challenge the formation and application of a policy?

The importance of different perspectives

The moral perspective

Early educators are likely to have a core set of values that may well define the types of practitioners we are. We use these either consciously or unconsciously in order to reflect on and consider the values that underpin our practice. It is therefore difficult, if not impossible, to separate day-to-day practice in our provision from the underpinning principles that drive us.

Therefore, the moral perspective helps us to consider if policy addresses equality and equity, inclusive practice, access and achievement for all.

The child's perspective

The child is the learner at the centre of what we do. An effective policy should therefore take account of key principles of curriculum design that reflect the child's needs in its broadest sense, including academic, social and emotional needs. Any policy should also listen to and respond to the child's voice, which means seeing things from the child's perspective. A policy should actually mean something to children and not just say it has listened to their viewpoints. For example, children's rights as enshrined in the United Nations Convention on the Rights of the Child (UN General Assembly, 1989; Clark et al, 2005) should be truly embedded in any policy.

The political perspective

Whether as professionals, students, parents/carers or practitioners, it is important to ask a question: what is the legitimate role of government in education? As critical and reflective practitioners, we need to understand and accept that change is a constant and can be a force for good (Fullan, 2001). However, we also need to recognise and challenge the extent to which political views (including those of differing political parties either in office or opposition) might influence and adopt changes. For example, it can be argued that successive governments in the UK have moved early education towards being centrally controlled thereby placing too much store on the process of regulation and inspection. Other commentators think differently and see the process as an opportunity for the profession to show its professional capability by having clear standards and effective ways to monitor quality. The key issue is not about who is right or wrong but about understanding the issues and participating in the debate.

The parent/carer perspective

The quality and effectiveness of early education is a significant predictor of future success and stronger still is the impact of the home (Sammons et al, 2008). Therefore, whether a person is a practitioner or policy maker, it is important to question and reflect on whether high-quality early years provision can support all young learners (and their families) and help to remove the potential barriers to learning. It is also important to ask if a policy reflects the views of all parents, because it is usually those from higher socio-economic groups who are heard the most. In which case, should a professional be an advocate for parents and the rights of all parents? Should they therefore attempt to view any policy through the eyes of all parents and consider how it may affect families in the local community?

The learning perspective

It is very important to understand and recognise the key theories about children's early learning as these have a pronounced impact on policy. Indeed, it would be unusual for any policy not to take account of models of early learning. For example, this could involve having a clear understanding of the influence of the social world which the child inhabits and considering the original work of a key theorist such as Bronfenbrenner (1979). This is not to say his views are the only interpretation of how children learn; other views need to be considered. The key issue is to understand and challenge what is meant by effective early learning.

The international perspective

Examining a policy from an international perspective can provide different viewpoints, which can allow a rigorous comparison to be made between policies in different parts of the world. For example, there is a growing body of international research evidence that indicates that parents play a crucial role in enhancing educational outcomes for children (Sylva et al, 2010, 2012). There is far less evidence regarding the impact of early interventions where practitioners directly engage with parents (DfE, 2012). Nevertheless, an international commitment to early intervention with parents continues to gather momentum. It is therefore important to consider policy and practice from other nations. This may highlight differences but also some of the common issues with regard to working with parents.

An example using the model

In the example given in Table 6.1 of the EYFS Progress Check at age 2 it can be seen that the *moral perspective* would allow us to consider if this policy embodies principles of inclusive practice and equality for all children. Although this is a universal requirement for all children attending settings, the moral lens may cause us to question how this might be provided for children not accessing early years provision. Could this also be a way of making children feel failures at a very young age and does it allow for the diversity of very young children? The *child's perspective* in developing the check is important and advice is provided about supporting children to participate in the celebration of their achievement. However, how well is this achieved in all settings? The *political perspective* may lead us to understand that the purpose of the check is primarily economic as identifying needs early and dealing with these is more cost effective to society and reduces the need for more expensive specialised services later on. From the *parent perspective*, the check can cement partnerships between home and setting and support parents in enabling their child to develop to their full potential, but conversely they may feel that potential problems are being identified too early and that their parenting is being judged. The *learning perspective* may ensure that the policy is based on sound theories of child development and learning but we could perhaps ask what training is being given to staff in carrying out the check.

The importance of interconnections

Although it is important to view policy through different perspectives, it is essential to remember they are interconnected. It is therefore important to compare one perspective with another and see how they relate to each other. As this is done it is possible to consider if there is one aspect carrying more weight than another. For example, consider the political influence over the child's rights or ask if the policy is driven by the needs of a particular group of parents or the views of particular educators.

Table 6.2 *Critical questions when exploring a policy*

What is the aim of the policy?
Why is it being proposed?
Who was consulted as it was formed?
Who is it for?
When will it be reviewed and how will it be evaluated/researched so as to consider its impact?
Now look at the policy through:
the moral perspective
the child's perspective
the political perspective
the perspective of the parent
the learning perspective
the international perspective

The role of the student in practice

We hope that this chapter has allowed you to realise the importance of those studying early education looking critically at the design and development of policy. University education is important as it provides a detailed exploration of what has influenced and shaped early education and it allows you to critically examine what goes on and importantly to ask questions that unpack issues and allow learning to take place. Therefore, you are gaining the skills to interpret and critically examine a policy and understand the ideologies on which policy is based, and as part of your studies to share ideas with other students and enter into what we call *the policy debate*. As you do this you will be clarifying issues and sourcing information as well as evaluating, reflecting, organising and analysing material. You will also be gathering information, drawing things together and engaging in analysis and reflection – in which case, you will be using critical analysis to explore policy and practice.

Policy has a pronounced effect on practice and influences professional roles in a setting. Developing a policy – however well intentioned – does not make it work. It needs to be closely examined as to its implementation on the ground, and policy makers need to be aware that changes to policy and practice have to be carefully managed. Therefore, a practitioner has to develop ways to translate policy and regulations into meaningful actions in their own settings and community. The skills and knowledge that you have gained will allow you to play an important role in achieving this within settings. Through your studies you will gain the knowledge and understanding to interpret government policies in a way that will be useful to the culture and values of your own setting.

Critical question

» *As a student practitioner, what would you consider are your responsibilities in relation to understanding policy?*

Chapter reflections

» *Sometimes policy can be highly effective and may be welcomed by professional groups and parents.*

» *Sometimes a policy can result in pleasing no one because it may not have been thought through and the implications may not have been mapped against the perspectives identified in this chapter.*

» *Policy should be viewed as something to be accepted as part of a professional response to change, but it should also be interrogated and tested in practice.*

Further reading

Updates on policy and practice in the UK nations.

www.gov.uk/government/policies/childcare-and-early-education

This is the government website which provides details of general policies, practices and updates. It allows you to navigate to web links which tell you about changes in policies such as the way early education is regulated and inspected.

In Scotland, information is available from: www.educationscotland.gov.uk/learningandteaching/earlylearningandchild-care/about/index.asp

This site also allows navigation to regulation and inspection policy from the Scottish Care Inspectorate: www.education-scotland.gov.uk/learningandteaching/earlylearningandchildcare/about/qa/index.asp

In Wales similar information can be obtained from: http://gov.wales/topics/educationandskills/earlyyearshome/?lang=en

In Northern Ireland, information can be obtained from:

Department of Education (Northern Ireland) (DENI) (2012) *Learning to Learn. A Framework for Early Years Education and Learning.* [online] Available at: www.deni.gov.uk/articles/learning-learn (accessed November 2016).

Other useful reading includes:

Department for Education (DfE) (2015) *Pedagogy in Early Childhood Education and Care (ECEC): An International Comparative Study of Approaches and Policies.* Research brief, by S Wall, I Litjens and M Taguma. [online] Available at: www.oecd.org/unitedkingdom/early-childhood-education-and-care-pedagogy-review-england.pdf (accessed November 2016).

Myers, R G (2005) *In Search of Quality Programmes of Early Childhood Care and Education.* Paper prepared for the 2005 EFA Global Monitoring Report: Early Childhood Care and Education (ECCE). [online] Available at: http://unesdoc.unesco.org/images/0014/001466/146677e.pdf (accessed November 2016).

References

Apple, M (2003) *The State and the Politics of Knowledge.* London: Routledge Falmer.

Baldock, P, Fitzgerald, D and Kay, J (2013) *Understanding Early Years Policy.* 3rd ed. London: Sage.

Bronfenbrenner, U (1979) *Bronfenbrenner, The Ecology of Human Development: Experiments by Nature and Design.* Cambridge, MA: Harvard University Press.

Brookfield, S (1995) *Becoming a Critically Reflective Teacher*. San Francisco, CA: Jossey-Bass.

Carey-Jenkins, D (2015) Whose Curriculum Is It Anyway? in Reed, M and Walker, R (eds) *A Critical Companion to Early Childhood*. London: Sage: pp 193–205. [online] Available at: https://study.sagepub.com/reedandwalker (accessed November 2016).

Clark, A, Kjorholt, A T and Moss, P (2005) *Beyond Listening: Children's Perspectives on Early Childhood Services*. Bristol: Policy Press.

Department for Education (2014) Statutory Framework for the Early Years Foundation Stage. [online] Available at: www.gov.uk/government/uploads/system/uploads/attachment_data/file/335504/EYFS_framework_from_1_September_2014__with_clarification_note.pdf (accessed January 2017).

Fullan, M (2001) *Leading in a Culture of Change*. San Francisco, CA: Jossey-Bass.

Merriam, S B, Caffarella, R S and Baumgartner, L M (2007) *Learning in Adulthood: A Comprehensive Guide*. 3rd ed. San Francisco, CA: Jossey-Bass.

Ofsted (2015) *Inspection Outcomes of Early Years Providers by Staff Qualifications*. [online] Available at: www.gov.uk/government/uploads/system/uploads/attachment_data/file/468869/Inspection_outcomes_of_early_years_providers_by_staff_qualifications.pdf (accessed November 2016).

Sammons, P, Sylva, K, Melhuish, E, Siraj-Blatchford, I and Taggart, B (2008) *Influences on Children's Cognitive and Social Development in Year 6 (EPPE 3–11)*. Nottingham: DCSF.

Sylva, K, Melhuish, E, Sammons, P, Siraj-Blatchford, I and Taggart, B (2010) *Evidence from the Effective Pre-School and Primary Education Project*. London: Routledge.

Sylva, K, Melhuish, E C, Sammons, P, Siraj-Blatchford, I and Taggart, B (2012) *Effective Pre-School, Primary and Secondary Education 3–14 Project (EPPSE 3–14). Final Report from the Key Stage 3 Phase: Influences on Students' Development from Age 11–14*. London: DfE/Institute of Education, University of London; Birkbeck, University of London. University of Oxford Research Report: DFE – RR202.

UN General Assembly (1989) *Convention on the Rights of the Child, United Nations, Treaty Series*, 1577(3). [online] Available at: www.refworld.org/docid/3ae6b38f0.html (accessed November 2016).

7 Learning in a digital age

MICHELLE ROGERS AND LINDA TYLER

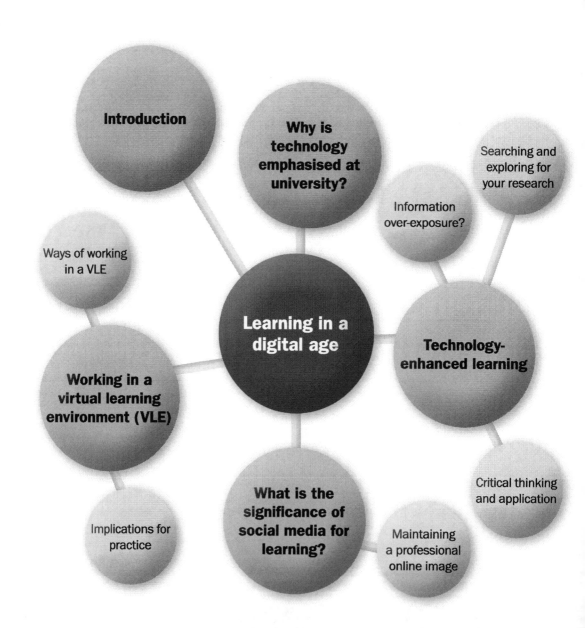

Introduction

Why is technology emphasised at university?

Searching and exploring for your research

Information over-exposure?

Ways of working in a VLE

Learning in a digital age

Technology-enhanced learning

Working in a virtual learning environment (VLE)

Critical thinking and application

Implications for practice

What is the significance of social media for learning?

Maintaining a professional online image

The number one benefit of information technology is that it empowers people to do what they want to do. It lets people be creative. It lets people be productive. It lets people learn things they didn't think they could learn before, and so in a sense it is all about potential.

Steve Ballmer, 2005

Introduction

This chapter will consider the approaches to learning and practice and how both can be supported using current technologies. Your higher education institution will probably have some form of online learning environment that we will also address. This chapter is not a *how to use technology guidance* but will act as a catalyst for action and thinking on how you can engage with technology to optimise your potential. This will influence how you use technology within practice with children and families, being mindful of your own, colleagues', children's and their families' digital identities, and an awareness of safeguarding identities online.

Critical questions

» *What do you already know about technology?*

» *Define the vocabulary in the table below. Try to do this without looking in a dictionary or online glossary.*

» *Consider how you may apply each of the technologies.*

Think about the technology you have used today – what sorts of things are you including as

Area	Definition	Application
ICT		
Digital technologies		
Technologies		

technology? Defining the vocabulary above will help you understand each area of use in the table above. The Department for Education Early Years Foundation Stage (DfE, 2014) identifies digital technologies as including microwave ovens, washing machines, credit cards, car keys and many more everyday objects. You may not have highlighted the same areas of technology that are currently recognised within the EYFS guidance (DfE, 2014); however, these will be considered later in the chapter when discussing technology and practice in early years settings.

Why is technology emphasised at university?

Since about 2005, higher education has been transformed by the use of technology, and in recent years, the transformations have been more widely spread across universities globally competing for students who have no intention of ever visiting the campus where their studies are based. This shift in approach to accessing learning opportunities within higher education is and will continue to drive the changes in universities throughout the world. Learning *in* universities was once the only way of accessing higher education. However, more diverse pathways of gaining a degree are available to students, from distance learning (whereby students gain online access only) to flexible and distributed learning approaches (which support a balance of distance and face-to-face contact). Learning in higher education now is more exciting than ever before as universities are tuning into students' needs and their ways of working, and are adapting to enable learning through more mobile and student-centred technology.

Decebo (2015) recognised that institutions that are:

> *beginning to think about learning through a more connected and participative process using leverage technology and apply[ing] it to learning in new and innovative ways are considerably better positioned than those who continue to hold on to old school approaches to learning.*

Universities can no longer be seen as traditional sites of learning, as students access a range of technologies that support their experience as a learner, classrooms are becoming virtual and libraries across the globe are open to those who would wish to explore them. For some, a *flipped learning* (Little, 2015; Love et al, 2015) approach is considered whereby content is delivered prior to the session remotely, via streamed online content, with the opportunity to engage in face-to-face *real-time* discussion taking the place of the traditional three-hour chalk-and-talk lecture, or the 'death by PowerPoint' experience which may spring to mind when thinking about traditional university lectures. This is a new era for higher education, and students for the first time in higher education are the consumer (Woodall et al, 2012).

Various strategies and projects have centred on new technologies in support of innovative learning and teaching, and because of this many universities within the UK have seen increased investment, both financially and human. This has enabled both staff and students to consider how technologies can be used to enhance learning experiences. The UK Professional Standards Framework (UKPSF) supports a sector-wide approach to ensure that the quality of learning and teaching aligns with the opportunities of current and new technologies in pushing this agenda forward. If you are already used to learning in a Virtual Learning Environment (VLE) you might already be aware that innovative teaching strategies may incorporate different aspects of VLE tools to facilitate enhancement. As a possible owner of technologies already, a strategy such as Bring Your Own Devices (BYOD) is one which you will benefit from.

In June 2015 three billion people were believed to be using the internet (MilliWatts, 2015). The internet is the world's largest shop, library and discussion space. MilliWatts (2015) recognised that research accounted for 62 per cent of users, followed by shopping (58 per cent), banking (50 per cent) and looking for jobs (45.5 per cent). The widely held belief that the internet is predominantly for social engagement and interactions remains unclear, with this purpose only accounting for 15.2 per cent of users.

Searching and exploring for your research

It is widely recognised that working online gives students a wealth of sites to visit and explore. Some sites are more valuable and constructive than others, and through the use of search engines, fine tuning what is being searched for is undoubtedly a skill in its own right. On entering a course of study for the first time, the amount of information that students will never have been introduced to before is overwhelming. A Google search on *child development*, for example, completed in 0.58 seconds gives a return of 14,500,000 results (23 October 2015). If you spent two minutes looking at each of these sites it would take you just over 55 years, certainly way beyond the average three years for a degree course. The internet is growing, storing more information daily. However, in sourcing information students have to be mindful of several things regarding the credibility of internet sites. Some sites can contain information that gives particular views on issues, may have an identified and possibly covert bias, and have other agendas in providing the information to such a massive audience.

In order to fine-tune searches it is essential to consider key words that may be associated with individual searches; for example, a search of *child development* amended to *child development birth Vygotsky* identifies 145,000 searches (23 October 2015). Google's algorithms, which use ranking systems, identify three categories to sort each search; these are popularity, suitability and sites which have paid to have their site moved to a higher ranking than it normally would have been. It is still not safe to assume that the primary sites recognised are those sites which are likely to be the most credible; the criteria do not recognise the validity or the robustness of the site. For research, there are specific search engines which filter research (see the following activity on filtering) into articles and peer-reviewed articles. Platforms such as Google Scholar do this automatically; however, the information portrayed via Google Scholar also needs to be rigorously considered (see the following activity on validating information). Without doubt, the internet is the largest and most diverse resource available to any student and how you use it and what you use it for are significant considerations.

Critical thinking and application

ACTIVITY

Filtering

Clear the history of your browser on your computer, laptop or tablet. Set a diary date for one month in your electronic calendar, or set a reminder on your phone. Once the month is up and the alarm alerts you to this, sit down and consider your browsing history. Can you categorise these sites into genre, for example learning, research, social, and functional? How many sites have you visited? Consider if these sites are specific searches or are they secondary sites you have stumbled upon in a clicking frenzy. Conducting purposeful searches will ensure you have saved hours in the pursuit of quality research.

Critical question

» *Evaluate the website http://zapatopi.net/treeoctopus/ in terms of the validity and robustness of the information given. Complete the table below to support your evaluation.*

Question	Prompt	Your thoughts on using this site
Who?	are the authors?	
What?	is the purpose of the site?	
When?	was it last updated?	
Where?	is the source reliable?	
Why?	would you use this site for collection of valid information?	

What is the significance of social media for learning?

Khatri et al (2015) and Luo and Zhang (2013) reported that social media sites are those that have the most traffic; the average person in the UK spends one hour and 40 minutes a day posting and lurking in their four most popular social media accounts. For students, this has consequences. Predominantly, the impact upon students is the time available to spend on research and studying. Recent trends acknowledged by academics have shown that some courses are now being taught through social media sites. Students have already become used to navigating social media, and have significant social presence and confidence in using these platforms. Forward-thinking lecturers have recognised this and built their learning groups within the network concept. This principle of online communities is not new to education and is a significant element of any successful online experience, further explored by Vazou et al (2015) and Swift (2014).

Continuous evaluation of what is posted on social media sites about you and from you, and images uploaded by you of others produces a profile that communicates who you are to the outside world. The conflicting spaces of online learning and social networking need to be balanced carefully in order to protect your identity as a professional early years worker. No one would advocate the withdrawal of social networking accounts, but the necessity to protect and safeguard your identity is of paramount importance. Your induction at university should cover issues such as protecting your identity online and what is acceptable to post and what is not.

Maintaining a professional online image

Do not have one account which everyone you know can access. Compartmentalise your friends, your family and work colleagues. Each of these groups has a perception about you, due to the environments and ways in which you engage with them.

It is flattering when parents in early years settings ask you to *friend* them. However, to them you are a professional and the links you have with them should be through any network the setting chooses and not your private networking accounts.

Not all groups identified will need to see images of you out with your friends. You choose who sees what. Online posts and images are forever available to access somewhere. Embarrassing posts or images stay in the 'ether' of the internet. Do all your posts and images portray you as the professional you would want future employers to see?

Keep updated with the security setting of any network you are part of and review these frequently. Do you know the difference between private and social spaces and can you make changes according to the group you are communicating with?

Critical questions

Thinking about your digital footprint and your social networking accounts, review the photographs and images uploaded onto your accounts. If you can answer yes to all/any of the self-audit questions posed below, others' perceptions of you may be influenced negatively.

» *Are you embarrassed by any of the images on your sites?*

» *Have you set privacy controls to protect what people see? Why was this?*

» *What if at an interview a potential employer showed you a picture, or quoted a statement from your social network site?*

» *Do you think that you are being portrayed as something other than a professional and potential employee?*

Working in a Virtual Learning Environment

Your academic identity can be forged within the online spaces your institution chooses to use, and the above self-audit is something that you may find useful to consider for your ongoing use of the VLE. Networking in a VLE, regardless of the platform, is a collaborative experience between the student, course peers and the teaching team. This online space, when used at its best, supports the co-construction of ideas and principles, the very heart of what higher education is about. The VLE will have many tools for students to use. Frequently, research identifies that tutors often stick with tools that are tried and trusted. These may be discussion boards, online journals or wikis. Either way, the tools are beneficial and require individuals to navigate and use them in order to support the optimum online experiences students can have. They are tools, however, and tools have a purpose. The purpose of these tools is to assimilate asynchronous discussion, which are those discussions that are not in *real time*. For example, a tutor might post a question and when someone logs in they see the question posed in the discussion board and post their answer. The discussion does not take place in real time and can have an ongoing life, students adding to it when they feel they can contribute, supported by the affordances of reflective spaces. The reflective spaces give students the opportunity to read posts, think about them and see what others have contributed. This may then shift their thinking and support a deeper reflective version of their original thoughts.

Virtual spaces allow flexibility for interaction at a time and date to suit individual needs; this contrasts with synchronous discussion, which happens in real time and requires everyone to be logged into the online space at a given time. Synchronous discussion can be cumbersome for large groups and difficult to manage if broadband is not fully functional. The nature of being *here and now* ensures this space is less equipped to be able to support the reflective spaces; these would need to be facilitated outside the classroom by peers or the teaching team. Research has demonstrated the benefits of working collaboratively online. However, Nicol (2009) recognises the challenges that this may cause students who are new to this approach to learning. Nevertheless, he concedes that within the first year of study, students need to develop an understanding of and responsibility for the way in which they gain a sense of control over their own learning, and recognise that a willingness to participate in all learning environments will prove beneficial to their ongoing studies. Such learning environments may consist of, for example, online spaces, lecture halls, classrooms and a range of early years placements, none of which are more important than the others.

Ways of working in a VLE

A beneficial tool for the online community is the co-constructed development of a protocol. The protocol considers such aspects as the ethicality of being an online learner, what you communicate and how you communicate it; for example, is it acceptable to use text speak, or smiley faces? Being part of an online community brings with it individual professional and personal responsibility (Rogers, 2015). Working online brings ethical responsibility, which may not have been considered in any depth before. The intonation (smiles, frowns, pauses between words, emphasis on certain words) of face-to-face speech is lost online, therefore communication within the online environment needs to be considered carefully in order not to offend, or cause distress. These are aspects of how the community will communicate and interact and it is important that there is both a shared understanding of the points considered and a way in which they can be agreed and reviewed on an online basis. As the community continues to develop and evolve, it is likely that the protocol will become more complex and sophisticated as knowledge grows and individuals within the community gain a sense of ownership within their online environment. The development of an online agreement about how to work online effectively can have many benefits and clarify expectations of the group regarding what is acceptable and what is not. Tutors may suggest the development of such a document; however, if this is not the case a proactive student who values an ethicality might suggest this to peers for future action. Keppell et al (2006) suggest that such actions build lifelong skills which enhance employability for all participating students.

Research conducted by Dennen and Hao (2014) identifies that the majority of students now access learning via mobile technologies. Selwyn (2005) recognises the fluidity of mobile technology and the different set of affordances with which it supports learning.

He argues alongside JISC (2015) that mobile devices are an added dimension to learning which ensure total flexibility in how, when and where students approach their learning. Preparation for this is timely as universities make strides forward in supporting students in terms of the affordance of fluidity to access learning at a time and way that suits individuals. Using tablets, laptops and smart phones to record and take notes is a simple and effective way to ensure students are able to capture as much information as they can from the sessions. This harvesting of notes and lectures supports students in gaining information they may have missed when writing. Ethical considerations are important when recording in groups. Permission should be gained from the lecturer and other students in order to be able to record, and there should be explicit agreement regarding where the session recordings will be stored, who will be able to access the resource and the time frame for when the resource will be deleted. Thought and transparency on where such recordings will be stored and for how long is an important consideration and one which must be clarified for all those contributing.

Implications for practice

By engaging with the activities in the sections above, you have begun to consider how you can enhance your approaches to study. These skills and knowledge will also be contextualised to the ECEC environments in which you find yourself as part of your course. For those students engaged with placement settings, thinking of how the affordances of technologies are used with children, families and colleagues is critical. Lyons and Tredwell (2015) argue that when technology is embedded within the curriculum, children's learning opportunities are enhanced, which brings about an actual increase in their attainment. For example, increased language and literacy achievements were identified by Penuel et al (2009); an increase in mathematical concept knowledge was also acknowledged by Clements and Sarama (2007). For children who had access to touch screen technologies in pre-school, increased achievement was seen in vocabulary and phonological awareness (Chiong and Shuler, 2010). However, facilitating such learning opportunities cannot take place within ECEC if early years workers are unsure of the affordances and opportunities the vast range of technologies available to children afford them. Aubry and Dahl (2014) recognise the lack of confidence and competence in technology of not only parents, but also practitioners in ECEC. This skills shortage is one which needs to be addressed urgently as children become more aware of technology through the environments in which they interact. Neither practitioners nor families can keep children safe and instil safety in the online environment if they have limited knowledge and confidence to interact with it.

The digital footprint of children is now an important responsibility of the ECEC sector. Through social media networks, children's images will often be uploaded and shared, and this is the overall right at present of parents to be able to share such images. However, it is important to consider how as an advocate for children you can highlight the possible risks and responsibilities adults have in safeguarding children online, and also recognise the impact of such acts on the children themselves.

Critical question

» Considering the first activity at the beginning of this chapter, now think about the range of technologies available to you in the setting you are currently in. Complete the table below.

What technologies are available for the children?	Age range?	In which activities might you consider purposeful to use these technologies?	How would children's learning be supported or enhanced by these technologies being embedded?

CASE STUDY

Jo's story

Jo works in the pre-school room of a private nursery. The staff team have been exploring how they can make the voice of the children heard within the planning they are undertaking to explore the current outdoor area and revamp it. Children have identified various drawings of what they would like within their outdoor play space. Jo and the team have given the children interactive postcards. (A5 in size, they have a cover which can be written on, and an on/off button which allows them to record four minutes of speech. Batteries have very limited use and are not rechargeable.) They have not done this before and the idea held by some of the adult team is that the interactive postcards will be wasted upon an activity like this, and that they should be used for literacy sessions only.

Critical questions

» What are your thoughts on this case study?

» Using technology in context is important for children, due to the recognised benefit for development and learning and the quality of their engagement with everyday lives, and also for them as future and lifelong learners. In light of your reading, can you consider reasons for using the technology with the children in the case study?

» While you are on placement, seek permission to access the policies within the setting. Identify which policies recognise firstly the well-being of children and secondly, the part of the policy document which identifies the protocol for use of photographs and images. What do you feel is significant about these policies?

Chapter reflections

» Technology enables a diverse range of students to access Higher Education.

» Using the Internet for research purposes requires a critical approach to prevent inadvertently citing information which is not credible.

» Maintain a professional image when using social media and protect your identity as an early years worker.

» When using the VLE become familiar with all the available tools to maximise your participation.

» Be aware of ethical protocol when using the VLE.

» Share your expertise of technologies with practitioners and parents when on placement.

Further reading

Chiong, C and Shuler, C (2010) *Learning: Is There an App for That? Investigations of Young Children's Usage and Learning with Mobile Devices and Apps.* New York: The Joan Ganz Cooney Center at Sesame Workshop. [online] Available at: http://pbskids.org/read/files/cooney_learning_apps.pdf (accessed November 2016).

Gibbons, A (2015) Debating Digital Childhoods: Questions Concerning Technologies, Economies and Determinisms. *Open Review of Educational Research*, 2(1): 118–27.

References

Aubrey, C and Dahl, S (2014) The Confidence and Competence in Information Communication Technologies of Practitioners, Parents and Young Children in the Early Years Foundation Stage. *Early Years*, 34: 94–108.

Ballmer, S (2005) Alamo Community Area Information System, Unlimited Potential Grant Announcement. San Antonio, TX.

Chiong, C and Shuler, C (2010) *Learning: Is There an App for That? Investigations of Young Children's Usage and Learning with Mobile Devices and Apps.* New York: The Joan Ganz Center at Sesame Workshop. [online] Available at: http://pbskids.org/read/files/cooney_learning_apps.pdf (accessed November 2016).

Clements, D H and Sarama, J (2007) Effects of a Preschool Mathematical Curriculum: Summative Research on the Building Blocks Project. *Journals for Research in Mathematics Education*, 38(2): 136–63.

Dennen, V P and Hao, S (2014) Intentionally Mobile Pedagogy: The M-COPE Framework for Mobile Learning in Higher Education. *Technology, Pedagogy and Education*, 23(3): 397–419.

Department for Education (DfE) (2014) *Early Years Foundation Stage Guidance*. London: DfE.

Docebo, S.p.A. (2015) The New 70:20:10? The Changing Face of Learning. [online] Available at: www.docebo.com/elearning-lms-resources/papers-researches/ (accessed November 2016).

Gibbons, A (2015) Debating Digital Childhoods: Questions Concerning Technologies, Economies and Determinisms. *Open Review of Educational Research*, 2(1): 118–27.

JISC (2015) Mobile learning: A practical guide for educational organisations planning to implement a mobile learning initiative. Bristol: JISC. [online] Available at: www.jisc.ac.uk/full-guide/mobile-learning (accessed February 2017).

Keppell, M, Au, E, Ma, A and Chan, C (2006) Peer Learning and Learning-Orientated Assessment in Technology-Enhanced Learning Environments. *Assessment and Evaluation in Higher Education*, 31(4): 453–64.

Khatri, C, Chapman, S, Glasbey, J, Kelly, M, Nepogodiev, D, Bhangu, A and Fitzgerald, J and STARSurg Committee (2015) Social Media and Internet Driven Study Recruitment: Evaluating a New Model for Promoting Collaborator Engagement and Participation. *PLOS ONE*, 10(3): e0118899.

Little, C (2015) The Flipped Classroom in Further Education: Literature Review and Case Study. *Research in Post-Compulsory Education*, 20(3): 265–79.

Love, B, Hodge, A, Corritore, C and Ernst, D C (2015) Inquiry-Based Learning and the Flipped Classroom Module. *PRIMUS*, 25(8): 745–62.

Luo, X and Zhang, J (2013) How Do Consumer Buzz and Traffic in Social Media Marketing Predict the Value of the Firm? *Journal of Management Information Systems*, 30(2): 213–38.

Lyons, C and Tredwell, C (2015) Steps to Implementing Technology in Inclusive Early Childhood Programs. *Computers in Schools*, 32(2): 152–66.

Milliwatts (2015) *Global Internet Report: Mobile Evolution and Development of the Internet*. Internet Society.

Nicol, D (2009) Assessment for Learner Self-Regulation: Enhancing Achievement in the First Year of Using Technologies. *Assessment and Evaluation in Higher Education*, 34(3): 335–52.

Penuel, W R, Pasnik, S, Bates, L, Townsend, E, Gallagher, L P, Llorenet, C and Hupert, N (2009) *Pre-school Teachers Can Make a Media-Rich Curriculum to Prepare Low-Income Children for School Success: Results of a Randomised Controlled Trial*. New York: Education Development Centre; Menlo Park, CA: SRI International.

Rogers, M (2015) ICT: A New Way of Thinking, in Reed, M and Walker, R (eds) *Critical Companion for Early Years*. London: Sage, pp 58–66.

Selwyn, N (2005) Reflexivity and technology in adult learning. Seminar.net – *International Journal of Media, Technology & Lifelong Learning*. [online] Available at: http://seminar.net/files/NeilSelwyn-ReflexityAndTechnology.pdf (accessed November 2016).

Swift, L (2014) Online Communities of Practice and Their Role in Educational Development: A Systematic Appraisal. *Community Practitioner: The Journal of the Community Practitioners' & Health Visitors' Association*, 87(4): 28–31.

Vazou, S, Hutchinson, A and Webster, C (2015) Empowering Teachers to Integrate Physical Activity: Online Communities of Practice. *Research Quarterly for Exercise and Sport*, 86: A6–A7.

Woodall, T, Hiller, A and Resnick, S (2012) Making Sense of Higher Education: Students as Consumers and the Value of the University Experience. *Studies in Higher Education*, 39(1): 48–67.

Zapato, L (2014) The Pacific Northwest tree octopus. [online] Available at: http://zapatopi.net/treeoctopus/ (accessed November 2016).

8 Exploring creativity

ALISON PROWLE AND FRANCES BRETT

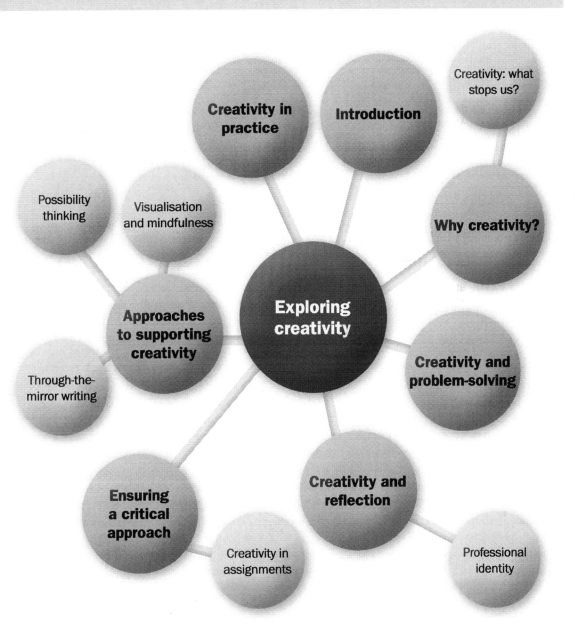

Creativity is intelligence having fun.

Attributed to Albert Einstein

Introduction

This chapter explores the role of creativity within your early childhood degree course. Academic life provides multiple opportunities for creative responses, and creativity can be a powerful tool for learning, development and practice. However, without explicit permission to be creative, you may feel constrained by perceptions that this is not something academia values and feel worried that if you take a risk you may achieve a low grade.

However, there is a growing recognition that creativity forms a vital part of academic life. Jackson and Burgess (2005) suggest that creativity is present in all learning contexts; we all need to be creative (inventive/adaptive) in a world that is constantly changing. While creativity is rarely discussed directly, tutors *do* value creativity, originality and flair in their students' learning. This chapter uses case studies which provide examples of students' creative responses in academic work to explore the benefits of creativity, relating these to the following themes:

*   problem-solving;
*   critical reflection;
*   communicating meaning within a community of practice;
*   practice-based learning.

Why creativity?

So, what exactly is creativity? It is important to note at the outset that creativity means different things to different people. For some, creativity will involve being inventive, challenging established ideas and taking risks. Others might think of creativity more in terms of creating and conveying new meanings.

This chapter represents creativity as a learning journey: the way in which we bring together different elements of our lives and make meaning from them. A creative response suggests the possibility of looking at the familiar in a new way, or linking the unfamiliar to something we already recognise and understand – in both cases, we create an opportunity to see with fresh eyes. Tools such as role play, image making, expressive writing and modelling, all facilitate a *stepping aside* in order to see more clearly the element we are dealing with. For example, just as a child wearing a superhero outfit might feel freed to fully be that character by wearing the clothes and engaging in imaginative role play, so you might enter more fully into a parent's experience if you are invited to role-play a parent attending a meeting with a health visitor. The experience may potentially enable you to draw upon how you *feel* as well as what you *think*, accessing other layers of your knowledge and understanding other than the purely cognitive; this in turn can support you in working through a problem (why does that parent behave as they do?), developing critical reflection (what would have happened if I had acted/spoken differently?), communicating your ideas in ways that speak to others more directly (a model or picture may convey more than words) and thus linking our understanding of theory to our practice. In short, creative approaches can support the self-reflective disposition that will inform and strengthen you as a developing academic student and early childhood professional.

Creativity: what stops us?

De Bono (1970) suggests that young children in their innocence are highly creative, partly because they are not so constrained by the views and ideas of others, allowing them to identify fresh and creative ways of looking at things. As we get older, this creativity can become constrained, and patterns of thinking and communication become more fixed. As tutors we very often hear students say, '*But I am not very creative*'. We need therefore to broaden our definitions of creativity and to recognise the multiplicity of ways in which creativity is expressed. Moreover, as we study early childhood, we need to be aware both of our own creative potential and also that of the children we work with.

To dig a little deeper, it could be argued that even before we access any creative tools we also need to be able to understand – or at least, trust – the creative process – our own in particular. What do we mean by this, and how can it be developed? Simply being offered opportunities to take a different path towards outcomes (a completed assignment, our viewpoint, a behaviour management solution), with a focus on the journey itself, can immerse us in a creative way of being that then informs our intended outcomes when we address them. The following sections explore how creativity plays a role within many aspects of our academic journey and how we can harness the potential to be creative within ourselves and others.

Critical questions

»   *List all the ways in which you are creative in everyday life. Are there any skills or dispositions that you display in these creative activities that could support you in your academic work?*

»   *Think about a time when you were at your most creative and write an account of this: what was the context? What helped you to be creative? What were the outcomes of your creativity (personal benefits as well as the product)? Are there any insights here that can help you within your academic studies? Present your findings as a table similar to the one below.*

Examples of creativity in my everyday life	How this could support my academic work
Example: I use Pinterest images to create mood boards for the rooms in my house.	*I could use Pinterest to collect images, quotations and ideas that represent my thinking about the use of the outdoor environment in early childhood.*
Example: I enjoy experimenting with new recipes.	*What is the recipe for a happy and healthy childhood? This could be an appendix to your assignment on children's well-being.*

Creativity and problem-solving

In order to enable you to begin to recognise and explore your creativity, this section uses case studies as examples of creative tools and processes in action, and the reflective response that these have elicited.

We live in a complex world that is forever throwing up new challenges. This is certainly the case in early years where there are shifting policy landscapes, social change and restrictions relating to resources, all of which mean that we need to discover new and innovative solutions. Working to improve quality in settings requires people at all levels to use initiative when making decisions and to think differently. The skills and qualities that we associate with creativity and ingenuity are required to help us work more effectively with others in generating new ideas and solving problems. Using creativity as a problem-solving tool can generate new ideas (divergent thought) and then support the selection of the idea with the most potential (convergent thought) for a solution (Guilford, 1950). This implies that when using creativity to problem-solve you need to cultivate what might appear to be contradictory mindsets: both imaginative and emotional, but also rational. Critical reflection occurs when you stand back and recognise your new perspective.

In an attempt to explain the process of critical reflection, Mezirow (1975) studied women returning to education in the 1970s and developed *transformational learning theory*. He proposed that students must engage in critical reflection that enables them to view themselves, others and different cultures from a new perspective. The trigger for this transformational learning was often a critical incident (referred to as a disorientating dilemma), sometimes occurring naturally in students' lives, but also frequently being instigated by a prompt from a tutor. Mezirow concluded that there are ten phases to transformational learning:

1. a disorienting dilemma;

2. self-examination;

3. a critical assessment of epistemic, socio-cultural or psychic assumptions;

4. recognition of a connection between one's discontent and the process of transformation;

5. exploration of options for new roles, relationships and actions;

6. planning a course of action;

7. acquisition of knowledge and skills for implementing one's plan;

8. provisional trying of new roles;

9. building of competence and self-confidence in new roles and relationships;

10. a reintegration into one's life on the basis of conditions dictated by one's new perspective.

He recognised that some phases would be more relevant to some students than others, depending on their unique circumstances.

CASE STUDY

Using creative approaches to explore complex situations and solve problems

Within this example, students were considering aspects of their own practice where they would like to make a change. In many cases, the chosen focus was something that was troubling the student, and alternative forms of representation were used to share the *story* of the focus with their peers as a way of accessing alternative perspectives and gaining additional insights to support their problem-solving.

In the example below, foundation degree student Jakki Watkins (used with permission) explores what for her and her team was a difficult move into a new building. Jakki chose model making to create a visual representation of her focus, namely, *'How can I create an enabling environment for children at a time of change and transition for the setting?'* The process of creating the model was for Jakki very emotional. *'I realised I was focusing so much on what we had lost'*, she said. *'I was not viewing the move as a positive one for staff or the children.'* When presenting to her peers, Jakki realised that she had represented the past in technicolour and the future very blandly.

To accompany the model, she developed a poem.

A poem to accompany this reflective model.

> *I am trying to be positive as we move to the new build,*
> *But find myself mourning the large, lush green fields.*
> *Our space has been condensed in quite a major way*
> *With so many issues that will affect our children's day.*

Not having a separate cloakroom will disrupt routines,
Wet coats and boots in the classroom, is that the best hygiene?
Activities in the classroom will often be disrupted,
All for the lack of a cloakroom, it really is absurd.

We also have the question of a room without doors,
'You've got nicer toys today, can we come and play?'
With no windows to open and a door that is not secure,
It's best not to think about the carpet on the floor!

We are starting our new journey with our children you see,
Support each other and explore with me...
New ideas, new space, new toys, new face,
Exciting times ahead in our new space.

We will move forward of this I am sure,
To new ideas, new initiatives to explore.
We will use our knowledge to create a space
We will enable as much as our old place.

We will follow the theory that Maslow proclaimed,
And an enabling environment will be our aim.
The children will flourish with adults who care.

During the following weeks, Jakki considered her focus from a number of different perspectives, using Brookfield's lenses to explore colleague, child and theoretical standpoints as well as considering the role that her own personal and professional history, beliefs and values played within her framing of the 'problem'. This culminated in her reviewing and changing the model to reflect aspects previously unconsidered such as the children's ideas for the new build. As a result, Jakki and the children redeveloped the model to incorporate these new ideas.

Jakki writes:

> This second model represents the changes being made within the initial transition period; developing our environment while supporting our children in making a new environment fit for purpose.

The following poem was written after six weeks in the new build by Jakki and a colleague to express how thoughts and worries were changing as they settled into the new environment:

> Well! After all my negativity,
> It is not as bad as I thought it would be.
> The children are coping without a door,
> The middle room has a lovely floor.
>
> Maybe the playdough has christened the carpet,
> But the loo door is fine if you jar it!
> How lucky are we with such a lovely view –
> Low windows so the children can enjoy it too!
> As long as they are safe and warm,
> Are they worried how we adorn?

Reflecting upon the process, Jakki writes:

> This has helped me understand that when dealing with change, patience and understanding is necessary to appreciate the bigger picture... I felt that making a physical model helped to clarify and express what I was feeling about our situation at the time. It stimulated my thinking to a much deeper level, which as a result inspired me to produce some poetry to support the models. I believe the mixture of the two allowed me to examine my personal and professional beliefs and values.

Critical questions

» *How did Jakki engage others within the creative process of making and subsequent meaning making?*

» *Having read Jakki's account, what professional challenges that you are currently facing may be supported by creative problem-solving?*

» *Can you apply Mezirow's phases to Jakki's learning?*

Creativity and reflection

This section focuses specifically on how creativity can be used to enhance critical reflection and introduces some tools to support this. Robinson (2001) suggests that creative thinking means moving outside our habitual patterns of thought. As explored within Chapter 11, reflection on self and on practice is an important disposition for students of early childhood to explore and develop. Using alternative forms of representation to explore aspects of our professional identities and our practice can offer a useful starting point for critical reflection. This is perhaps most powerfully seen when reflecting upon our own professional identity.

Professional identity

Professional identity is multi-faceted and can be defined as a professional self-concept based on attributes, beliefs, values, motives and experiences (Ibarra, 1999). Wenger defines identity as what we know, what is foreign and what we choose to know, as well as how we know it (Wenger, 2000, p 239). As Beijaard (2006) points out, people develop their identity in interaction with other people (a social constructivist perspective), but express their professional identity in their perceptions of '*who they are*' and '*who they want to become*' as a result of this interaction (cognitive psychological perspective). Hence you can explore your professional identity by using what Brookfield (1995) refers to as different lenses, for example:

- An *autobiographical* lens can help you draw insight from your own personal and professional background, exploring your own beliefs, values and experiences.

- A *colleague* lens can enable you to draw upon insights from trusted others.

- A *child* lens can enable you to engage with children's views and can lead to more responsive practice.

- A *socio-cultural* lens (Hanson, 2012) helps you to understand how cultural norms and experiences impact on your values and identities.

- A *theory* lens can assist in relating insights from the other lenses within a theoretical context, thus contributing to further meaning making.

Hence, by applying insights gained through using a lenses approach to Johari's Window (Luft, 1969) in Figure 8.1, you can reduce the *blind* spot and enhance the *open* area of knowledge about self. Using a creative approach, such as storytelling or role play, can be an effective way of enabling you to explore your developing professional identity from different perspectives, leading to new insights and understanding.

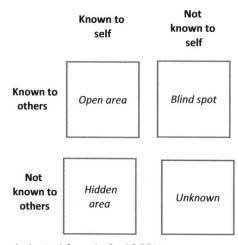

Figure 8.1 Johari's Window (adapted from Luft, 1969)

Ensuring a critical approach

Students sometimes express concern that if they are creative, this may impact negatively on their ability to be critical; however, creativity offers opportunities to explore connections and develop new ideas. In this way, it offers an additional *lens* through which to view your academic work and a new vehicle for communicating this. Of course, creativity alone cannot achieve a critical approach, and academic work needs to be supported by wide reading, a questioning approach and an ability to analyse and synthesise. However, creative approaches can often add that additional *spark* to an already impressive assignment, showing individual interpretation and flair that goes above and beyond the scope of the task.

Creativity in assignments

University tutors sometimes refer to a '*creative response within your academic work*', often mentioning this in relation to the sought-after A grade. What exactly does creativity mean in this context? It is firstly important to mention that creativity alone cannot compensate for other forms of academic rigour. It goes without saying that an A grade piece of work will fully meet the requirements of the task and robustly address the learning outcomes; it will be thoughtfully underpinned with relevant academic literature and will demonstrate criticality in the use of these sources; it will be written in an appropriate academic style and will be referenced according to academic conventions. However, often an A grade assignment will do all this and more, and it is this idea of *more* that we sometimes refer to as creativity. For example, a student may make innovative links to ideas and practice within their work, they may adapt existing models and paradigms or identify new solutions to problems, or they may offer new interpretations of existing data and concepts. To return to the point made at the outset of the chapter, the creative response is one that offers fresh insight through making new connections.

Approaches to supporting creativity

There really is no limit to the different ways in which creativity can be expressed, and people express their creativity differently. For some people, it is the process of planning an essay, bringing together ideas in a new way that unleashes their creativity. For others, creativity will be sparked by talking with others, by reading or by times of personal reflection. Finding what works for you is important. The section below explores just three possible approaches to enhancing your creativity.

Through-the-mirror writing

Bolton describes through-the-mirror writing as '*intuitive spontaneous, similar to initial drafting... Reflective practitioners write for self-illumination and exploration, not to create a product.*' The process of writing, Bolton argues, enables new insights as '*We know a great deal more than we are aware, absorbing information unwittingly, and data we do not use and think we have forgotten, and challenging material shoved into boxes mentally labelled do not open*' (Bolton, 2014). The writings can then be shared within a safe environment to gain others' perspectives. The use of words, metaphors and images can help you to see beyond what is visible and to explore emotional aspects of a situation or problem, often resulting in new and important insights. These insights can also clarify situations so that possible solutions are more easily identified.

Possibility thinking

Craft, writing in the context of children's creativity, first coined the term *'possibility thinking'* (Craft, 2000). Craft was keen to map out how creativity could be understood as an everyday occurrence and as an inherent capability in all, rather than the preserve of a gifted few individuals. Her theoretical account of creativity as possibility thinking (or, in other words, *what if?* and *as if* thinking) was driven by a belief in the power of questioning and imagination.

You can use these approaches to enable your own critical thinking, using creative tools to enable the questioning of *what if?* As Cremin and Craft (2006) identified, in order to enable possibility thinking with children, practitioners need to stand back and also allow time and space for children to explore endless possibilities. Children can be supported to think critically as staff take the time to pose prompts based on Socratic questioning after the possibilities seem to have been exhausted, such as *'what gave you that idea?' 'Do you think this would work in every situation?'*

Visualisation and mindfulness

Visualisation could be defined as being able to visualise for ourselves – in our minds or as words or images expressed externally – a new set of possibilities as a powerful means to shift our thinking. Adopting Craft's possibility question, *What if?* and following this to its conclusion: *If I did that, what would it look/feel like/what would be the result?* is an opportunity to picture (literally, if wanted!) the new reality.

Mindfulness (Kabat-Zinn, 1994) is the practice of bringing one's attention to the internal and external experiences occurring in the present moment, thus enhancing awareness of self. Mindfulness derives from a Buddhist tradition and can be developed through the practice of meditation. According to Siegel (2010), practising mindfulness can help fine-tune brain connections and develop new neural pathways. This in turn can help unlock creativity, enabling new ways of thinking and expression.

Creative approaches and responses can leave you feeling empowered but also vulnerable. It is important to remain aware that the moment we open up a way of working that offers access to emotions at a deeper level, then – alongside the possibility of experiencing surprising and joyful insights – there is also the possibility of unleashing more unsettling emotions and becoming overwhelmed.

As in any effective group work, it is key to establish ground rules and a way of working together that prioritises trust and acceptance – as well as clear, practical ideas as to how to support each other both within and beyond the group. For example, it may be useful to enlist the support of your tutor in order to define and list where support and guidance can be obtained if needed, including a list of relevant contacts. Reading this chapter in conjunction with that on Safeguarding (Chapter 12) would be valuable.

Creativity in practice

As a student of early childhood you will engage in extensive work-based learning, which is an excellent opportunity to consider creative approaches in action. In those settings where creativity is actively fostered, you may see some of the principles outlined in this chapter realised: for example, the environment may model a range of expressive media, the materials to engage with these and scaffolded support to develop skills in using these; it may honour the need for children to take time and revisit their ideas; and it may emphasise the value of the *process* as much as the final outcome. You will have the opportunity to observe how children respond to these elements and how this impacts upon their ability to make meaning through creatively connecting materials and ideas according to their own design. All of these opportunities will provide you with ideas to enhance both your own creativity and that of the children you work with. Some students find that it is useful to keep a journal where you can note down ideas and insights (both written and through doodling!).

Chapter reflections

» *Taking a creative approach can be a valuable way of enabling you to develop as a problem-solver, critical thinker, reflective practitioner and academic writer.*

» *The tools outlined can support your progress in this area. However, the most important point to revisit is that we need to give ourselves – and each other – the permission to be creative in order to find our way to new insights and understanding.*

» *This is important not just for ourselves, but for all those we work with, especially the children.*

» *If we genuinely support creativity across our learning communities of students and educators, and our communities of practice – the children, families, practitioners and other professionals that we work with – there is less danger that our practice, as individuals and as a professional community, will stand still.*

Further reading

De Bono, E (2009) *Lateral Thinking: A Textbook of Creativity*. London: Penguin.

Csikszentmihaly, M (2013) *Creativity: The Psychology of Discovery and Invention*. New York: Harper Collins Publishers.

References

Amulya, J (2011) What is Reflective Practice? *Community Science*. [online] Available at: www.communityscience.com/images/file/What%20is%20Reflective%20Practice.pdf (accessed November 2016).

Beijaard, D (2006) Dilemmas and Conflicting Constraints in Teachers' Professional Identity Development. Paper presented at *EARLI SIG Professional Learning and Development Conference*.

Bolton, G (2014) *Reflective Practice Writing and Professional Development*. 4th ed. London: Sage.

Brookfield, S (1995) *Becoming a Reflective Teacher*. San Francisco: Jossey-Bass.

Callan, S and Reed, M (2011) *Work-Based Research in the Early Years*. London: Sage.

Craft, A (2000) *Creativity across the Primary Curriculum*. London: Routledge.

Cremin, B and Craft, A (2006) Pedagogy and Possibility Thinking in the Early Years. *International Journal of Thinking Skills and Creativity*, 1(2): 108–19.

De Bono, E (1970) *Lateral Thinking: Creativity Step by Step*. New York: Harper & Row.

Department for Education (DfE) (2007) The Early Years Foundation Stage. Effective Practice: Creativity and Critical Thinking.

Guilford, J P (1950) Creativity. *American Psychologist*, 5(9): 444–54.

Harvey, L and Knight, P T (1996) *Transforming Higher Education*. Buckingham: SRHE/Open University Press.

Ibarra, H (1999) Provisional Selves: Experimenting with Image and Identity in Professional Adaptation. *Administrative Science Quarterly*, 44(4): 764–91.

Jackson, N and Burgess, H (2005) *Creativity in Social Work and Social Work Education*. Higher Education Academy.

Kabat-Zinn, J (1994) *Mindfulness Training as a Clinical Intervention: A Conceptual and Empirical Review*, by Ruth A. Baer. [online] Available at: www.wisebrain.org/papers/MindfulnessPsyTx.pdf (accessed November 2016).

Mezirow, J (1975). *Education for Perspective Transformation: Women's Reentry Programs in Community Colleges*. New York: Center for Adult Education, Teachers College, Columbia University.

Moon, J (1999) *Reflection in Learning and Professional Development*. London: Kogan Page.

Pinker, S (1997) *How the Mind Works*. New York: W. W. Norton & Company.

Robinson, K (2001) *Out of Our Minds: Learning to be Creative*. Oxford: Capstone Publishing.

Siegel, D J (2010) *Mindsight: The New Science of Personal Transformation*. New York: Bantam Books.

Wenger, E (2000) Communities of Practice and Social Learning Systems. *Organization*, 7(2): 225–46.

9 Working with others at university

LINDA TYLER AND MICHELLE ROGERS

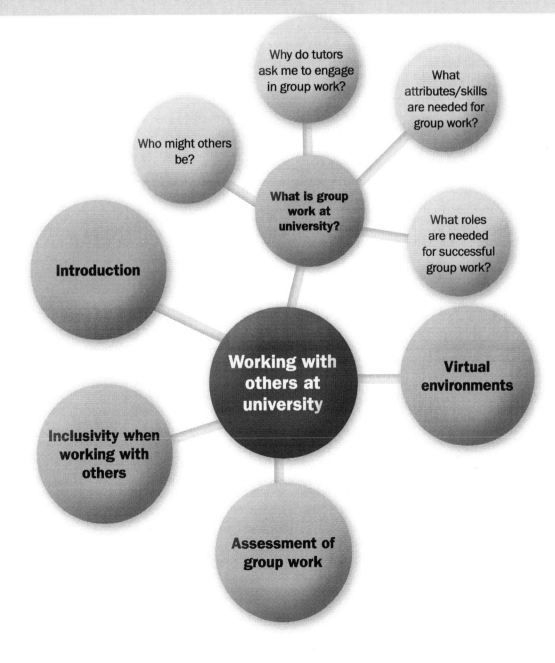

Introduction

This chapter considers collaborative working with peers, tutors and others within the university environment. Group work can, at times, be challenging; group dynamics can seem to be counterproductive to learning and you may wonder why you are being asked to work in this way. This chapter helps you benefit from these challenges by sharing insights into how similar challenges can exist in settings and how developing the skills to overcome them within university can support you to work with confidence on placement or in the workplace (see Chapter 10 for more detail on successful work-based learning). It will also help you develop good communication skills within a group, face-to-face and online. As Rogers and Tyler (2015) explain, working collaboratively is not exclusive to a physical environment but is relevant in a Virtual Learning Environment (VLE) as well (see Chapter 7 for more information on how to use technology for learning).

Critical questions

» *What are your expectations of group work at university?*

» *What do you think your role may be in a group work environment?*

» *What do you think the tutor role will be during group work sessions?*

RESEARCH FOCUS

Drawing on wider literature, Savin-Baden and Major (2004) note that when considering how teams learn in higher education, three models emerge as dominant:

1. The Post-Industrialist model describes the process whereby decisions that were once made by following a strict hierarchical order are now made by the consensus of the team.

2. The Social Constructivist model draws on social constructivist theory proposed by theorists such as Vygotsky (1978), proposing that we are capable of performing at higher intellectual levels when working with other members of our community, including tutors. Bruner (1985) agreed, stating that co-operative learning methods improve problem-solving strategies because we are confronted with different interpretations of the situation/problem.

3. The Popular Democratic model is based on the premise that in a multicultural environment there will almost inevitably be differences of opinion; these should be faced and explored rather than smoothed over. Building on this, Lafont (2012) proposed that learners experience tensions when their psychological constructs do not match either the conditions in which they find themselves or the ideas of their peers.

Although these models have different theoretical underpinnings, they all support the notion that working together in groups is essential to the learning process.

What is group work at university?

Whether in university or in the workplace, group work means working effectively with others on a common task: It means taking actions which respect the needs and contributions of others; contributing to and accepting the consensus through negotiating a solution to achieve the objectives of the group and ultimately success with the task. A common theme in these actions would appear to be communication.

Jaques and Salmon (2007) highlight that learning in groups allows greater scope to negotiate meaning and express our own ideas. They also recognise that group learning helps students to establish far more effective relationships, not only with their tutors but with each other. Slavin (2001) proposed that the four major theoretical perspectives on the achievements of group learning were motivation, social cohesion, cognitive development and cognitive elaboration. The motivational perspective presumes that task motivation is *the* most important part of the learning process, and that other processes, such as planning and supporting, are driven by an individual's desire to succeed. Figure 9.1 shows how tutors aim to set tasks to complete in placement that are engaging and motivational. It has to be a task that is relevant

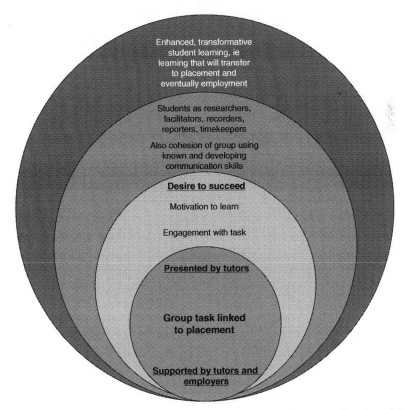

Figure 9.1 *How group work can enhance student learning. Diagram developed by Tyler and Rogers from Slavin (2001)*

to your future employment and a task that employers can also see the value of. The group's dynamics and knowledge radiate outwards once the task is set. The figure highlights how the skills developed as shown in the outer edge are suited to the workplace.

CASE STUDY

Within a practice-based learning module students were asked to consider Gypsy, Romany and Traveller (GRT) children in terms of their culture, the way that the children learned best and how their nomadic lifestyles impacted on their education, health and social care. The students were given a case study linked to a local GRT site and identified some of the health, education and care issues faced by this group and considered how they could best offer support if they were working with others in the nearest children's centre. Each student group could choose the issue that most interested their group, eg health (of babies and young children or pre- and post-natal care of the mothers), education (either pre-school or school) and care (social, safeguarding etc).

Many students started the task with negative, often stereotypical, perceptions of GRT families but these changed as their research developed and their interest and understanding of the GRT culture grew. Feedback from this task was positive, as shown in the end of module evaluation highlighted in the following *student voices*.

STUDENT VOICES

I think I can now work better in a group. I feel I can contribute to group discussions better than I could before, and I enjoy sharing my findings with my group. I have also learned to keep to deadlines because I don't want to let the group down.

I have developed my skills within group work, as well as participating in groups as we all had a go at leading the group on different weeks.

Nevertheless, as with all other tasks, there are those who are harder to motivate and engage. When a group is imbalanced in terms of commitment then those who are working hard can struggle to accept the students who appear to 'drag their feet'. In the student group mentioned above, the frustration this caused to those students who worked hard was evident.

STUDENT VOICE

The only disadvantage is some members of the group not turning up for some of the lectures and then not engaging fully in the work of the group.

Thankfully, negative feedback is less common. Students quickly become aware of each other's strengths and weaknesses and accept them, but they are less accepting of students they perceive to be 'lazy'. By the final year of studies some students can find they are not easily accepted into groups they may have previously let down.

Why do tutors ask me to engage in group work?

The Framework for Higher Education Qualifications (FHEQ; QAA, 2008) decide the benchmarks against which all further education and higher education degrees have to be mapped as well as the attributes and skills that any degree must include for developing the future workforce (see Chapter 5 for further information). In terms of communication and working with others, the following descriptors outline what you are expected to be able to do:

1. communicate information, ideas, problems and solutions to both specialist and non-specialist audiences;

2. possess the qualities and transferable skills necessary for employment.

Group work will support you to develop and demonstrate your ability to meet these descriptors.

The Code of Practice for Work Based Learning (QAA, 2011) should also be considered. When your learning is based at university, you may feel reasonably confident in what and how you are learning; however, this is not always the case when your learning takes place outside the university. It is therefore important to ensure that the learning you do both in university and on placement is synchronised to enhance the development of your employability skills. Thus we see that both the FHEQ (QAA, 2008) and the Code of Practice (QAA, 2011) both emphasise communication as an important skill needed for placement.

It is clear that your success as a student in university and within the workplace is dependent on a cycle of communication, requiring you to work with your peers, tutors and the employers providing your placements. As Figure 9.2 below shows, you will develop confidence within a group situation at university, which will help you become self-assured and knowledgeable on placement. This developed self-assurance and knowledge, alongside employer advice, is brought back into your group following each placement. Communication skills, confidence and knowledge develop ad infinitum following each placement. As you discuss your experiences within your group and with your tutors, not only does *your* skill set develop but the group skill set also grows. This can be really powerful and group work can become the *beating heart* of many student discussions or tasks.

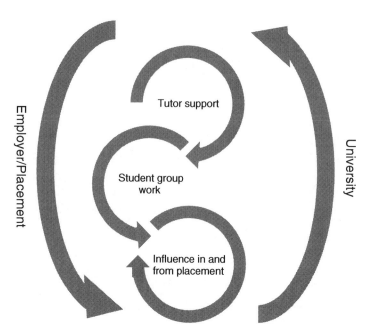

Figure 9.2 *How tutor support of student group work can influence student performance in placement*

Who might *others* be?

As early years settings generally work in a less hierarchical way than many other businesses, the requirement to work well together and to lead by example is particularly important. Initially as a student on placement, you may be well supported in understanding the need for and value of communication in the many roles expected of you. However, an eye should be kept on future professional development, including promotion. As a key person, room leader or group manager, there is an expectation that you will be able to speak up confidently in meetings on behalf of children who may need the involvement of outside agencies, for example doctors, speech and language therapists, social workers and educational psychologists. Parents will look to you as the person who, next to themselves, knows their child best. As an early years graduate who has worked closely with the child and their family, you will be expected to collaborate with these services for the benefit of the child. To be able to do this, there is a need to know how groups work, what works best when sharing within a group and sometimes how to persuade seemingly more knowledgeable people that your way might be better. There is a need to be factual but assertive and persuasive at these times; however, the need to listen is also crucial.

Figure 9.3 provides an overview of how groups function and is still relevant today (adapted from Adair, 1986). As the overview shows, the functions do not differ greatly from the group spirit shown by many sports teams.

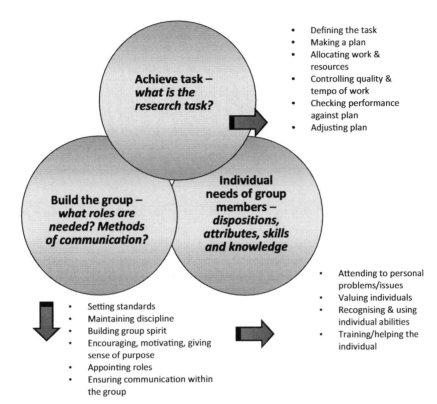

*Defining the task
*Making a plan
*Allocating work & resources
*Controlling quality & tempo of work
*Checking performance against plan
*Adjusting plan

*Attending to personal problems/issues
*Valuing individuals
*Recognising & using individual abilities
*Training/helping the individual

*Setting standards
*Maintaining discipline
*Building group spirit
*Encouraging, motivating, giving sense of purpose
*Appointing roles
*Ensuring communication within the group

Figure 9.3 *Adair's model of group functioning adapted by Tyler and Rogers to show group functioning in a digital age in higher education*

When tutors ask you to come together as individuals to form a group, they recognise that you probably do not know anyone and that you may be feeling rather anxious about working with 'strangers'. However, you will be supported to work in several groups within your first few weeks. The use of *icebreakers* will help you make friends and also enable you to recognise those *personalities* that you feel you may work best with.

The forming, storming, norming and performing model of group development was first suggested by Tuckman (1965) who proposed that four phases were necessary and inevitable in order for groups to develop and grow, face up to challenges, tackle problems, plan work and find answers to the task set.

In order for you and your group to develop through these stages, there is a need to put ground rules in place at the *forming* stage. This will give you a mechanism to deal with some of the difficulties you will face in the *storming* phase. Sometimes the storming phase cannot easily be resolved with some group members. Consider the following case study:

CASE STUDY

You are working within a mixed cohort group. Some students you have come to know well but others not so well. Things are going reasonably well. Your group has developed ground rules, appointed a group leader and you have had regular meetings, both virtual and physical. However, as time has gone on problems have arisen as two group members aren't contributing as they should. One has stopped attending meetings and has not followed up on any assignments yet. You and the rest of the group are getting annoyed as your hard work is being compromised by these group members.

Critical questions

What would you do? Consider the actions in Table 9.1.

» *Which one do you think you would select? Why?*

» *What would be the resultant impact on you? The group?*

» *Perhaps you might select them all? If so, organise the actions below to show what order you might put them in.*

Table 9.1 *Options for action*

1.	Find out if the group members not contributing have genuine reasons for not doing the work.
2.	Ignore the group members and do their work for them.
3.	Contact the group members and refer them back to the agreed ground rules that the whole group established. Remind them of what they have to do to complete the task but ask them if there is any reason they cannot complete it. You do this in writing, virtually or physically (email or letter), the email or letter is signed by the rest of the group and it contains a date for a response.
4.	Report the group members to the tutor explaining what the problem has been and what steps the group has taken to try to re-establish contact and get contributions. *If you choose this action, what evidence do you think the tutor might want to see that confirms these group members have not contributed their share of time and work?*
5.	Do you have some ideas of your own?

» *Why is working with others in university important?*

» *What skills might be needed for successful group work?*

» *What types of role might each student within a group adopt?*

What attributes/skills are needed for group work?

Social and group skills learned in student groups are important for employment success. As Fellenz (2006) notes, and as has already been outlined in this chapter, group work is important in developing social learning experiences because it enhances the development of skills and knowledge which are relevant to real world practice. Whether higher education is your first experience of working in a group, or you have had many such experiences prior to university, you will probably have questions or reservations about it.

Critical questions

» *Do you generally co-operate with others? Do you lead, follow, contribute, guide, advise or just observe?*

» *What do you consider is a personality strength of yours? What do you consider your personality weakness? How might your answers to this question impact on a group's dynamic?*

» *What do you see as important roles when working in groups?*

What roles are needed for successful group work?

The roles needed for successful group work will depend upon the goals of the task given and the size of the group. Roles can be fixed or rotating but rotating roles does support the development of different skills which will eventually be required for the workplace. Figure 9.4 below illustrates important group roles necessary for tasks to be successfully completed. This is not exhaustive and could be added to. For example, if the group were being asked to develop a *play space* for children then perhaps a *resources collector/researcher* bubble may be added.

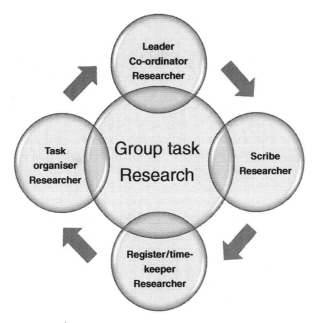

Figure 9.4 *Roles for group work*

The arrows in Figure 9.4 indicate that each week roles can be rotated. It was famously stated that *'there is no 'I' in team'* and therefore to ensure that all group members feel equally important and respected, rotating roles would make the most sense. Of course, if you recognised that one of your personality traits was *shy* in one of the questions above then leading the group in week one may not appeal to you. However, observing and understanding the group's dynamics over a number of weeks will help you develop the confidence to lead at some point. It is important to recognise you are all working towards the same goal and hope to achieve the best grade possible.

Virtual environments

Much of the content of this chapter is focused on physical meetings for group tasks. However, it would be wrong to exclude digital technologies and their uses within group work situations due to the growth in this type of learning. According to Lave and Wenger (1991), a Community of Practice (CoP) is a group of people who share a focus. They recognise that a community can evolve naturally because of the members' common interest in a particular domain or area, or it can be created deliberately with the goal of gaining knowledge related to a specific field. Lave and Wenger (1991) continue by stating that it is through the process of sharing information and experiences within the group that the members learn from each other, and have an opportunity to develop personally and professionally. Of course, this CoP ideology could apply to both physical working environments and virtual working environments; a community of practice is not defined by the medium through which members connect.

When we are face-to-face with others it is easy to recognise if someone is anxious, happy/unhappy, listening, supporting, contributing and most obviously, present! However, when using digital technology it can be harder to gauge the personalities, attributes, contributions and presence of others. Nevertheless, Bates (2014 online) notes that communities of practice can be very effective as working contexts can be complex, uncertain and ambiguous. Bates (2014) continues by stating that communities of practice are likely to become more rather than less important in a digital age but that it is probably a mistake to think of them as a replacement for traditional forms of education. The use of technologies, Virtual Learning Environments (VLEs) in higher education is discussed more fully by Rogers and Tyler in Chapter 7.

Alongside more traditional and formal tutor-supported VLEs, some students working in groups have found it useful to use less formal areas for their groups to work within, for example Facebook. This offers the flexibility for 'meeting up' at a mutually convenient time or to meet a task deadline, while also taking out travel and other costs if the meeting/deadline is on a non-teaching day. One of our students who worked on the GRT case study recognised that:

> *Working through our FB page when not in uni means that there are less excuses given about convenience or other clashes. We all meet the deadlines posted and it is clear to see that we have all done what we were asked to do. On teaching days, we like to meet up and talk about it at break times but on non-teaching days we all have other commitments. One of our group is a new mum and two of us have jobs in nurseries so it isn't always easy to get together.*
>
> Anonymous module evaluation feedback, 2014

Studies have found positive correlations between social networking website use and student engagement with their tasks/research. These studies focused on Facebook and Twitter usage. However, there are serious implications for posting 'unprofessional' comments on Facebook. A survey carried out in 2014 found that 93 per cent of employers checked social media profiles to better recognise the type of person they might be employing, with 67 per cent of these recruiters using Facebook (Jobvite, 2014). Keeping clean and professional profiles is paramount to your future success in the job market. Be vigilant not to post anything you wouldn't mind an employer or potential employer seeing and remember that digital security systems can be breached (this is discussed in more detail in Chapter 7).

Assessment of group work

As with all other work given within higher education institutions, there will be a need to assess and sometimes grade your group efforts. In instances where the group is tasked to deliver a response, individuals within the group generally receive the same grade. Sometimes however, as highlighted earlier in the chapter, groups struggle to engage all the members. This is rare but there will be safety nets in place to ensure fairness of grading whereby lower grades can be awarded to those who have not 'pulled their weight'. However, tutors will need evidence that this is the case.

It is important that each week you keep a register of attendance of both physical and virtual meetings; you should also keep a diary of what tasks are given and what responses were received. You should also show that you have tried really hard to engage using a written format (for example, emails) with these 'reluctant' students to find out if there are any circumstances which may present a barrier to their work. The tutor(s) will get involved to help resolve the situation at this point.

Critical questions

» *If you were a room leader, key worker or setting manager and you met resistance with a co-worker, what would you do first?*

» *If your first approaches/ideas did not work what would you need to do next?*

» *Who would have the ultimate responsibility for the next steps?*

Inclusivity when working with others

To be inclusive we should value the contribution of all students regardless of their backgrounds and appreciate the contributions and perspectives that everyone can bring. It is not about providing a *one-size-fits-all* approach but ensuring that all students are able to access all learning whatever the mode/style of learning used (Thomas, 2002).

Group work is often utilised by tutors to explore a theme. If the group work focus is unfamiliar to all participants then no individual is perceived as having an advantage during collaborative sessions. Montgomery (2009) proposed that this approach makes all students '*equally* unsure' and that it encourages a structured approach to discussion to give all group members a chance to speak. In effect it is an inclusive approach to group work.

At its best group work supports the development of collaboration, communication, time management and presentation skills that are transferable to the workplace. However, sometimes inclusion of those perceived to be different (identity-based exclusion) can cause the group and/or the person problems in one way or another (Chavez and Weisinger, 2008). Inclusion based on, for example, ethnicity, disability, age, religion, gender or perhaps previous educational experience can be stressful for some group members. Anyone who is in a minority within a group can feel excluded or unwelcome. Tutors are required to ensure that *all* students will benefit from group work activities and as a result to facilitate activities which will benefit all within the groups (Fuller et al, 2004).

During the first taught session of the GRT activity discussed above, it was disclosed to us that indeed one of our students was a Romany gypsy (an ethnic minority group). This student was extremely proud of her heritage and wanted to share this with her peers to help curb some of the preconceived ideas that people had of her culture. As many students began to realise the uniqueness of GRT communities, they began to support inclusion of GRT resources within the early years settings that they visited. The results and impact were truly inspiring. Acceptance of this student's culture by the whole group was crucial to her own group work experience and the group's assessment outcome.

Chapter reflections

»   *Group work has many benefits in terms of transferable skills related to working in both academic and employment settings.*

»   *There will always be challenges associated with group work, particularly when students do not understand why they are being asked to work in this way or the importance of their full engagement.*

»   *There are always safety nets put in place by tutors to support groups with uneven contributers to ensure fairness when allocating grades.*

»   *Students and tutors should be aware of the needs of all students and take an inclusive approach.*

Further reading

Musgrave, J and Stobbs, N (2015) *Early Years Placements: A Critical Guide to Outstanding Work-based Learning.* Northwich: Critical Publishing Ltd.

If you are interested in finding out more about the GRT culture, use the following website as a starting point: www.gypsy-traveller.org/ (accessed November 2016).

References

Adair, J (1986) *Effective Group Building.* Aldershot: Gower.

Bates, T (2014) The role of communities of practice in a digital age. [online] Available at: www.tonybates.ca/2014/10/01/the-role-of-communities-of-practice-in-a-digital-age/ (accessed November 2016).

Belbin, M (1981) *Management Groups: Why They Succeed or Fail*. London: Heinemann.

Bruffee, K (1999) *Collaborative Learning: Higher Education, Interdependence, and the Authority of Knowledge*. 2nd ed. Baltimore/London: The Johns Hopkins University Press.

Bruner, J (1985) Vygotsky: An Historical and Conceptual Perspective. *Culture, Communication, and Cognition: Vygotskian Perspectives*. London: Cambridge University Press, pp 21–34.

Chavez, C I and Weisinger, J Y (2008) Beyond Diversity Training: A Social Infusion for Cultural Inclusion. *Human Resource Management*, 47(2): 331–50.

Department for Education (DfE) (2014) *Statutory Framework for the Early Years Foundation Stage*. [online] Available at: www.gov.uk/government/uploads/system/uploads/attachment_data/file/335504/EYFS_framework_from_1_September_2014__with_clarification_note.pdf (accessed November 2016).

Fellenz, M R (2006) Towards Fairness in Assessing Student Group Work: A Protocol for Peer Evaluation of Individual Contributions. *Journal of Management Education*, 30(4): 570–91.

Fuller, M, Healey, M, Bradley, A and Hall, T (2004) Barriers to Learning: A Systematic Study of the Experience of Disabled Students in One University. *Studies in Higher Education*, 29(3): 303–18.

Heiberger, G and Harper, R (2008) Have You Facebooked Astin Lately? Using Technology to Increase Student Involvement, in Junco, R and Timm, D M (eds) *Using Emerging Technologies to Enhance Student Engagement: New Directions for Student Services, Issue #124*. San Francisco, CA: Jossey-Bass, pp 19–35.

Higher Education Research Institute (HERI) (2007). *College Freshman and Online Social Networking Sites*. [online] Available at: www.gseis.ucla.edu/heri/PDFs/pubs/briefs/brief-091107-SocialNetworking.pdf (accessed November 2016).

Jaques, D and Salmon, G (2007) *Learning in Groups: A Handbook for Face-to-Face and Online Environments*. London: Routledge.

Jobvite (2014) Social recruiting survey. [online] Available at: http://time.com/money/3510967/jobvite-social-media-profiles-job-applicants/ (accessed November 2016).

Lafont, L (2012). Cooperative Learning and Tutoring in Sports and Physical Activities, in Dyson, B and Casey, A (eds) *Cooperative Learning in Physical Education: A Research-Based Approach*. London: Routledge, pp 136–49.

Lave, J and Wenger, E (1991) *Situated Learning: Legitimate Peripheral Participation*. Cambridge: Cambridge University Press.

Montgomery, C (2009) A Decade of Internationalisation: Has It Influenced Students' Views of Cross-Cultural Group Work at University? *Journal of Studies in International Education*, 13(2): 256–70.

Quality Assurance Agency for Higher Education (QAA) (2008) *Framework for Higher Education Qualifications*. Gloucester: QAA for HE.

Thomas, L (2002) Student Retention in Higher Education: The Role of Habitus. *Journal of Education Policy*, 17(4): 423–42.

Tuckman, B (1965) Developmental Sequence in Small Groups. *Psychological Bulletin*, 63, 384–99. The article was reprinted in *Group Facilitation: A Research and Applications Journal*, No 3, Spring 2001.

Savin-Baden, M and Howell Major, C (2004) *Foundations of Problem-Based Learning*. Maidenhead: Open University Press.

Vygotsky, L (1978). *Mind in Society: The Development of Higher Psychological Processes*. Cambridge, MA: Harvard University Press.

Part B
Applying learning to the workplace

10 Learning in the workplace

NICOLA STOBBS AND JACKIE MUSGRAVE

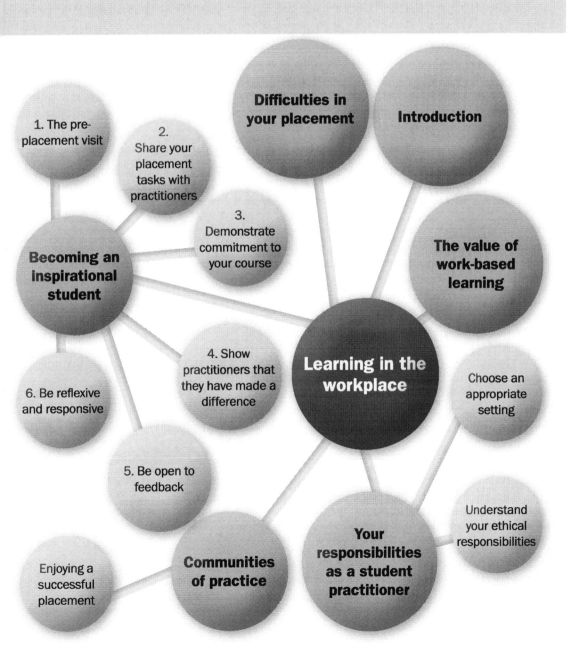

She became more like a colleague than a student.

A practitioner

Introduction

This chapter introduces key issues relating to your role as a student practitioner in early years settings and the skills you will need to be successful. Firstly it is important to remember that you are a guest in the setting and that status brings with it responsibilities in relation to your role working with children, practitioners and possibly parents. In addition, you have responsibilities to yourself as an emerging professional practitioner to make the most of the learning opportunities available to you in your setting. This chapter includes advice and suggestions on how you can develop the skills and confidence necessary to communicate and negotiate with staff to achieve your learning goals on placement. For example, as a guest in the setting it is important that you have a clear understanding of ethical issues relating to confidentiality, courtesy and appreciation of your place in the setting. Working in a setting gives you a golden opportunity to see how the theory you have learned applies to practice. Equally, it is important for you to explore how practice links to theory and how you can apply critical thinking to interrogate aspects of practice. There is also an opportunity to have a positive impact on the setting, creating such a good impression that you can approach the lead practitioner for a reference on completion of your course. The final section of this chapter provides answers to some of the questions that students frequently ask about placement.

The value of work-based learning

There has been a long tradition of early years students working in settings in order to learn, observe and practice aspects of children's care and education. In an increasingly competitive job market, having an opportunity to experience the world of real work can help to develop your employability skills. Such skills include:

- interpersonal and communication skills, eg developing relationships with children, colleagues and parents;

- sensitivity, ie knowing how and when practitioners may be open to suggestions of how to adapt their practice;

- demonstrating commitment to regular and consistent attendance;

- applying theory to practice, as well as practice to theory (Lohmander, 2015);

- specific workplace knowledge, eg understanding how settings are run and developing knowledge of the working process (Rauner, 2007, cited in Flämiga et al, 2015);

- contributing to a '*community of practice*' (Lave and Wenger, 1991), eg by inspiring practitioners to reflect on their own learning as they support you in yours.

All of these will help you develop a full curriculum vitae (CV), as discussed in Chapter 15, which can be used for job applications. It is beneficial to settings to have university students because practitioners appreciate that you are likely to have new ideas to share with them.

Sharon gives an example of how having a student in the setting can provoke deeper thinking about practice.

PRACTITIONER VOICE

Good students enthuse all of us. In the staffroom there is often some lunchtime banter and the conversation frequently turns to discussion about a child, everyone bandying ideas around. A student may ask a question that gets us thinking, it stimulates discussion. For my staff this gives them a bite of the academic cherry. Even going through questionnaires makes you think of things you hadn't thought of.

Your responsibilities as a student practitioner

Below are some key responsibilities that you should consider before, during and after your placement.

Choose an appropriate setting

Some universities place students in a setting and others ask that you find your own placement. If the latter is the situation in your university, then try to sort this out as soon as you can as placement settings quickly become unavailable if they have committed to giving someone else a placement. Even if you know that you want to be a Reception teacher in the future, for example, it is still worth undertaking placements with a range of ages so that if you have a child in your class who is not following a normal developmental trajectory you are aware of the steps that come before and can start from where the child is currently at, then build from that. If you have no idea of what a setting is like, undertake some research; look at past Ofsted reports and talk to students in other year groups who may have experience of it.

While it is short-sighted to choose a setting only because its location is close to your home, practical implications must nevertheless be taken into consideration. Make sure that you work out a plan to get to your setting on time every day and that you are prepared to conform to their policies and procedures; for example, some settings have an *indoor/outdoor policy* where you could be outside all day; some settings have a *slipper policy*, particularly those where there are crawling babies; some will give you a uniform and others may not have a uniform at all, but still follow an implicit dress code. All these cases require some initial inquiries to ensure that you do not feel out of place.

One of the most important requirements regarding your choice of placement, however, is their Ofsted rating. Recommendation 11 of the Nutbrown Review (2012) states:

> Only settings that are rated 'Good' or 'Outstanding' by Ofsted should be able to host students on placement.

Check this before every placement, even if you have been to the setting previously, as they may have had an inspection which resulted in a *requires improvement* grade, meaning that you will not be able to return until they have been re-inspected and the grading has improved.

Understand your ethical responsibilities

'Safeguarding is everyone's responsibility' is the argument that is outlined in the Working Together to Safeguard Children guidance (HM Government, 2015). As a student practitioner you have an ethical and legal responsibility to understand your role in safeguarding children. This is discussed in much greater detail in Chapter 12. You have a moral responsibility not to cause any harm as a consequence of you working in the setting. An example of how you may cause harm is by breaching confidentiality, because maintaining confidentiality is a key characteristic of a professional practitioner. Therefore, ensure that you do not discuss children or the setting on social media, or share confidential details with friends and family. If you arrive at the setting and find that you know a child already, tell the practitioners straight away so that they do not think you have become inappropriately overfamiliar with the child or its family.

Although the least you can do as a student undertaking an early years placement is to do no harm, ideally you should be aiming to do good.

Critical questions

» *How do you feel about your upcoming or most recent placement?*

» *What do you consider are your strengths that will help you have a successful placement?*

» *How important do you think higher qualifications are for raising the quality of children's early years experience?*

Communities of practice

One of the main theoretical perspectives that can be applied to practice in placements is that of *Communities of Practice* proposed by Lave and Wenger (1991). They argue that communities of practice are everywhere and we are probably involved in a number of them already. These communities have a common purpose, identity and commitment, and come together to share specialist knowledge, resources and experiences unique to them, enabling members to learn from one another. You may have a learning group that requires you to work with others on your course that could be defined as a community of practice, where, in the security of trusting relationships, you discuss your experiences of being an emerging practitioner. You may share ideas, resources, successful approaches to behaviour management or a new experience which enabled you to see the connection between theory and practice, for example. While you share your experiences you will also benefit from the experiences of others. These types of communities take time and commitment to build, but once established the gains for members can be more than the sum of their individual parts.

In communities of practice there will be some members who are *core members*: those who are the instigators and enablers, while others will be more peripheral, perhaps moving nearer to the core over time as they show growing alignment with the group identity, demonstrating their competence by using the vocabulary of the community and their shared understanding of norms and routines. Lave and Wenger (1991) noted that learning in these cases results as part of social participation, rather than the accumulation of knowledge and facts.

In our research for this chapter into why some students seem to have a more successful placement than others, it was apparent that while some students were able to learn *from* the effective practice of the practitioners, the more successful students learned *to* practise *like* the effective practitioners and became part of the community of practice. They became skilled at using the distinctive vocabulary and tools of the profession as opposed to watching from the sidelines.

Critical questions

» *Can you think of groups that are communities of practice other than in early years settings?*

» *Which communities of practice do you belong to now? Can you identify whether you are a core member or on the periphery?*

Some examples from the research we undertook for this chapter illustrate how this theory can be seen in practice and how it can help you to develop the skills. As a student new to work-based learning, you may be under the impression that to become a core member of your setting's community of practice your success depends on your ability to form good relationships with the children. However, what is of equal importance is your relationship with the staff team. Having the skills to communicate effectively and negotiate how you can support one another is subtler and more involved than merely choosing the appropriate place and time to discuss practical questions such as what time the lunch break is or what to do if you are ill. It requires a blend of emotional intelligence and application of the theory of communities of practice.

Enjoying a successful placement

Some students become a genuine member of a setting's community of practice – as one practitioner commented, 'She became more like a colleague than a student'.

Other students, however, seem to leave placement feeling that they never really had the opportunity to show what they were capable of, or of building meaningful relationships with the practitioners:

> ...don't be put off by what practitioners think of you. As long as you take part, show initiative, talk to staff and get involved with children, your experience should be a pleasant one ☺. Easier said than done...

This student sounds as if she had the key elements for a successful placement: showing initiative, talking to the staff and getting involved with the children, but there seems to be something missing in terms of her relationship with the practitioners.

It is possible to categorise students into three different types:

* Type 1: the child-like student;

* Type 2: the neutral student;

* Type 3: the inspirational student.

A Type 1 student

A Type 1 student does not think like a practitioner and consistently needs to be told what to do. The practitioner already has a room full of children to care for and a Type 1 student just adds to the workload. Not surprisingly, a Type 1 student does not manage to become part of the community of practice.

A Type 2 student

A Type 2 student is typified as one who helps out with the physical routines of the setting, for example wiping down tables at lunchtime or assisting with putting on the children's coats. While this type of student is appreciated for their practical help, they do not become a core part of the staff team. This student may be the one who *learns by observing and listening* to the practitioners, but does not *learn to use* the same vocabulary as them and thus misses out on establishing themselves as someone with a shared identity. The practitioners do not see the student as someone they can learn from and thus, while remaining pleasant, regard the student as *'just a student'*.

A Type 3 student

This inspirational student moves into a high level of participation in the community of practice (Lave and Wenger, 1991), able to get right into the core and inspire the practitioners to improve practice in a relationship where both parties are able to learn from one another.

Becoming an inspirational student

The following six steps will help you maximise the likelihood of having a rewarding experience and enable you to move away from the periphery of the community and closer to the core.

1. The pre-placement visit

Organising a pre-placement visit shows that you take your course seriously and want to be professional about expectations on both sides. The following quotes from practitioners emphasise that first impressions are formed in the pre-placement visit:

PRACTITIONER VOICE

If they're committed, they come for a pre-placement visit.

Those who bother to ring up and make a pre-placement visit and ask to have a look around, you can tell they will be ok.

2. Share your placement tasks with practitioners

Gain the respect of practitioners through sharing details of the tasks you need to complete while on placement. This demonstrates your commitment to becoming a professional practitioner.

PRACTITIONER VOICE

Many students do not have any specific tasks to do when in the setting. When asked, they answer 'no, no tasks, I've just come for experience'. It would help if they had some specific tasks as it helps focus them. I often feel as if students on placement are here because they 'have to' be here rather than because they 'want to' be here.

Critical questions

»   What specific terminology have you come across that is specific to early years practice?

»   Why is it important to use this language on placement?

»   Why is it important to be organised in your own mind about what you need to do on placement?

»   Make a table of the placement tasks you are expected to achieve to share with the practitioners, with a space for notes and suggestions from them regarding how and when these might be achieved.

3. Demonstrate commitment to your course

You can show commitment to becoming a professional practitioner by asking for the practitioners' support in the completion of your tasks. Staff members are likely to be very busy, which might make you hesitant in asking for their time, electing instead to be *another pair of hands*, like the Type 2 student. You may feel that you are low down on the setting's hierarchy:

STUDENT VOICE

It was nerve wracking going into placement because I didn't know what to expect. Would I be welcomed by the staff? Would I just be expected to do the student-type jobs like photocopying and making displays?

How to be assertive enough to make your requirements clear, while at the same time not appearing too demanding, is a common dilemma for students.

RESEARCH FOCUS

The dynamics of being a burden

Hamel and Jaasko Fisher (2011) discuss the *'dynamics of being a burden'* – the worry students have that they will be a nuisance to practitioners by asking for help when it is clear the practitioners are very busy already, which results in them keeping quiet about their queries and observations. However, use of the '*practitioner lens*' (Brookfield, 1995; see Chapter 10 for further details of the use of Brookfield as a tool for reflection) sheds some light on why this is not necessarily the best policy to adopt.

Placement involves both practitioners and students taking risks; there is the possibility of error, of appearing naïve, a loss of status and worry about upsetting others. Although you may feel nervous about being on placement, practitioners may feel that you are judging them in a harsh and negative light. They may feel that their knowledge of theory is a bit rusty and that you will inadvertently expose this shortcoming. If you show a desire to learn from them, this may put their mind at ease and allow them to open up to you without fear of judgement. Students who seek practitioners' advice are implicitly complimenting them on their expertise. If you do not take the initial risk by asking a question you may prevent the practitioner from taking a risk too, in giving a response. You may never feel as if you had a supportive relationship with the practitioners and could become anxious and depressed about being a burden, withdrawing further into yourself. In an ironic self-fulfilling prophecy, the practitioners may eventually come to resent you for taking them away from the children as they have to think of ways to occupy you, resulting in you actually becoming the burden you so desperately wanted to avoid.

Critical questions

» *Why is having a student on placement a potential risk for practitioners?*

» *If you were a practitioner who had not studied academically for a long time, how might you feel about a student watching your practice?*

» *Explain in your own words how fear of becoming a burden can result in a self-fulfilling prophecy. How can you avoid this happening?*

4. Show practitioners that they have made a difference

Early years practitioners are not paid a huge amount of money but one of the rewards that may offset this is feeling that they have made a difference.

PRACTITIONER VOICE

We have had students who have been interested and wanting to understand how we do observations and use the information to meet individual children's needs, how the setting works overall. They have worked alongside us, asked relevant questions. We can see the children respond well to them. When you have a student with a positive attitude, it makes you feel that you want to help them more – give information, make the environment and planning more enabling – to help them with their own goals.

The quote illustrates how important it is to try to learn the routines of the setting and work alongside the practitioners, using this time to ask questions that go beyond the *here and now* but relate to the wider picture. Using the unique professional language that characterises early years working, such as the language of the EYFS guidance, understanding adult to child ratios, the observation cycle and knowledge of child development will move you closer to the core group of the community of practice. If you need to negotiate access to other stakeholders, for example parents or professionals from other agencies who come into the setting, you are far more likely to achieve this if you have built positive relationships with practitioners where they can see that you are well on the way to becoming the professional you aspire to be.

5. Be open to feedback

While no one enjoys being observed making mistakes or initiating an activity that the children do not respond to, being able to accept helpful feedback is a key characteristic of a professional practitioner and the fifth step to becoming a part of the community of practice.

PRACTITIONER VOICES

She was happy to discuss and adapt, for example, I told her that sometimes she wasn't pushing the children enough. She was willing to take criticism and didn't take it personally. To be a good student you have to understand that criticism isn't against you – it's just to help you make your practice better.

The dreadful students have no humility – they are unteachable. Maybe their parents were teachers. If you're giving feedback to students and they're nodding, but the next day they've not implemented anything, there is nothing more annoying.

The last quotation is interesting because, as well as being able to be teachable, it hints at the sixth step of how to become a core member of the community of practice, which is discussed next.

6. Be reflexive and responsive

A key skill in building your relationship with practitioners is to go beyond stereotypes and be open to new ideas (reflexive), even if you already feel that you have a good knowledge of early years practice. It is particularly important to make sure you do not hold views that include some misconceptions that those outside the community of early years practitioners may hold. These include thinking that early years practice:

- is just playing with children all day;
- means leaving as soon as the children do;
- does not involve linking theory and practice.

Being able to adapt your practice in light of your developing understanding (responsivity) will clearly demonstrate your appreciation that working with children requires commitment and professionality.

Critical questions

» *How can you demonstrate to practitioners that their support is enabling you to make progress with your studies?*

» *How will doing this further your own development?*

Difficulties in your placement

Hopefully, you will have a really valuable and successful placement. However:

> *It is possible, even likely, for a student undertaking a placement in a poor setting to pick up bad habits, witness inappropriate practice, or for them to feel lost and confused when there is a lack of support. This could be a tremendous waste of that student's potential, and ultimately detrimental to the young children they will work with.*

(Nutbrown, 2012, section 28)

As is implied in this quotation from the Nutbrown Review, it is not uncommon for students to experience difficulties on placement.

Here are some answers to questions commonly asked by our students. The answers are meant to be a guide only and you should always check with your own university or college tutor if you have a specific concern.

Q. *What if I don't like my setting?*

A. There will always be times when you feel as if you are not having the experience you hoped for; maybe the practice there does not fit with your ideal; maybe there is a high staff turnover and a community of practice has yet to be established. Maybe you do not like the physical features of the building, or any other number of reasons. The advice in all of these situations is the same; choose to be positive, remember that practitioners are usually doing their best and it is nearly always worth sticking the placement out. If you think the setting should not be on the university database as a recommended setting, talk it over with your placement co-ordinator at university.

Q. *What if I am concerned about a safeguarding issue?*

A. Before you go on placement familiarise yourself with the safeguarding policy of your university or college. The vast majority of students will never encounter a safeguarding issue on placement but if you are at all worried you should seek advice from your university or college tutor who will support you in whatever action you need to take (see Chapter 12 for further advice about your safeguarding responsibilities).

Q. *What if I can't do my work?*

A. Reasons why you can't do your work may be because you have not had the opportunity to complete placement tasks or because you found the work too difficult to write about. In either case try not to wait until the end of your placement before doing anything about it. If you have not been able to complete any placement tasks, get in touch with the placement co-ordinator at college or university, who may be able to contact the setting and explain your needs on your behalf. Make sure you outline the steps that you have taken yourself to try and broach the subject already.

Most courses will aim to help you see the link between theory and practice and your tutors will rely on you bringing examples of practice (eg child observations) to review in lectures to support you in this process. If you are not able to do this, seek their support before the first lecture so that you can be as prepared as possible to take advantage of every opportunity to increase your understanding.

Q. *What if I get a bad report?*

A. It is always disappointing when we feel we have not made as good an impression as we would have liked, but coping with this disappointment is part of becoming a well-adjusted adult. Consider if there is any truth in any of the feedback that was given. If there was, then resolve to take it on board and learn from it. Making an action plan and sharing this with your tutor will demonstrate your commitment to becoming a professional in practice.

Your university or college tutors will never take a bad report at face value but will always talk to you to hear your version of events. Your placement report will be put into context with all your other reports, so one disappointing one will not be blown out of proportion.

Chapter reflections

» *This chapter has highlighted your responsibilities as a guest in a setting.*

» *It is important for you to be aware of the impact that you can have on a setting and appreciate the learning opportunities that are available to you. You have the potential to become much more than 'just a student'.*

» *Genuine commitment to your course and the children is a good way to acquire a positive response from practitioners.*

» *Remember that you can learn from good and bad experiences, but hopefully by following the advice in this chapter you will have a really good experience that will equip you to become an excellent practitioner.*

Further reading

Hayes, C et al (2014) *Developing as a Reflective Early Years Professional.* Northwich: Critical Publishing Ltd.

Musgrave, J and Stobbs, N (2015) *Early Years Placements: A Critical Guide to Outstanding Work-Based Learning.* Northwich: Critical Publishing Ltd.

References

Brookfield, S (1995) *Becoming a Critically Reflective Teacher.* San Francisco: Jossey-Bass.

Department for Education (DfE) (2014) *Statutory Framework for the Early Years Foundation Stage.* [online] Available at: www.gov.uk/government/uploads/system/uploads/attachment_data/file/335504/EYFS_framework_from_1_September_2014_with_clarification_note.pdf (accessed November 2016).

Hamel, F L and Jaasko Fisher, H A (2011) Hidden Labor in the Mentoring of Pre-Service Teachers: Notes from a Mentor Teacher Advisory Council. *Teaching and Teacher Education*, 27(2): 434–42.

HM Government (2015) *Working Together to Safeguard Children.* [online] Available at: www.gov.uk/government/uploads/system/uploads/attachment_data/file/419595/Working_Together_to_Safeguard_Children.pdf (accessed November 2016).

Lave, J and Wenger, E (1991) *Situated Learning: Legitimate Peripheral Participation.* Cambridge: Cambridge University Press.

Nutbrown, C (2012) *Foundations for Quality. The Independent Review of Early Education and Childcare Qualifications. Final Report.* [online] Available at: www.education.gov.uk/publications (accessed November 2016).

11 Becoming a reflective practitioner

KAREN HANSON AND KAREN APPLEBY

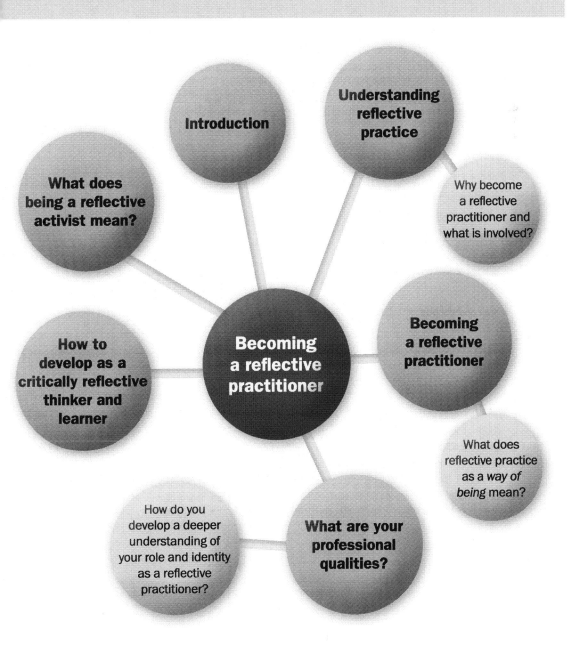

The self is not something ready-made, but something in continuous formation through choice of action.

John Dewey

Introduction

Reflective practice is examined as a *way of being,* which is an essential part of your identity; who you are both personally and professionally. It requires a willingness to look within yourself and to consider how your actions might be viewed by others. This chapter explores your developing role and identity as a reflective practitioner, and what this might mean to you. It examines your potential development as a critically reflective thinker, learner and activist who is motivated to *make a difference* for children, families and colleagues. Key themes are introduced and then revisited in greater depth as the chapter unfolds.

Understanding reflective practice

Reflective practice can be challenging, but to reassure you the emphasis here is on recognising and appreciating what you have to offer and already, your potential for growth, as a graduate practitioner. The examination of your own personal and professional qualities, your strengths and areas for development is essential to your role as a reflective practitioner. The identification and development of your personal position or perspective on what it means to be an effective reflective practitioner has many benefits for you and those you work with in practice. Knowing who you are and *how to be* is empowering because it can:

- enhance your confidence and resilience when engaging in real-life situations and facing potentially challenging issues in practice;

- support thinking and learning from what has worked and what can be improved;

- support working and learning with others including collaboration with children, families and colleagues;

- enable you to act on behalf of and advocate for children, young people, their families and your colleagues.

All of this helps you to develop both personally and professionally. Your motivation to learn, your engagement with academic learning experiences, and practice-based learning opportunities discussed elsewhere in this text play a significant role in your development as a reflective practitioner.

While recognising the significance of your own role and responsibility as a reflective practitioner, it is important to recognise that this must always be considered in relation to working and learning with others within professional communities of practice. This includes peers and tutors on your course as well as colleagues, children and their families in practice.

Why become a reflective practitioner and what is involved?

Critical questions

Close your eyes and try to remember the point in time when you decided you wanted to work with young children. Consider the following questions...

» *Where were you?*

» *Who inspired you to want to work with children?*

» *What were and are your reasons for wanting to work with children?*

» *Why have you chosen to study for a degree in early childhood?*

Your development as a reflective practitioner may start with you questioning why you want to follow a career in this field. Most people will state their reasons for wanting to work with children as being the potential for making a difference (Atkinson and Claxton, 2000). There is much evidence to support the significance of the early years of a child's life and the need for high-quality professionals who are committed to meeting children's needs. You may relate to this aspiration but you may also feel an emotional and social connection with children, find them interesting, enjoy observing, interacting, communicating and playing with them. Your reasons for choosing to study early childhood as an undergraduate may include the desire to find out more about children and how they develop. Past experiences may have nurtured an interest in a particular aspect of childhood such as special needs or child development.

The transition into higher education

Your previous studies will have focused quite considerably on developing knowledge and then being assessed on how well this has been understood and applied. Developing your knowledge about children and childhood is a significant part of your studies but in itself will not enable you to make a difference to children and families. You need to develop the ability to think critically (as discussed in Chapter 4) about different sources of knowledge, extract meaning and learn from them, and make sense of the knowledge for yourself in relation to your experiences with children and in practice. Taking responsibility for and owning this knowledge and constantly reviewing and developing it further will enable you to understand and explain what informs your actions, what you do in practice. This can be described as developing your *knowledge for practice*, which in turn will inform how you demonstrate this through your actions, your *knowledge in practice*. For an effective reflective practitioner, engaging with knowledge as a thinker and learner is an ongoing *way of being* (discussed later in this chapter). As an effective reflective practitioner, this in turn must inform what you do; your actions.

STUDENT VOICE

I used to think it was just about thinking over what I had done – thinking about things that had happened, but with no real result or action following the reflective process. Now I know how effective it can be in improving practice and actually changing what I think, say and do at work. It's not just about grand, massive revelations – it's the small everyday points that matter too. The small changes can make a massive difference to children!

Kim Fox
(Appleby, 2010, p 14)

Kim is highlighting the complex nature of reflective practice and being a reflective practitioner which includes three processes:

- reflective thinking (reflection);
- reflective learning;
- reflective action.

(Appleby, 2010, p 11)

Reflective thinking and learning inform reflective action (what you do). The significance of *changing what I think* can be explained using Mezirow's (1998) theory of *transformatory learning*. Developing a new and informed perspective can stimulate new insights into how you can make a difference for children and families. This learning then informs what you do, your actions in practice.

How can you make a difference for children through your reflective practice?

When asked in what ways we can make a difference for children, first-year early childhood undergraduates at the very beginning of their studies identified the following themes:

- allow children to have a voice... to express themselves in different ways;
- give all children your time... provide opportunities for all children;
- have one-to-one conversations with children in a safe environment;
- give children opportunities to develop through offering a range of opportunities within and outside of settings;
- knowledge of health needs;
- have procedures in place to support children's well-being;
- empower children as individuals;
- allow children to take risks;

- be effective communicators;

- ensure good team working and communication with staff teams;

- keep knowledge and skills up to date;

- communicate with other agencies... working together;

- reflect on daily practice.

At this early stage in their studies these students are already aware of their responsibility as developing practitioners. They are identifying some key principles which will guide their actions in practice with children and families. In addition to developing relevant skills and knowledge, the next step for these students is to learn how to examine the validity of these principles through a process of reflective thinking and learning. Seeking and reflecting on knowledge from different sources will help them to review their own interpretation of what children need and how this can be supported. The level of commitment to your own development is high but you need to consider whether this is what young children should expect from the early years profession.

Becoming a reflective practitioner

It is essential that you make a decision about your aspirations as an early years practitioner. Do you want to make a difference? If you do then you need to recognise the commitment required to become a reflective practitioner.

Critical questions

Think about the experiences or individual(s) who inspired you to work with children.

» *What was special about these experiences or individuals?*

» *How has this informed who you want to be and become as an early years practitioner?*

» *How would you like someone else to describe you and your practice?*

The following case study supports your developing understanding of the role of the reflective practitioner. It focuses on key points emerging from a Serious Case Review and considers what could have made a difference

CASE STUDY

Daniel Pelka

Daniel Pelka was seriously mistreated for months before he died at four years old at his home in Coventry in March 2012. A Serious Case Review (Lock, 2013) found that:

- Chances were missed to save the life of a four-year-old boy who suffered from 'terrifying and dreadful' abuse.

- Daniel was *'invisible'* at times to the people who should have helped him.

- No one *'listened'* to Daniel – no one enabled him to express and communicate what he was experiencing.

- Daniel's school, the social services and health professionals did not work together.

- Practitioners were *'overly optimistic'* about the reasons for his injuries.

When asked the question *'what could have made a difference for Daniel?'* first-year early childhood undergraduate students at the very beginning of their studies identified the following themes.

- Have the child's interest at the centre – hear the voice of the child – develop knowledge of the child.

- More observation and follow-up from professionals.

- Professionals working together… ensuring effective communication/sharing knowledge and planning action.

- Effective partnership working with parents… not taking things at face value – check out information with the wider professional team.

- Apply good listening, memory and communication skills, be open-minded but also 'mindful'.

- Be reflective about what you have heard and seen… questioning – analyse/take it apart/go deeper.

These students demonstrate a strong *voice* on what could have made a difference for Daniel. They demonstrate considerable insight into the issues stimulated by the outcomes of the Serious Case Review. They are thinking for themselves, offering their interpretation or position and considering the implications for practice. Their next steps will be to reflect on what that means for them as developing reflective practitioners; what they know and need to know; how they are going to continue to think and learn; how they will realise their learning in practice and therefore potentially make a difference for children. They are beginning the journey towards assuming the role of the reflective practitioner as a *'way of being'*; becoming a *'reflective activist'* whose actions are informed by considerable thought and learning from a wide range of sources (Hanson and Appleby, 2015).

Throughout your career in early years you need to be aware of and develop your vision of the reflective professional practitioner you aspire to be; your values and principles; your purpose and disposition in relation to self and others learning and how this informs what you do. None of us live up to this aspiration all of the time but this *identity* provides a moral compass that guides the way we are in relation to how we see ourselves and others and how this is realised in our practice. Having confidence in our professional identity and knowing that our decisions and actions reflect this can be very significant when faced with challenging situations. It is important, as discussed in Chapter 4, to recognise that thinking *critically* about ourselves and our practice does not mean being negative; rather, it is about questioning and identifying what can be learned. Your developing critical self-awareness can be likened to what Schön (1983) describes as '*professional artistry*'. You will be working with a diverse range of people and contexts and it will require you to be creative and divergent with your thinking and actions. You will soon discover that every day, every child, every family and every different context in which you work will require you to use your creative professional artistry to solve the issues that arise (Hanson and Appleby, 2016).

What does reflective practice as a *way of being* mean?

Dispositions and identity

As you progress with your academic studies and learn from experience in practice, you will become increasingly aware of the complex and diverse nature of the practitioner role and responsibility when working with colleagues from a range of professional backgrounds, children and families. In our experience this can be overwhelming at times and you can doubt your ability and effectiveness as a practitioner. Embracing reflective practice as a core *way of being* enables you to value your existing professional qualities and what you bring to the role while working on further developing your practice. A commitment to *doing good*, to learning and improving practice will support you when faced with challenging situations and circumstances.

Your identity as a reflective practitioner therefore involves continually seeking opportunities to improve your competence in practice. You need to learn from success and identify new targets. You need to think reflectively as a way of seeking knowledge not only from academic sources but also from your own learning journey, from others and the complex situations in which you will find yourself in practice. As this very much includes working with children and adults, this is likely to include thinking about social and emotional dimensions including relationships and your role in seeking understanding of yourself and others.

Therefore, the professional qualities of emotional intelligence will support your development as a reflective professional.

> *Emotional intelligence is what we commonly refer to as street smart, or 'common sense'. It has to do with the ability to read the political and social environment, and landscape, to intuitively grasp what others want and need.*
>
> (Stein and Book, 2000, p 14)

Emotional intelligence will support the development of your self-awareness and identity. Being able to recognise your own and others' emotions and understand why they are happening will enable a more informed critical reflective process.

What are your professional qualities?

Developing as a reflective practitioner involves knowing and valuing yourself and your qualities as well as planning for future development. We often talk about valuing children as individuals but can forget to apply this to ourselves and others in our professional communities.

Appleby and Andrews (2012) identify a number of professional qualities which support reflective practitioners within the context of professional situations, and are described in the next section.

Critical questions

Consider your existing qualities in relation to the following themes.

» *your 'way of being'/identity in practice: I am ...;*

» *values, beliefs and principles: I value ...; I believe ...;*

» *feelings: I feel ...;*

» *experience: I have experience of ...;*

» *skills: I can ...;*

» *knowledge: I know ...;*

» *personal characteristics: I am ...*

(Adapted from Appleby and Andrews, 2012, pp 63–4)

How do you develop a deeper understanding of your role and identity as a reflective practitioner?

You can also ask the same questions of peers and those you work with in practice. Knowing yourself and others supports effective use of individual and shared resources as well as enhancing the potential for effective collaborative working. A significant aspect of your *way of being* or identity as a reflective practitioner is being curious.

Are you naturally curious and open to suggestion from different perspectives? When referring to young children, how often have you heard or used the phrase, '*they're into everything!*'? It is completely natural for most young children to explore, experiment, test and discover. As children get older they usually develop a deeper inquisitiveness, which gives rise to that continual '*why?*' question. At this stage children are not seeking scientific reasoning; they merely want to engage more within the mysterious world they are encountering. Progression from this leads to intellectual curiosity, a curiosity that really does want to know the reason; an insatiable curiosity that tests and challenges; a curiosity that endeavours to make real sense of experiences by gathering as much evidence as possible to come to an independent conclusion. It is important that children's open-mindedness and flexibility is encouraged through stimulating curiosity and enjoying awe and wonder through new experiences.

Critical questions

» *Are you still curious?*

» *Do you explore – seek answers?*

» *Are you always satisfied with someone else's explanation or answer?*

» *In what ways might curiosity support you in making a difference for children and families?*

As we become adults our natural inclination to be curious can be affected by many factors. Dewey (1910, p 34) states our task is to:

> keep alive the sacred spark of wonder and to fan the flame that already glows ... to protect the spirit of inquiry, to keep it from becoming blase from over-excitement, wooden from routine, fossilized through dogmatic instruction, or dissipated by random exercise upon trivial things.

Critical questions

» *What does this statement mean to you? Can you relate it to any of your own experiences?*

» *What does Dewey mean when he refers to 'keeping the sacred spark of wonder alive'?*

As our educational experiences become more transmission based, where facts are fed to us through prescribed texts, and we are asked to remember and recapitulate details to validate our knowledge through examination, we become ever more reliant upon others to provide the answers. Significantly, Dewey is arguing that we all have the capacity to be curious, to think and learn for ourselves; that we can regain what has been lost.

Hanson (2012, p 48) states that some of the characteristics determining a reflective disposition are as follows:

• adaptability of thought and flexibility of action;

• listening to other people's ideas and willingness to try them;

• sharing of ideas;

• determination and commitment;

• self-awareness, being honest with yourself and colleagues;

• genuine attitude and having a conviction for the improvement of practice for the good of self and others;

• open-mindedness and willingness to be challenged;

• ability to challenge assumptions;

• having evidence-based values about the profession;

• knowledgeable about the theoretical underpinning of practice;

• critical thinking skills; the ability to question and argue.

Critical questions

» *Are you willing to question assumptions about children and practice, including your own? Think of some examples.*

» *Can you think of an example where you have been open to other perspectives and thereby gained a different and more informed perspective?*

How often do you question why things are done as they are? Why are things done at certain times of day? Why are there certain rules about resources being used in a particular way? Why can't the children have free choice? Why aren't the ideas of all the adults working with children considered when planning? Why are children given templates to draw around? Why are children only given primary coloured paint to use? How often do you ask questions of those who should know the answer? How often do those who should know the answers actually question the working practices of their setting?

How to develop as a critically reflective thinker and learner

Other chapters in this text offer invaluable advice on how to learn in higher education and from practice. All of this supports the developing reflective practitioner's skills and knowledge. Capturing and recording significant experiences, thoughts and ideas in ways that suit your personal learning preferences is an invaluable tool for stimulating reflective thinking and learning. This is likely to begin with a descriptive approach where you record your reflections on experience, questions and ideas as they happen, thereby creating a story or narrative. You may keep a written journal but also supplement words with diagrams and other images. While maintaining a professional approach, this should be a safe place where you feel able to express yourself without the pressure of being judged by others. Once established, this record enables you to revisit your initial thoughts and identify what can be learned from your experiences; what is and has been significant for you as a developing practitioner and how this learning might inform your practice. Reflecting on the content of your reading and learning from academic texts including books, journals and other sources will provide you with the opportunity to question and develop your initial thoughts and assumptions to inform deeper learning. Revisiting your reflective journal and adding further notes supports your thinking and learning and creates a richer picture of your learning journey.

Reflective conversation

Conversations with a purpose with peers, tutors and colleagues in practice provide an invaluable way of sharing your reflections and developing further knowledge and understanding. Making a positive contribution to peer learning group activities in face-to-face situations or online is a significant way of stimulating further reflective thinking, conversation and learning. These experiences also support the development of team working and communication skills so essential to effective practice learning communities.

Questioning your own and others' actions and being able to cope with honest responses can sometimes render us vulnerable. Dewey (1910, p 13) refers to this as experiencing '*mental unrest and disturbance*'. To be productive, it requires you and others involved to believe in the process, have an ability to manage the emotional challenges involved including potential impact on your self-identity and confidence and therefore to take a sensitively interrogative and appreciative approach.

Critical questions

»   *Are you willing to experience 'mental unrest and disturbance' in order to 'make a difference' for children?*

»   *How can you support reflective conversation with others?*

RESEARCH FOCUS

Being actively engaged in continual review

Hanson (2012, p 144) proposes that reflective practice is:

> An **active engagement** *in continual review and repositioning of assumptions, values and practice in light of evaluation of multiple perspectives, including the wider socio-cultural perspectives influencing the context; transforming and transcending self and practice in order to effect change and improvement.*

We have both been involved in and influenced by research into reflective practice; for example, Karen Hanson's (2012) research was influenced by the work of Brookfield (1995) who suggests the use of different *'lenses'* to gather the viewpoints and perspectives of others involved in the context where evaluations are taking place. It is natural for us to call upon our own perspective in the first instance. Even if we consciously make an effort to remain objective with our views, they will always be influenced by our personal history – our auto-biographical lens. Therefore, it is important to gain the views of others who are involved to determine a well-informed and objective evaluation. It could involve the perspectives of the children, practitioners, peers and tutors. It should always involve the theoretical knowledge gained about the issues being evaluated, through past and current research. It may require some reviewing of wider literature impacting upon the situation, for example policy documents. These different perspectives create a strong foundation for what Schön (1983, 1987) describes as reflection *'in'* and *'on'* practice. Hanson and Appleby (2016) further argue that the application of knowledge within the workplace to inform action, described by Thompson and Pascal (2012, p 322) as *'reflection-for-practice'*, is also essential.

Hanson's (2012) research revealed the need to consider the wider socio-cultural perspective. It is important that we gain an understanding of the *real world*s of the people we work with and the context in which we work. This can be very different to our own personal assumptions of the world, so taking into consideration the influences impacting upon the actions and lives of others is crucial for us being able to understand why things might be happening. The diagram in Figure 11.1 identifies the different perspectives you can consider when reflecting upon a given situation. Hanson (2012, p 144) states that if all five lenses (autobiographical, colleagues', childrens'/students', theoretical/literature and the peripheral socio-cultural) have been considered, a deeper '*evolutionary*' critical reflection process happens.

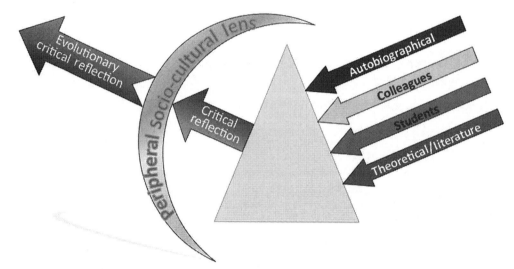

Figure 11.1 *Perspectives for critical reflection*

What does being a reflective activist mean?

Sometimes reflective practice is criticised as being self-indulgent *navel gazing*. There is a danger of this happening if the knowledge and information we have gained from our reflections are not used to good effect. To avoid this criticism there is a need to act upon our reflections and learning and to inform and justify our practice. Building on Hanson's definition of reflective practice (see above), Hanson and Appleby's (2015, p 33) concept of reflective activism:

- is perceived as a '*way of being*' for individuals and communities of practice. It builds on a strong value base that assumes personal/professional responsibility for improving the quality of provision for children and families;

- recognises the complex interaction between the individual and context;

- involves a pro-active stance in all aspects of reflective thinking, learning and action whereby practitioners question, examine and challenge different positions including their own;

- should be equally critical and meaningful and avoid a narrow interpretation that views reflective practice for external demands;

- is stimulated by a natural disposition to be '*curious*';

- involves actively engaging with the complexities and challenges within a diverse profession;

- recognises the significance of a reflexive approach which involves critical examination and '*theorisation*' of what you do and why in relation to the impact this has on self and others;

- requires a full critical evaluation of evidence gained from multi-dimensional reflections including the '*fifth socio-cultural lens*' (Hanson, 2012).

Critical question

» *Read Hanson and Appleby's (2015) chapter (see reference below). Consider your role as a reflective activist and your potential to think, learn and act for the benefit of children and families.*

Chapter reflections

» *Being a reflective practitioner is not a formulaic, technical or regulatory exercise. It is a way of being that develops from our values and beliefs about our role in providing the very best quality of provision for young children and*

» *Reflective practitioners are not complacent, but strive to improve professional knowledge, understandings and practice.*

» *Reflective practice involves being curious and asking questions so that assumptions are challenged.*

» *When making decisions, reflective practitioners take actions based on the multiple perspectives of work colleagues, and give consideration to the socio-cultural context.*

Critical questions

» *How deeply have you examined your own personal/professional journey?*

» *How has this informed your own identity and 'way of being' as a reflective practitioner within the context of professional practice?*

» *What is your current 'theory' of reflective practice?*

» *How are you making a contribution? For example, are you engaging in reflective conversation?*

» *Can you identify the impact you are having on self and others?*

Further reading

Hanson, K and Appleby, K (2015) Reflective Practice, in Reed, M and Walker, R (eds) *Early Childhood Studies: A Critical Reader*. London: Sage, pp 7–13.

This chapter examines the concept of 'reflective activism' in more depth.

Hanson, K and Appleby, K (2016) Reflective Practice, in Trodd, L (ed) *The Early Years Handbook for Students and Practitioners: An Essential Guide for Levels 4 and 5*. Abingdon, Oxford: Routledge.

This chapter examines reflective practice as a way of being.

References

Appleby, K and Andrews, M (2012) Reflective Practice is the Key to Quality Improvement, in Reed, M and Canning, N (eds) *Implementing Quality Improvement and Change in the Early Years*. London: Sage, pp 57–72.

Atkinson, T and Claxton, G (2000) *The Intuitive Practitioner: On the Value of Not Always Knowing What One Is Doing*. Buckingham: Open University Press.

BBC News (2013) Daniel Pelka review: He was an 'invisible' child. [online] Available at: www.bbc.co.uk/news/uk-2413486 (accessed November 2016).

Brookfield, S (1995) *Becoming a Critically Reflective Teacher*. San Francisco: Jossey-Bass.

Lock, R (2013) *Serious Case Review – Daniel Pelka*. Coventry: Coventry LSCB. [online] Available at: http://moderngov. coventry.gov.uk/documents/s13038/DanielPelkaSeriousCaseReviewSCR.pdf (accessed November 2016).

Dewey, J (1910) *How We Think*. Boston/New York/Chicago: D.C. Heath & Co.

Dewey, J (1933) *How We Think: A Restatement of the Relation of Reflective Thinking to the Educative Process*. Chicago: Henry Regnery.

Hanson, K and Appleby, K (2016) Reflective Practice, in Trodd, L (ed) *The Early Years Handbook for Students and Practitioners: An Essential Guide for Levels 4 and 5*. Abingdon, Oxford: Routledge.

Mezirow, J (1998) On Critical Reflection. *Adult Education Quarterly*, 48: 185–98.

Moss, P (2008) Foreword, in Paige-Smith, A and Craft, A (eds) *Developing Reflective Practice in the Early Years*. Maidenhead: Open University Press.

Schön, D A (1983) *The Reflective Practitioner*. London: Ashgate Publishing Ltd.

Schön, D A (1987) *Educating the Reflective Practitioner*. San Francisco: Jossey-Bass.

Stein, S and Book, H (2000) *The EQ Edge*. Toronto: Stoddart.

Thompson, N and Pascal, J (2012) Developing Critically Reflective Practice. *Reflective Practice: International and Multidisciplinary Perspectives*, 13(2): 311–25.

12 Safeguarding: understanding your responsibilities

STUART GALLAGHER AND SAMANTHA SUTTON-TSANG

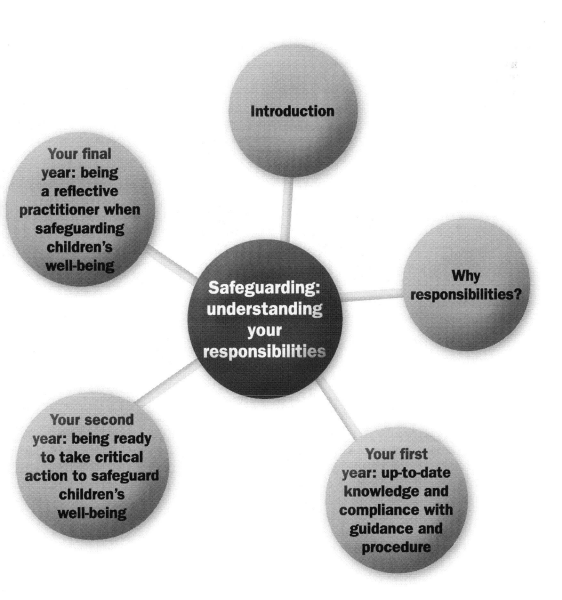

Deeds, not words, was to be our permanent motto.

Emmeline Pankhurst

Introduction

Learning how to safeguard the conditions of children's development is now seen as a non-negotiable aspect of early childhood professional development in higher education (DfE, 2012, p 20, para 2.11). This is especially so in the most acute cases of children's vulnerability to harm and the need to understand and act upon statutory duties to protect these children from maltreatment. Students need to understand how to safeguard the relationship with the host setting and the university to ensure adequate support is provided to enable them to take critical action to safeguard children's well-being. This chapter helps students to understand how to take advantage of opportunities to learn through reflective practice so that they can make a critical contribution to inter-agency children's safeguarding and child protection professional practices. This chapter presents safeguarding responsibilities as multi-dimensional relationships – with children and families, with settings and colleagues, with the university and peers, and with one's own academic and professional development.

Why responsibilities?

We need to talk about safeguarding and child protection. We do not do it often enough, and perhaps that is one of the reasons why we approach it with some anxiety – unnecessarily so. Of course, there is *necessary anxiety* when it comes to thinking about children's welfare, the harm they may be suffering, and the realisation that we are in a position to do something about it. That is understandable. But in this chapter we really want to address the unnecessary anxiety of safeguarding children in the early years, and our role in protecting children from serious harm, in order to prompt us to think about our *necessary responsibilities*. One goal of this chapter is to get us *thinking* about our responsibilities – as individuals, as teams, as the early years workforce, and as students and as practitioners – so that we can begin *talking* to one another about our concerns, our ideas, our challenges and our creative responses to practice so that children's well-being is safeguarded.

At times, unfortunately, safeguarding children is reduced to no more than a risk audit of childcare settings. Checks are made to make sure that children are not likely to be physically hurt when in the care of staff at a setting or a school. *Safeguarding*, at other times, incorporates categories of harm that are more usually associated with child protection, namely neglect, sexual abuse, emotional abuse and physical abuse. Safeguarding now includes the prevention of bullying (for example, online bullying), abuse (including racist and disability abuse), radicalisation, child sexual exploitation and child trafficking (see Ofsted, 2015a, p 6, para 10 for a fuller list). Preventing these from occurring is our responsibility.

Things can unexpectedly get in our way, though. Take the slogan, *Safeguarding is everyone's responsibility*, for example. It is a very good slogan. But, if safeguarding is everyone's responsibility, it can always be *someone else's* responsibility and no one will notice when I do nothing. And so, we are under-active. Or, again, if safeguarding is everyone's responsibility, then that means safeguarding the well-being of each child I encounter is *my responsibility*: '*Someone has got to do something about this, and that someone **is me**!*' Here, we are over-active. This chapter helps us to avoid being either over-active or under-active and supports us to be *active*, effectively contributing to young children's lives in a way that helps to secure children's well-being and welfare. In short, this chapter prepares us to be vigilant, not a vigilante.

The chapter is organised into three main parts. Each part is pitched towards the expectations the early years workforce may reasonably hold of us as early childhood students in each year of our degree. That may be two years for a foundation degree or three years for a BA (Hons) degree. These responsibilities are unpicked in more detail in each part of this chapter.

Your first year: up-to-date knowledge and compliance with guidance and procedure

Your first responsibility is always to ensure you read the relevant chapters and sections in the current edition of our statutory guidance, *Working Together to Safeguard Children* (DfE, 2015), the 'Safeguarding and Welfare Requirements' of the *Statutory Framework for the Early Years Foundation Stage* (DfE, 2014, section 3), *Keeping Children Safe in Schools and Colleges* (DfE, 2016) and attend all relevant training, especially that arranged by your own Local Safeguarding Children Board (LCSB). In this way, this chapter *is not* a one-stop shop for learning about safeguarding children's well-being and child protection in the field of early years practice-based studies. It is in the texts cited above that we access the most current definitions of key terms such as *safeguarding, neglect, children's sexual exploitation*, and so on, as well as details on what we should expect in terms of support from our employers or placement providers to help us safeguard children's well-being.

You must comply with these texts' instructions and guidance – this is *necessary*. However, reading them and noting them is not always *sufficient* to safeguard children's well-being and to protect them from harm. (Managing this dilemma is one of the practice responsibilities of reflective practice, by which you extend your ability to handle ambiguity and practice despite not knowing all of the unique and individual circumstances of individual children's private lives. The third part of this chapter discusses this dilemma.)

By reading this chapter, you are not relieved of your responsibility to engage with those essential texts. Instead, you are responsible for keeping an eye out for the latest edition of guidance, accessing and reading it, and doing what is needed in order to understand its implications for your own day-to-day work. You must use the opportunity of higher education to become familiar with important texts such as Ofsted's guidance to its own inspectors, *Inspecting Safeguarding in the Early Years: Education and Skills Settings* (Ofsted, 2016). You can impress your employer or placement provider with your knowledge of what Ofsted now inspects with regard to children's safeguarding and can be a valuable asset in the busy working childcare and education environments of practice placement.

Critical question

» *In the wake of a child welfare tragedy, such as the non-accidental harm of a very young child, a culture of blame may encourage you to point a finger at careless professionals. However mistaken this culture may be, to what extent is it your responsibility to keep up to date with statutory guidance and current policy in relation to children's safeguarding and child protection?*

Your second year: being ready to take critical action to safeguard children's well-being

In your second year, you are in a position to take action on behalf of children's welfare. You no longer have the excuse, '*I am only a student...*' Instead, with your knowledge and developing criticality, you can face practice dilemmas with greater confidence and say, '***Because I am a student, I know how to respond to this issue***'. The relationship between your studies (and the personal and academic tutoring support your college or university offers you) and your practice places you in a strong position to take critical action – action that *makes a difference* to vulnerable children and adults. For example, a serious case review (SCR) undertaken by Birmingham Safeguarding Children Board (BSCB, 2010) noted that:

> *Students may be well placed to identify both poor practice and potential abuse within settings and Colleges can play an important role in supporting them to make their concerns known, recording them appropriately and following up referrals to Children's Social Care.*

> (BSCB, 2010, p 9, paras 3.12–13)

In that particular SCR (BCSB, 2010), college students on placement, rather than either the setting's manager, the designated safeguarding officer or staff, raised specific concerns regarding the inappropriate actions of another student at an early years setting. Their concerns were valid, but not robustly acted upon. In the following paragraphs, the chapter presents a series of scenarios you may face at any point of a practice placement and details in general terms the reasonable responsibilities each of you would hold. These details should serve as a useful starting point to prompt your own critical action, to ensure robust action follows. (These details are intended as a guide only and are not intended to be interpreted as mandatory.)

I am concerned about the safeguarding practice of another student on placement

You should immediately share your concerns with your course leader or co-ordinator to discuss whether or not they merit further discussion with the setting's manager or school's headteacher or designated safeguarding officer. In these early discussions, sharing the other student's real name should be done only on a need-to-know basis. Depending on the quality of your evidence, the course leader or setting manager *may* need to know the name of the student you are concerned about. Let the evidence and your concerns guide your discussions, rather than the personal identity of the other student at the earliest stages.

I am concerned about the safeguarding practice of a teacher (or other practitioner) at my placement

You must follow the safeguarding policy of your school or setting. Normally, this requires you to inform the setting's manager or designated safeguarding officer of your concerns. Having done this, you must also inform your college or university course leader and ask that your concerns be formally recorded.

I am concerned about the safeguarding practice of the headteacher/ manager/designated safeguarding officer at my current placement

This is a dilemma, since the setting's manager or school's headteacher is the very person to whom you would usually go to share your concerns. What do you do when the person you should go to is the very person whose safeguarding practice concerns you greatly? The Birmingham SCR mentioned earlier (BSCB, 2010) tackled this very issue and highlighted that *'too much power and control resided with the manager who was seen as the expert in safeguarding'* (ibid, p 8, para 3.5). Faced with this situation, you must approach your own college or university's course leader and seek their guidance regarding whether or not your concerns merit *blowing the whistle* to your college or university. Choosing to follow a college's or university's whistleblowing procedure may prompt an investigation into the safety and well-being of children in a particular setting or school from a public interest approach.

I am concerned about the overall safeguarding policy and procedure of the school or setting where I am currently on placement

The recent guidance document, *Whistleblowing to Ofsted about Safeguarding in Local Authority Children's Services* (Ofsted, 2014), is useful in recommending next steps, given the sensitivity and seriousness of this scenario. Ofsted recommends that we should first seek third-party advice (such as from your course leader or college or university safeguarding officer) and also describes the steps that Ofsted will take to help you determine whether or not your concerns merit *blowing the whistle* to Ofsted.

I strongly suspect (or have evidence) that a child, young person or adult is being seriously harmed (or is at risk of being seriously harmed) at my current placement

You should contact the police and/or the placement's or school's local authority children's services department. Once you have shared your concerns appropriately, you should also inform your course leader of your actions, who may decide to inform the college or university also.

Critical questions

» *What or who will help you to take these steps?*

» *What or who will stop you taking these steps?*

» *Who might help you to develop good safeguarding practice?*

Your final year: being a reflective practitioner when safeguarding children's well-being

The primary purpose of this chapter is to help you take responsibility and to take effective action in matters that concern safeguarding children's well-being and protecting them from significant harm. A characteristic of third-year (Level 6) studies is *independence*, learning how to stand apart from the things you take for granted in order to examine them afresh. For example, '*Does early years practice enable me to do the work I really need to do to support children's learning and development? And if not, what can I do about that to bring about positive change?*' Here, safeguarding practice is presented as a field of study from which final-year early childhood undergraduate students can begin to stand apart, in order to ask questions about the robustness of the safeguarding and child protection systems of which they are a part.

Let's begin with an all-too-common example of a serious case review. We might hear people ask, '*How did that child manage to slip through the net?*' What is this net? It is another common cause of misunderstanding when it comes to safeguarding children, similar to the slogan dealt with earlier. This misunderstanding also prompts over-active or under-active responses to a safeguarding concern: either, '*There's a safeguarding net already – why should I bother to do anything?*', or '*The net failed?* **That's enough!** *I'm doing it alone from now on*'.

The mistake you may make is thinking the net is a physical thing, *separate* from you and your responsibilities. We fool ourselves into thinking that a net exists *out there*, doing the job of safeguarding children and protecting them from harm. Let us be clear: no prime minister, or director of children's services, wakes up each morning to sweep a huge net across the nation, expecting to catch within it all the country's vulnerable children. We are not talking about an actual physical net, leaning against the wall of 10 Downing Street.

Critical questions

Imagine a straight line with a point at each end. At one end, let's place early years practitioners who try and avoid the anxiety of safeguarding issues at all costs. At the other end, let's place the early years practitioners who consider themselves to be any vulnerable child's sole protector, willing to break every convention in the rulebook to secure a child's safety.

» *Where on that line would you place yourself? Why?*

» *How might you explain your reasons to another student?*

The child welfare practice landscape: safeguarding networks not nets

Safeguarding children's well-being does not rely on a net. Instead, it is the daily practical achievement of professionals understanding how their *own particular responsibilities* relate to the responsibilities of *other* welfare practitioners. We are talking about an interconnecting web of professional, personal and social responsibilities to care for children's well-being and to ensure they are not suffering significant harm. Re-imagining your responsibilities as part of a child's *network* of safeguarding support rather than a net may help us see our responsibilities more clearly. In this final part, the chapter aims to help you see why reflective practice will enable you to take responsibility for developing your own local network of safeguarding professionals, so that you understand how your own responsibilities relate to their responsibilities, to ensure children experience an effective network of safeguarding support.

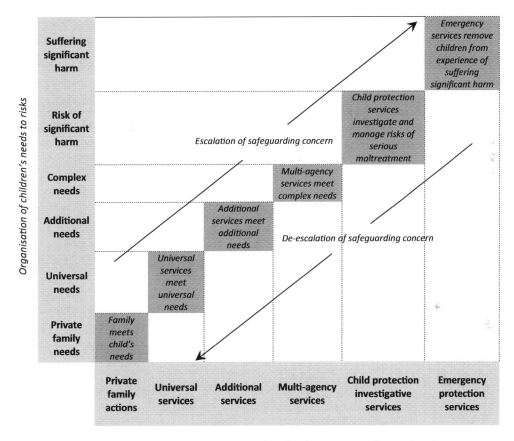

Organisation of resources from families to acute professional services

Figure 12.1 *A child welfare practice landscape*

Figure 12.1 represents a child welfare practice landscape. The left-hand axis organises categories of children's needs and risks while the bottom axis organises families and services that are designed as direct and proportionate responses to those categories.

Private family needs refers to needs that are particular to family life. Perhaps a child needs consolation following a minor accident or a number of siblings need help to organise a washing-up rota to avoid simmering resentment each evening. You will recognise these needs as related to the rough-and-tumble of private family life. And each family has its own unique way of responding to these needs through *private family actions*.

Universal needs are not restricted to family life and need to be satisfied beyond the family unit. For example, we all need to learn and to develop. We all need to have basic health to function as well as we can and the safety to move about our communities and further afield too. *Universal services* include those services designed to respond precisely to this kind of need: access to GPs and nurses, local police, children's centres, compulsory education and funded places in nurseries, for example.

Additional needs are more specific to individual people, going beyond what most people in most families would experience. For example, someone may have a particularly unusual health condition or struggle particularly with skills related to learning, such as reading or writing. In such cases, they need *additional services* (such as speech and language therapists or special educational needs professionals) in order to engage with tasks as an equal with others who do not share the particular additional need.

Complex needs are just that – they are difficult to sort out, to de-tangle. Needs appear tied in with other needs. For example, perhaps the unusual health condition relates to the quality of housing in which someone lives. Do they rely on prescribed medication to help alleviate their health condition or do they try to find new accommodation instead and hope that the health condition sorts itself out in time? And how might this change affect the children's school attendance? They need services to co-ordinate their interactions, to help identify pathways to an improved outcome. This is often the place for *multi-agency service integration*, common assessment and services that assess people's holistic lives. It can also be that point at which a local authority's children's service department considers a child to be a '*child in need*' (see Children Act, 1989, s17.1.a–b).

So far, the categories of need and their corresponding services fall into early help and early intervention services, addressed in terms of health equity, life chances and foundation years and safeguarding (Field, 2010; Marmot, 2010; Allen, 2011; DfE, 2011; Tickell, 2011).

The next category, *Risk of significant harm*, ups the ante somewhat. It moves away from needs to thinking about risks – to you and to others. For example, a child is experiencing neglect, or some other maltreatment and abuse, perhaps emotional, physical, sexual or even a combination of these. Given the risk the child is exposed to, it will require the authority of a social worker and the protection plans that they can make on the child's behalf. In the case where a child is *suffering significant harm*, it requires a service that can offer immediate protection by removing the child to a place of safety.

What enables services to organise and re-organise around children's needs and the risks they may experience is *formal assessment* by professionals. Following the *Framework for the Assessment of Need* (DoH, DfEE and HO, 2000, now covered by DfE, 2015), these assessments often take heed of children's developmental needs, the child's family and environmental factors as well as the child's parent's or parents' capacity to parent.

The shaded cells that rise from left to right in Figure 12.1 represent adequate service provision in response to identified and assessed need. This is *effective work*: children's well-being needs are met by appropriate services. When circumstances change, needs can become more acute or may become less acute and more manageable. Child welfare service provision can respond to such change in circumstances through the *escalation* and *de-escalation* of concerns across the service provision (represented by the arrows in Figure 12.1). For example, multi-agency meetings can agree that the robust intervention of social services is necessary in a particular case (escalation of concern) and, following investigation, the social worker may be satisfied that their intervention is unnecessary under the circumstances (de-escalation). In summary, what Figure 12.1 represents is the safeguarding network. *Everybody's responsibility* is visible.

What enables you to adapt to changes in circumstance is *co-operation* within services and families. The Children Act 2004 (see section 10.1–3) indicates that the responsibility of early years students really is to co-operate with children, families and other organisations to work out how best to safeguard children's well-being. Co-operation must not be understood by children and families as '*Do as I say*'. You must beware of taking positions of moral superiority. Instead, those of us working with children and families need to take responsibility for being seen as '*agents of hope and support*', who offer '*meaningful, hands-on, practical support*' and are most definitely '*not part of the problem*' (Featherstone et al, 2013, p 14).

How might you ever be part of the problem? In her review of the child protection system, Munro (DfE, 2011) noted practitioners' fixation with *doing things right* – we place our trust in blind obedience and compliance with procedure when faced with safeguarding concerns. So, one potential problem with the safeguarding network is that we use procedure to keep us safe but not necessarily to keep children safe. Munro instead proposed that we should be determined *to do the right thing*, where we learn how to help children by reflecting on awkward questions such as, '*Is following procedure actually going to help this child?*' What we develop through positive engagement with the awkward answers is what Munro calls *a learning culture* in children's safeguarding and child protection practice, where we begin to look at adapting our practice rather than applying a one-size-fits-all approach (see, in particular, DfE, 2010, p 14, para 1.17 and p 15, para 1.18).

Critical question

> *Imagine a straight line with a point at each end. At one end is total obedience to rules and compliance with procedure. At the other end is reflection and creativity – a willingness to learn how to adapt rules and provide help to children.*

» *Reflect on your professional competence when faced with difficult safeguarding and child protection questions and situations: what position are you likely to adopt and why?*

Figure 12.2 now points to another problem with the so-called net. Unlike the shaded cells of Figure 12.1, we are now more interested in what can happen in the *unshaded cells*. The greater number of unshaded cells suggests that there may be a greater chance of children's safeguarding needs corresponding with *inappropriate and disproportionate* services, following poor or inaccurate assessment of children's needs. For example, the Cleveland Inquiry (Butler-Sloss, 1988) discovered that paediatricians' poor assessment of children's needs and a local authority's social services department's poor practice had led to more than one hundred children being taken from their parents into state care – *unnecessarily so*, given the evidence. Figure 12.2 shows that the children addressed by the Cleveland Inquiry in reality experienced universal through to perhaps complex needs but, having had these needs assessed by child protection services operating in a vigilante mode, the children were removed from families rather than supported, more appropriately, by universal to complex services. Although these events took place some decades ago, the danger of causing harm to children and families through poor assessment remains today.

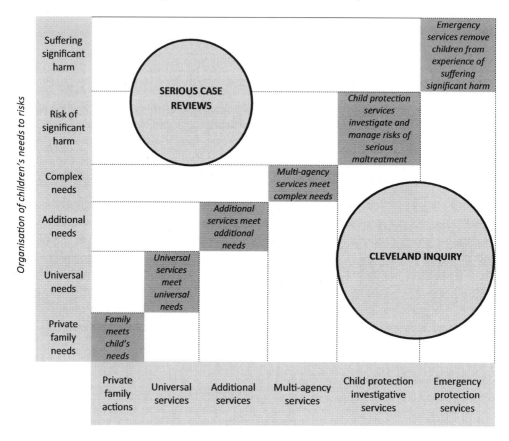

Organisation of resources from families to acute professional services

Figure 12.2 *Examples of failure in the safeguarding net*

Conversely, regular analysis of serious case reviews shows that significant numbers of children who suffer significant harm, often very young children, are *not known* to child protection agencies and are instead being supported by services designed to offer early help services, such as early years services:

> *Our findings indicate that approximately half of the children at the centre of the review are not known to children's social care [...]. [T]wo thirds of all serious case reviews concern children under the age of five (and half are for infants under twelve months). [...] Many of the very young children do not come to the attention of children's social care, so the role of GPs, midwives and health visitors, and other early years provision like Sure Start Children's Centres, is crucial for this highly vulnerable group.*
>
> (Brandon et al, 2010, p 52, para 6.2)

This situation is shown in Figure 12.2 by the circle indicating children at risk of significant harm and children who suffer significant harm but who are supported by families, universal services and so on – services that are simply not designed to address this scale of need adequately. This group too sits within the unshaded cells of the net, evading the safety of the shaded cells that indicate appropriate safeguarding networks. Recent and ongoing service cuts and restructuring in local authority children's services and the voluntary sector serve only to exacerbate this situation. Figure 12.2 illustrates that appropriate assessment, rather than over-activity or under-activity, upholds an effective safeguarding network.

Horwath (2007) argues that such practice mistakes may relate, at least in part, to the 'missing domain' of assessment: the *practitioner domain*. Where professionals unwaveringly stick to established procedure, or dare not divert from their manager's or supervisor's instructions and expectations, then the net will struggle to provide adequate services to meet children's actual needs. What this means is that we each have a responsibility to reflect on our own temptation to do things right (follow rules) at the expense of doing the right thing by children (reflecting on these rules to see how they may need to be changed so that children receive help). Ofsted consider the ability of a team to collaborate in such a way as to safeguard children effectively to be a characteristic of *outstanding leadership and management* in schools and early years settings (see the Ofsted inspection handbooks for further detail – Ofsted, 2015b, p 34 and Ofsted, 2015c, p 43). Where Munro (DfE, 2011) called for a learning culture, Ofsted calls this collaboration a *culture of vigilance* (see Ofsted, 2015a, p 34).

Critical questions

The Birmingham serious case review (BSCB, 2010, para 7.4) recommends that managers of nurseries 'create a culture where the voice of everyone in the staff team is valued and heard including students on placement'. How can you take responsibility to hear and value others' perspectives in order to reflect on the safeguarding policies and procedures that direct your work?

» *What skills, knowledge and understanding do you need to support you in developing the confidence to learn to challenge practice and ensure that your voice is heard? Putting the mistaken idea of a safeguarding net aside, who is your safeguarding network?*

» *How will you contribute to developing a 'culture of vigilance' (Ofsted, 2015) to work collaboratively within a team when in practice?*

Chapter reflections

» *When on placement you will face safeguarding and child protection responsibilities.*

» *As you progress through your degree, you should develop the skills necessary to prepare for practice as well as the ability to distinguish between the needs and risks of children's welfare.*

» *Keeping abreast of current safeguarding documents can develop an understanding of children's safeguarding (see reference list).*

» *Continuous academic and professional development through critical action and reflective practice is vital in ensuring that you are effectively able to work with children and families in an ever-changing landscape.*

» *Working in the early years, you are uniquely placed to take critical action when faced with safeguarding and child protection concerns. Therefore, it is vital that you are vigilant in your practice on a day-to-day basis. You must develop the confidence to challenge, using the frameworks for assessment and monitoring to identify concerns and take critical action to safeguard children's well-being.*

» *We must all move from the necessity of compliance with procedure to a position where we can question whether or not our rules are sufficient in safeguarding all children's well-being. We must be willing to play our part in a learning culture (DfE, 2011), to find our place in a local safeguarding network of effective practice.*

Further reading

Powell, J and Uppal, E L (2012) *Safeguarding Babies and Young Children: A Guide for Early Years Professionals.* Maidenhead. Open University Press.

References

Allen, G (2011) *Early Intervention: The Next Steps. An Independent Report to Her Majesty's Government.* London: Cabinet Office, HM Government.

Birmingham Safeguarding Children Board (BSCB) (2010) *Serious Case Review: Under Chapter VIII 'Working Together to Safeguard Children'. In Respect of the Serious Injury of Case no. 2010–11/3* (Report by Jane Wonnacott).

Brandon, M, Bailey, S and Belderson, P (2010) *Building on the Learning from Serious Case Reviews: A Two-Year Analysis of Child Protection Database Notifications 2007–2009* (Research Report DFE-RR040). Norwich: University of East Anglia.

Butler-Sloss, Judge E (1988) *Report of the Inquiry into Child Abuse in Cleveland 1987* (Cm 412). London: Her Majesty's Stationery Office.

Department for Education (DfE) (2010) *The Munro Review of Child Protection. Part One: A Systems Analysis.* London: DfE.

Department for Education (DfE) (2011) *The Munro Review of Child Protection: Final Report – A Child-Centred System.* London: DfE.

Department for Education (DfE) (2012) *Foundations for Quality: The Independent Review of Early Education and Childcare Qualifications. Final Report.* Cheshire: DfE.

Department for Education (DfE) (2014) *Statutory Framework for the Early Years Foundation Stage: Setting the Standards for Learning, Development and Care for Children from Birth to Five. Published March 2014. Effective September 2014.* London: DfE.

Department for Education (DfE) (2016) *Keeping Children Safe in Schools and Colleges: Statutory Guidance for Schools and Colleges* (Ref DfE-00140-2016). London: DfE.

Department of Health, Department for Education and Employment and the Home Office (DoH, DfEE and HO) (2000) *Framework for the Assessment of Children in Need and their Families.* Norwich: Her Majesty's Stationery Office.

Early Education (The British Association for Early Childhood Education) (2012) *Development Matters in the Early Years Foundation Stage (EYFS).* London: Early Education.

Featherstone, B, Morris, K and White, S (2013) A Marriage Made in Hell: Early Intervention Meets Child Protection. *British Journal of Social Work*, 44(7): 1735–49.

Field, F (2010) *The Foundation Years: Preventing Poor Children Becoming Poor Adults. The Report of the Independent Review on Poverty and Life Chances.* London: Cabinet Office, HM Government.

Horwath, J (2007) The Missing Assessment Domain: Personal, Professional and Organizational Factors Influencing Professional Judgements when Identifying and Referring Child Neglect. *British Journal of Social Work*, 37(8): 1285–1303.

Marmot, M (2010) *Fair Society, Healthy Lives: Strategic Review of Health Inequalities in England, Post-2010* (The Marmot Review). London: Marmot Review.

Munro, E, Taylor, J S and Bradbury-Jones, C (2014) Understanding the Causal Pathways to Child Maltreatment: Implications for Health and Social Care Policy and Practice. *Child Abuse Review*, 23(1): 61–74.

Ofsted (Office for Standards in Education, Children's Services and Skills) (2014) *Whistleblowing to Ofsted about Safeguarding in Local Authority Children's Services: Policy and Guidance for Whistleblowers* (ref no 100036). Manchester: Ofsted.

Ofsted (2015a) *Inspecting Safeguarding in Early Years, Education and Skills Settings: Guidance for Inspectors undertaking Inspection under the Common Inspection Framework* (reference no 150067). Manchester: Ofsted.

Ofsted (2015b) *Early Years Inspection Handbook: Handbook for Inspecting Early Years in England under Sections 49 and 50 of the Childcare Act 2006*. Manchester: Ofsted.

Ofsted (2015c) *School Inspection Handbook: Handbook for Inspecting Schools in England under Section 5 of the Education Act 2005*. Manchester: Ofsted.

Ofsted (2016) *Inspecting Safeguarding in the Early Years, Education and Skills Settings: Guidance for Inspectors undertaking Inspection under the Common Inspection Framework* (ref no 160047). Manchester: Ofsted.

Tickell, D C (2011) *The Early Years: Foundations for Life, Health and Learning: An Independent Report on the Early Years Foundation Stage to Her Majesty's Government*. London: DfE.

13 Learning to be an ethical practitioner

CARLA SOLVASON

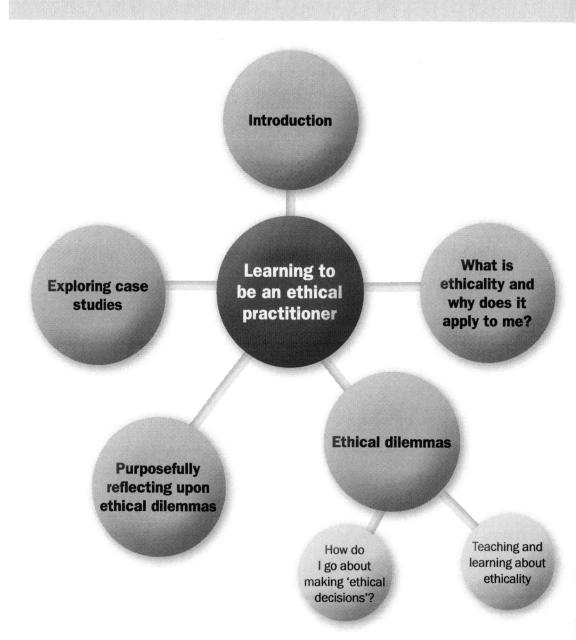

- Introduction
- Learning to be an ethical practitioner
- What is ethicality and why does it apply to me?
- Exploring case studies
- Purposefully reflecting upon ethical dilemmas
- Ethical dilemmas
  - How do I go about making 'ethical decisions'?
  - Teaching and learning about ethicality

Ethical conduct in the world consists not of being able to recite principles but in being willing really to engage with the messiness and complexity of the world to make things better.

(Beckett, 2009, p 67)

Introduction

This chapter encourages you to view yourself as an ethical professional and to recognise your ethical responsibilities throughout your studies and your practice. The topic of ethicality within early years is often seen as an aspect research, that is its *place*. Outside of research, within day-to-day practice, we frequently mention the terms safeguarding and confidentiality, but not general *ethical practice*. It is important not to view ethicality as something that is related to your research only, but to recognise it as a way of being that should underpin all aspects of your practice.

What is ethicality and why does it apply to me?

Ethical practice as a term is surprisingly absent from the discourse of early childhood studies. The meaning of the term *to be ethical* is usually taken for granted and rarely unpacked. Aubrey et al (2000, p 155, my emphasis) state that '*ethics means **the moral philosophy or set of moral principles** underpinning a project*'. Here we can substitute '*a project*' with '*our practice*'. Ethicality is about the beliefs and principles that comprise the foundation of our practice with young children. You will notice the use of '*moral*' used by Aubrey et al, because ethicality is about acting in a 'right' or 'good' way. Behaving ethically is about doing 'the right thing' by other people and showing sensitivity towards their position and their feelings. It is about showing empathy and understanding. As an early years practitioner, yours is a position of care and you have a responsibility to try to act ethically, despite how '*messy and complex*' (Clifford, 2008) situations often are.

It is important to begin to develop ethical sensitivity from the very outset of your studies and your practice. A large measure of your time studying to become an early years practitioner is actually spent within settings, dealing directly with children, families and colleagues; and with all of the complications that this entails. As an early years student you could, and in all likelihood will, encounter a range of small-scale ethical dilemmas from the very beginning of your studies. These could range from inappropriate comments made on social media, to concerns about children, to issues with colleagues. It is important that you feel prepared to tackle these situations, or that you at least have a good idea where to start. James et al (2005) discuss how practitioners like yourselves, with the moral obligations of public service, must have a '*good character*' if they are to shape the character of the young. This is a huge responsibility for you as trainee practitioners, and something that can often be taken for granted.

Critical questions

»   *Do you feel that you have already encountered 'ethical dilemmas' in your studies or your practice?*

»   *What were these and how did you reach a decision about how to respond?*

» *Were you content that you made the 'right' decision?*

Ethical dilemmas

Ethical dilemmas such as *conflict of interest* apply just as readily to those training in early childhood as they do to those studying subjects such as business or law. As an early years practitioner, you need to consider what you should do when your concerns for a child's needs conflict with the desire of the parents, or how you might respond when governors are pushing for a course of action that you know will be detrimental to the experience of the children. On a smaller and more feasible scale, what would you do when you are drawn into a friend's social network conversation that discusses one of your colleagues in a less than favourable light (as Katie encounters below)? You need to feel prepared and stop to consider the 'good' or the 'right' way to respond.

CASE STUDY

Katie's dilemma

Katie has been in university for six weeks now and the last week was spent in practice at a childcare centre. There were two other students from Katie's course at the setting and she got on with them very well. As a result she became part of these students' groups on Facebook. On the Sunday after her practice Katie browses Facebook and realises that the two students that she was on placement with have been posting critical and unpleasant remarks about one of the practitioners at the children's centre. They did not like her and have been making a number of demeaning comments about her appearance and personality. Worse still, they have named both the practitioner and the setting. What should Katie do?

Critical questions

» *Consider the individuals involved in this scenario and how you might respond if you found yourself in a similar situation.*

» *How useful would the four stages in Table 13.1 below be for guiding your response?*

How do I go about making 'ethical decisions'?

Unfortunately, an *off the shelf* set of rules for making ethical decisions simply doesn't exist. McAuliffe and Chenoweth (2008) offer some useful points for consideration when faced with an ethical dilemma. They suggest the four stages of action shown in Table 13.1 below.

Table 13.1 *Staged response to an ethical dilemma*

Stage One	Consider the **responsibility** that you hold in terms of this dilemma. Who might it affect – children, parents, colleagues?	**Define exactly what the dilemma is and the possible outcomes**. If you do not act then what is the worst-case scenario? If you have recognised this as an ethical dilemma then there are likely to be negative repercussions if it is not acted upon.
Stage Two	**Consult** with significant others who might be able to offer insights into the situation. These will usually be those with greater knowledge and experience within the area, but may alternatively be someone with no contextual knowledge and so impartial. Such a person is often referred to as a *critical friend*.	By doing this your worries can be **legitimised** and supported, instigating next steps, or alternatively they may be abated. You may come to realise that you are worrying for no reason.
Stage Three	Show sensitivity to your **context** – particularly the individuals within it. Consider the socio-cultural aspects (rules, relationships, traditions) which will influence your plan of action.	**Gather the information that you need** to make an informed decision. Consider different approaches which might be taken. What is common practice within your setting? What is policy?
Stage Four	**Critically analyse** the decision that you have reached regarding action. This is another good stage to **consult** with a critical friend.	**Carry out the course of action** that you have decided upon and reflect upon the response. If this is not satisfactory it may mean beginning the process again, at Stage One.

Based upon McAuliffe and Chenoweth (2008)

Teaching and learning about ethicality

Although the need to behave in an ethical manner is intrinsic to the skills of practitioners, this is rarely a formal element of your training. Straightforward processes such as confidentiality are explicitly introduced, but qualities such as care, compassion, sensitivity and empathy are rarely explored in depth in our seminar discussions. James et al (2005, p 19) make a valid point when they ask 'How can the prospective teacher be ethical when he or she does not know with any certainty what it is to be ethical?' Haddad (2005) suggests that some key terms such as being *mindful*, or *self-aware*, or recognising *human dignity*, are key to reflecting upon ethical issues in practice. And Noddings (1984) explains why reflecting upon actual experiences and not only upon *case studies* is necessary:

> ... the actions of one-caring will be varied rather than rule-bound; that is, her actions, while predictable in a global sense, will be unpredictable in detail. Variation is to be expected if the one claiming to care really cares...

Part of caring, Noddings argues, is recognising the individuality of people and contexts and that no two responses to situations will ever be the same. You should not be afraid to bring your experiences to teaching sessions in order to discuss and better understand them. Confidentiality is not breached simply by discussing issues; discussion is not the same as being critical of individuals, which is explored more fully in the next session.

Exploring the literature makes it clear that ethicality or *morality* within teaching has been more fully explored in other countries, for example the USA (Cummings et al, 2001; Fleischmann, 2006; Tuana, 2007) and Australia (Walker et al, 2012), than it has in the UK. Tuana (2007) produced a significant piece of research, which discussed the absence of *'moral literacy'* from American teenagers' education. In this article Tuana argues that moral literacy should take an equal standing with subjects such as literacy or numeracy, yet it is seldom touched upon within secondary schooling. To what extent has acting morally, or ethically, been a part of your own educational experience?

Engen and Kaha (2000) argue that it is not the content of teaching sessions that makes a difference, but the way that tutors act. They contend that the *'hidden curriculum'* that teachers, often subconsciously, nurture, is more important than actual session content. They note that:

> In short, our messages in the classroom do much more than simply transmit information, they build – or disrupt – community, and they teach about citizenship and moral vision in ways we too often ignore.
>
> (Engen and Kaha, 2000, p 22)

Jarvis (1995, p 25) makes a very similar point when he notes that *'the manner through which teachers interact with learners is probably more important that the actual teaching methods employed'*. So these theorists suggest that your university tutors should be modelling, rather than actually teaching, the *good character* that they hope all early years practitioners will develop.

Critical questions

» *What are your thoughts about this? How much do you learn from the content of sessions and how much from the way that the tutor delivers the content?*

» *Now, relate these reflections to your own practice with young children – what significant points can you draw?*

Purposefully reflecting upon ethical dilemmas

The best way to develop your ethical understanding is to discuss and reflect upon actual situations as they arise with someone that you trust, or to *talk through* issues within your reflective writing. But discussing real-life occurrences does need a clear set of ethical guidelines. The following approaches can help to change a potentially unprofessional outburst into a useful professional reflection.

1. Focus upon the *issue* or *dilemma* that has caused difficulty, not upon the individuals involved. Never use names, instead generalise, so that your discussion will be about a practitioner, a student or a parent; it won't be about Ruth, or Steve, or Charlie's mum.

2. Try not to judge. Although it is likely that these situations have become dilemmas because they have caused an emotional reaction in you, such as hurt or outrage, try to accept that initial, human reaction and then step back from the situation to view it more objectively. It is vital to consider the factors acting upon the other individuals involved and their differing perspectives of the situation. Talking with someone who is less emotionally involved will often help you to gain a clearer view of the different perspectives.

3. Focus your reflection upon devising a way forward. Raising (or writing about) an issue in a negative manner is counterproductive. Considering the situation and then suggesting positive action in relation to your own practice turns your discussion from a tirade into a purposeful reflection.

Below are two reflections upon the same situation. These are the types of reflection often recorded within a placement journal that you might use in your written work. Both students have replaced the child's name with a made-up name (a pseudonym) to maintain anonymity and both have been careful not to use the name of the setting in order to discuss this incident in a confidential way. These examples clearly show that just following ethical processes and procedures in your writing is not enough to make a piece of work ethical in nature.

CASE STUDY

Approach 1

I tried to talk to Kali's mum at the end of the day about Kali's reading at home. Kali has taken a few books home but doesn't seem to have read any of them. Nothing has been written in her home reading record for months. When her mum came in to collect her I tried to tell her how important it was for Kali's language development that she make time at home to hear her read. Her mum was quite rude and dismissive. She didn't seem interested in supporting Kali's development at all.

Approach 2

Kali has taken a few reading books home but doesn't seem to have read any of them. Nothing has been written in her home reading record for months. I wondered why this might be and brought it to the attention of the lead practitioner. The lead practitioner told me that Kali's mum is on her own looking after three children (the eldest two are teenagers) while working full time and has been struggling since the loss of her own mother four months ago. Her mother had been a great help to her with the children and she was finding it hard to adjust to the loss. I discussed some ideas with colleagues about possible ways forward.

When Kali's mum came to collect her the next day she seemed in a rush. I made a point of telling her how well Kali had done with her reading in the setting over the last few weeks and that she had now moved on to the next set of books. She was really pleased to hear that. I told her that she didn't need to feel that she was the only one that could fill in the reading record that Kali took home and that if Kali's older brother or sister heard her read it would be great for them to write a few comments. Kali's mum said that was great, Kali's big brother had been reading with Kali each night before bed, but was not sure whether or not he was 'allowed' to write in her book.

Table 13.2 *Analysis of the two approaches*

Unethical response	Ethical response
Angered outburst	Reasoned and thoughtful reflection
Only one view presented	Information sought about different perspectives
A criticism of the mother	

If you carefully consider these responses you can begin to clearly recognise ethical (caring and empathetic) and unethical (insensitive) responses. *Are you able to complete Table 13.2 above by pulling out the key behaviours from the examples?*

Returning to the three guidance points above, it would be fair to say that Approach 1, although thinly disguised as reflective writing, is in fact an emotional outburst. This piece of writing does not consider the issue, that the child's reading record is not being completed; instead, it focuses on a criticism of the mother as she has not acted in a way that the student considers to be appropriate. Approach 1 offers no empathy or understanding, no care or support for the parent or child and no possible way forward. Approach 1 is simply a criticism of the parent used in such a way as to portray the superior understanding of the student.

Approach 1 demonstrates how, in such situations, our emotions can often take over our reasoning; this is why talking to someone who is not emotionally involved in the event can be extremely helpful. Sometimes it is difficult to see things from different perspectives and talking to someone on the 'outside' of the situation always helps. This approach is also promoted by McAuliffe and Chenoweth (2008) in their response guidance. Make sure that this is someone whose opinion you respect and avoid identifying a friend that you know will agree with you. An appropriate *critical friend* will be able to offer a detached and rational view and may be able to offer insights into the situation that you had not considered. Your tutors will be happy to talk through such situations with you.

Although the second reflective piece is considering precisely the same issue, the response could not be more different. Starting with the same issue of the reading record not having been completed, the focus of Approach 2 is to identify the reasons for the problem, the precedents. Having taken the time to talk to colleagues, the student has then reflected upon how both mother and child can be best supported, reaching a potential solution. Not only does she present this solution, but by showing sensitivity to the vulnerable position that the parent is currently in, she frames it in as positive and supportive a manner as possible. Her approach is one of sharing something positive with the mother, there is no hint of 'telling off' in this dialogue. The key difference between these two approaches is the time made to reflect upon the issue and within that reflection to carefully and sensitively consider the alternative perspectives of all individuals involved. The second reflection is mindful of the '*dignity of the parent*', to use Haddad's (2005) terminology.

But sometimes it is difficult to make time for careful consideration as the professional demands placed upon practitioners seem to increase almost daily. From planning, to assessment, to record keeping, to information sharing and working collaboratively, there are rarely enough hours in the day to take stock. Despite best intentions the need for haste can sometimes sabotage thoughtful reflection. In the Snapchat and Twitter age replies are formulated within seconds, meaning that frequently there is no time to stop, review or edit one's thoughts. Czarniawska (2013) discusses how within the current electronic generation thoughts are often 'burped' out without temperance. How can you find time to slow down and systematically consider your thoughts and actions? How can you make the time to act mindfully?

Critical questions

» *Have you ever posted something in haste on social media that you have later regretted? If so, how did you feel?*

» *Does your online, public persona reflect that of the ethical professional that you strive to be and that you would like potential employers to see?*

RESEARCH FOCUS

Making time for mindfulness

It may seem strange for a chapter discussing early years education to refer to a science and engineering article, but Fleischmann's (2006) exploration of teaching ethics within an American university's school of engineering is extremely thought-provoking. In this article she unpacks many of the issues that I have just begun to touch upon in this last section, such as the 'problem' of living for the present, influenced by the rapid technological shift over recent times. Fleischmann explores some key literature which outlines a shift away from historical principles over the last century towards a life of '*the present*', which does not retain the underpinning foundations of honour and respect for others that it has had in the past. She touches upon Bloom's (1987) depiction of young people today living in an '*impoverished present*' starved of '*an understanding of the past and a vision for the future, both of which come out of the human tradition that is passed from generation to generation in the form of shared values and standards of human behaviour*' (Fleischmann, 2006, p 383). She concludes that in a world where students want answers, not reasons for them, the teaching of ethics has become more difficult than ever.

Critical questions

»   *What are your thoughts on these ideas presented by Fleischmann?*

»   *Are you content to simply take on board what you have been told is the 'right' answer, or do you feel it is important to explore the issue more deeply and be sure that you understand why?*

By modelling the creation of time and space to explore emotional responses and reasons why, we demonstrate that these aspects are just as worthy of consideration as other skills and knowledge. We should all try to find the time and space in our seminars and in our activities with children to introduce the language of ethicality: care, empathy, mindfulness, kindness and sensitivity. Regardless of the ever mounting pressures of assessment, we should not lose sight of '*the ethic of concern for persons that forms the very essence of education itself*' (Jarvis, 1995, p 25).

Exploring case studies

Although it has been stated above that it is best to explore real-life examples emerging from your own practice, some of you may be fortunate enough not to have encountered such situations so far. For this reason, some examples are given below of the types of ethical dilemmas, involving children, colleagues, parents and fellow students, that you are likely to come across in your practice experience.

CASE STUDIES

1. Safeguarding concerns

You are on practice in a nursery, in the toddler room. You have been working with these children for two weeks and you feel that you are getting to know them quite well. Thomas is just over two years old and appears to have a voracious appetite, although he looks quite underweight. During snack time he is prone to snatch food and has even taken food from the other children. You notice practitioners telling Thomas off quite sharply for this and hear one practitioner tell Thomas that he will have to miss his next snack time because of his behaviour. You feel uneasy about this situation and the way that this is being dealt with.

2. Policy breach

You were employed by one of your placements, a pre-school, on a part-time basis, because they were impressed by your interaction with the children. You thoroughly enjoy working at the nursery due to its caring ethos and you regularly encourage your friends to come and do their placements there. One of your best friends at university is currently on placement with you. This friend is going through a very difficult break-up with his girlfriend. Although very unsettled, he is managing to control his emotions and get on with his placement. You have noticed, though, that he is texting whenever he is out of view of the other practitioners. Because you are aware of his situation he assumes that you will understand his need to text, even though there is a *no mobile phones* policy at the setting. He has been relying on you a great deal for emotional support at this time and you are wary of confronting him about this.

3. Confidentiality

You have only been at your new placement three days and you are quite shocked by the way that a number of practitioners at the setting talk about the families. Some of the practitioners are friends with parents of the children in the setting and see them socially. They will openly discuss private details about those parents in front of both yourself and the children. Sometimes these have included comments about drunkenness and even promiscuousness. This appears to be the 'norm' within this setting due to the social relationships in existence. Comments made have implicated a sense of 'fun', not concern about the parents under discussion.

Critical question

»   Use the three guidance points suggested previously to unpack each of these case studies: what is the actual issue, what factors may be influencing different perspectives, and what are possible ways forward?

Chapter reflections

As an early years practitioner you have a responsibility to carry out 'ethics work'. Banks (2009, p 62) defines this as 'the work that goes into being caring, attentive and compassionate in situations where this would not be our natural response'. It would not be a stretch of the imagination to suppose that many who choose a career in early years do have a caring nature, and this will enable an ethical or moral response to a situation as a matter of course. But sometimes doing 'the right thing' can be more difficult. You may have conflicting principles, or, as Beckett (2009, p 67) points out, 'the morally correct course of action is often not clear'. That is when ethics becomes work.

While this chapter cannot provide full 'answers', it should help you recognise your own responsibility to engage in 'ethics work' and to endeavour to do what is 'good' or 'right'. Sometimes the best course of action will not be clear and sometimes you will make mistakes, everyone does, but it is dealing with human frailties and foibles that makes a caring and understanding approach so important for us all.

Further reading

Banks, S (2009) From Professional Ethics to Ethics in Professional Life: Implications for Learning, Teaching and Study. *Ethics and Social Welfare*, 3(1): 55–63.

References

Aubrey, C, David, T, Godfrey, R and Thompson, L (2000) *Early Childhood Educational Research: Issues in Methodology and Ethics*. London: Routledge.

Banks, S (2009) From Professional Ethics to Ethics in Professional Life: Implications for Learning, Teaching and Study. *Ethics and Social Welfare*, 3(1): 55–63.

Beckett, C (2009) Ethics that Work? A Critical Review of Ethics and Values in Teaching and Practice – Papers from the Ethics and Social Welfare Conference, London, 10 November 2008: Editorial Introduction. *Ethics and Social Welfare*, 3(1): 54–76.

Cummings, R, Dyas, L, Maddux, C D and Kochman, A (2001) Principled Moral Reasoning and Behavior of Preservice Teacher Education Students. *American Educational Research Journal*, 38(1): 143–58.

Czarniawska, B (2013) Cyberwork: Cybernization and Cyborgization in News Agencies. Paper presented at the *8th Researching Work and Learning Conference*, Stirling.

Engen, D E and Kaha, C W (2000) Moral Conversations. *College Teaching*, 48(1): 22.

Fleischmann, S T (2006) Teaching Ethics: More than an Honour Code. *Science and Engineering Ethics*, 12: 381–89.

Haddad, A (2005). Applying the Scholarship of Teaching and Learning to Ethics Education in Occupational and Physical Therapy, in *Educating for Moral Action: A Sourcebook in Health and Rehabilitation Ethics*. Philadelphia, PA: F.A. Davis Publishers, pp 305–10.

James, A, Davison, J and Lewis, M (2005) *Professional Values and Practice: Achieving the Standards for QTS*. London: Routledge.

Jarvis, P (1995) Teachers and Learners in Adult Education: Transaction or Moral Interaction? *Studies in the Education of Adults*, 27(1): 24. [online] Available at: Academic Search Complete (accessed November 2016).

McAuliffe, D and Chenoweth, L (2008). Leave no Stone Unturned: The Inclusive Model of Ethical Decision Making. *Ethics and Social Welfare*, 2(1): 38–49.

Moore, T (1993) Care of the Soul. The Benefits – and Costs – of a More Spiritual Life. *Psychology Today*, May–June: 28–30, 76–77.

Noddings, N (1984) *Caring: A Feminine Approach to Ethics*. London: University of California Press.

Tuana, N (2007) Conceptualizing Moral Literacy. *Journal of Educational Administration*, 45(4): 364–78.

Walker, S, Brownlee, J, Whiteford, C, Cobb-Moore, C, Johansson, E, Ailwood, J and Boulton-Lewis, G (2012) Early Years Teachers' Epistemic Beliefs and Beliefs about Children's Moral Learning. *Teachers and Teaching: Theory and Practice*, 18(2): 263–75. doi: 10.1080/13540602.2012.632267.

14 Doing your research project

MAGGI SAVIN-BADEN

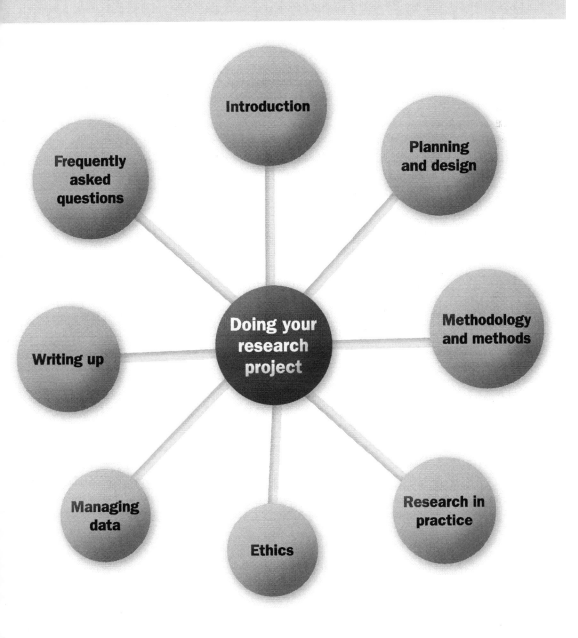

Learning is but an adjunct to ourself
And where we are our learning likewise is.

Shakespeare (1597)
Love's Labour's Lost, Act IV Sc III

Introduction

This chapter explains the importance of planning and organising research and enables you to consider the importance of research in practice. It begins by explaining the design and planning stage and presents different research methodologies. The chapter suggests research methods to use and provides guidance on the ethics procedure. The final part of the chapter recommends ways of managing data and writing up your project.

Your research project

When undertaking research it is important to ask a number of questions that will enable you to develop a clear research question and design for your research. Often people who undertake a research project assume that *interviewing* is qualitative research, or that *surveys* are quantitative research, and fail to understand the need to have a strong design and clear methodology.

Critical question

»   *What are your concerns about undertaking research?*

Planning and design

Beginning your research project with a good design helps to keep the focus of your research clear and enables you to keep it on schedule. Figure 14.1 will help you to think through all the different areas you need to plan and design.

Your research question

It is often difficult to focus on a manageable research question. The easy option often seems to be to think of something you are interested in, rather than looking for gaps in the research. By examining what has not been explored already it will then be possible to develop a problem statement, and from that develop a research question. For example, how do people manage stress in the Early Childhood Centres and what would help them to feel less stressed? You could measure stress but it would not really tell you what to change. A way to ensure you have a workable question is to ask yourself the following questions:

- What do you want to know?

- How will you find this out?

- What is manageable?

- How will you ensure your study is robust?

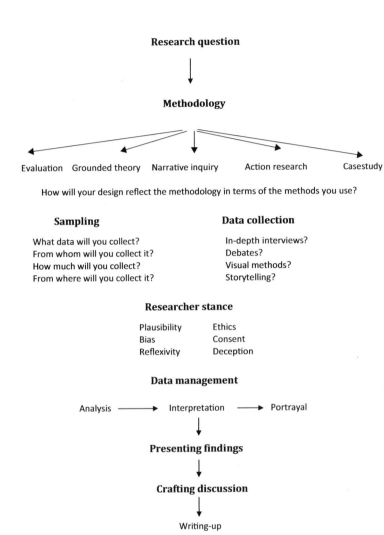

Figure 14.1 *Planning your research project*

What is a research question? It is a question that highlights what is to be studied and indicates what the researcher wishes to know about it. For example:

* How do rural students experience online courses?

* What factors do early childhood students perceive as barriers or opportunities for their learning?

* How do students learn with and through others in placement settings?

Undertaking a literature review

A literature review is an overview of the research studies and literature that relates to the topic you are studying. You need to remember that you cannot include everything and so you will need to be focused. Perhaps consider just finding 25–30 articles and reviewing

15–20 that are the most relevant to your study. Your literature review should contain critical analysis of previous research studies, and sometimes non-research-based literature, on the topic you are investigating. The literature review is more than just a description of what has been undertaken already. As a researcher you need to indicate which are research studies, which studies are qualitative, quantitative or mixed methods and what is an opinion piece. Furthermore, your literature also needs to provide an analytical argument and draw conclusions, so that you are not just reporting who said what, but putting your research questions in the context of the existing literature.

Questions to ask yourself when doing a literature review.

- What do you already know about the topic?
- Has anyone else ever conducted the same study?
- What do we still need to know about the topic?
- Why is this research worth doing?

Critical question

» *How soon do you think you need to start planning your literature review?*

Methodology and methods

When starting out on a research project, people often struggle with understanding the difference between approaches.

- Quantitative research focuses on cause and effect relationships and thus this form of research makes assumptions (hypotheses) and then tests them to prove what is or is not true. By using the correct techniques you will be able to gain correct answers; for example, by measuring and then changing calorific intake you can work out the most effective weight-loss diet.

- Qualitative research is used to learn about, describe and explain people's perceptions: so conduct research with people, rather than on them. For example, the researchers might ask people through interviews what they felt the impact of eating chocolate was on their health.

Mixed methods combines qualitative and quantitative research, so you might undertake a survey to explore people's opinions about chocolate and then interview a few of those with differing views.

Often people get confused between methodology and methods; but there is a clear difference:

- **Methodology** is the particular kind of research undertaken. It refers to the rationale and the philosophical assumptions that underlie the study, whether qualitative, mixed methods or quantitative. A qualitative example would be ethnography or phenomenology. Some researchers call these research strategies, research designs, research approaches or research traditions.

- **Methods** are the tools used to collect data, such as interviewing or focus groups, that need to fit with the methodology. It is no good doing a quick 15-minute interview if using narrative inquiry, as you will have little narrative and no story!

When choosing methodology you need to think about:

- What is the relationship between the methodology and the context, or topic, of the research?
- What type of data will you collect?
- How will you analyse and interpret data?
- What are the ethical issues and how will you tackle them?
- How will you ensure your data are plausible?

Methodological options

It is important to choose a methodology as this frames your whole project and helps you to choose the right methods. For example, if you wanted to know about people's stories of becoming a parent you would choose narrative inquiry. If you wanted to see if a new assessment system worked in a nursery, you would choose action research. Some of the methodologies are as follows:

Action research

This is about changing and improving practice and is a method based on cycles of action and reflection. A spin-off from this is *participatory action research* (Carr and Kemmis, 1986), which involves examining an issue from the perspectives of the community members most affected by that issue.

Arts-based research

This approach uses art to collect data and explore meaning, using emotion, intellect and physical movement to create research and art together.

Case study

There are many different types but case study is useful for testing whether theories and models actually work in the real world.

Ethnography

This is an approach that involves intensive fieldwork to gain a detailed and comprehensive view of a social group and its setting. A more recent approach is *virtual ethnography*, which seeks to understand what people *do* on the internet (Hine, 2000).

Evaluation

Evaluation approaches are used to study an organisation or curriculum in such a way that it contributes to a review of policy and decision-making within the organisation.

Grounded theory

Grounded theory is a research approach that developed in the late 1960s which has the overt purpose of generating theory from empirical (first-hand) data.

Narrative inquiry

This uses stories for collecting data and researchers in this area seek to tell stories of people's lives, and then present them as narratives of experience.

Phenomenology

Phenomenologists are researchers who seek to examine meanings of phenomena (observable events) through exploring people's lived experience.

Pragmatic qualitative research

This approach draws upon the practical methods available in order to answer a given research question and researchers aim for a description of an experience or event as interpreted by the researcher.

Critical question

» *What do you think will be the difficulties if you mix up your methodologies?*

Research in practice

Having worked out which methodology to use, you then need to consider how to collect data. This is referred to as fieldwork and part of designing this part of the project involves working out who to include (sampling).

CASE STUDY

Doing research

Before I (Maggi) did any real fieldwork I just thought I could easily slot in two interviews at lunchtime and two after work, and that they would be interesting. No one had said how it really might be. I am not saying it was awful, just most of the time it was not how I thought it would be. I assumed four interviews in a day would be fine, that I would easily get 20 interviews and four observations done in a week. I was wrong. People told me things I felt they should not have. Some turned up late, others arrived early. People said they could spend 30 minutes with me and stayed for two hours. Nothing prepared me for the sheer intensity of fieldwork; your nerves feel as if they are on fire. The excitement and the adrenaline, but also the questions and worry involved in fieldwork, are something that is still, for me, a surprise.

Data collection

Collecting data needs to reflect your methodology. For example, if using participatory action research, rather than just using semi-structured interviews it is better to use interview debates with participants in their own setting, so that exploring ideas and sharing perspectives reflects the methodology undertaken. When you are planning to collect data you need to decide who to include and what your reasoning for this is.

Sampling

There are two main ways of sampling; *theoretical sampling* and *purposeful sampling*. Theoretical sampling is designed to generate theory, carried out during data collection and grounded in data; as such it is most frequently associated with grounded theory. Purposeful sampling is based upon the research tradition and research question, the goal being to understand something when generalisation is unnecessary. For example, interviewing eight different early years educators from different nurseries in different counties would give you a wide sample size.

Data collection methods

There are a wide range of approaches to collecting data, which include quantitative methods. If you use quantitative methods such as a survey it is vital to ensure that you are clear about which statistical tests you will use to analyse these data before you collect them. The main qualitative methods used tend to be:

Interviews

There are many types and styles of research interview (Patton, 1990); the most common ones are:

- **The informal conversation interview** – this relies on the spontaneous generation of questions so that questions arise from the context, with the result that data gathered from each interview will be different.

- **The semi-structured interview** – a list of issues or questions are explored in the interview. You can ask open-ended questions such as *'Tell me about your experiences of teaching here'*. It is important to avoid *why* questions as they can be threatening. You can also use follow-up questions such as *"You said the Government "made you angry", can you tell me some more about that?'*

- **The standardised open-ended interview** – here interviewees are asked the same questions using the same words.

Focus groups

A focus group is a gathering of individuals, who through conversation with each other, provide information about a specific topic, issue or subject. Focus groups have been used for evaluating products during marketing campaigns, providing political perspectives and providing feedback on screenings of films. In contrast, a group interview involves an interviewer who asks questions with a group. In practice the interviewer asks a question and individuals respond in turn.

Observation

Observation can provide a researcher with information about the participants within a natural environment that could not be gained using another data collection approach. One of the greatest disadvantages of observation, however, is that a researcher's presence might have an effect on the situation, but often people just get used to you being there. However, it is important never to observe people at work without their consent and never imagine you could do a better job than those you are observing; your task as an observer is to analyse and understand – not to judge.

Before you collect any data you need to ensure your project passes an ethics board and gains ethical approval.

Ethics

Ethics are the moral principles that govern behaviour. Bogdan and Biklen define ethics in research as the '*principles of right and wrong that a particular group accepts*' (1992, p 49). Some of the areas that bear consideration include:

* **Consent**: Informed consent provides information to a participant about the potential risks and benefits of participating in a study. There is often an assumption made by researchers, once consent has been gained and a form signed, that this consent is both informed and lasts for the duration of the project. However, consent can never be something that is fully informed, as participants rarely completely understand what they have signed up for or indeed what is published as a result of what they have said, even if they have signed a form stating that they do. Nevertheless, it is important to have a consent protocol in place.

* **Plausibility**: This is a technique for ensuring you take a critical approach and acknowledge the complexities of managing 'truths' in research. This way of ensuring rigour has been called *triangulation* in the past but this is now seen as too rigid and related to quantitative approaches so has been superseded by other terms, the best probably being plausibility.

* **Bias**: In research, bias often is considered to be negative and something to be removed, although some researchers believe this to be impossible. Researchers should be prepared to engage with biases – the researcher's own biases as well as those of the participants. How will you develop a better set of biases?

* **Reflexivity** helps researchers to consider their position and influence during the study. An important way of becoming reflexive is to keep a research journal where you tell the story of a research journey and reflect upon the way you collected data and the ways in which you were challenged.

- **To whom does the data belong?** It is important to send back the transcription of data to the participants (called participant validation) and also provide an overview of how you have brought the data together (called member checking).

- **Agreements**: Be sure that everyone knows what they have signed up to and the consequences. Do not agree to anything you cannot ensure will happen, such as sharing data and publishing together with fellow researchers.

What is an ethics committee?

A Research Ethics Committee (REC) typically comprises a group of five or more lecturers, experts and administrators who review and potentially approve research proposals. They also review research instruments (including surveys and interview protocols) and materials for participants (including requests for participation and informed consent forms). Guidance on ethics can be found on the British Education Research Association website or you can use the EECERA guidelines (www.eecera.org/documents/pdf/organisation/EECERA-Ethical-Code.pdf).

Ethics and children and vulnerable groups

Children or other vulnerable groups include those people who are not legally able to provide informed consent due to age or incompetence, or who are in an unequal relationship with the researcher. This group also can include individuals with disability, who are members of a minority group or who have language difficulties. What counts as vulnerability is contested since there are many reasons why research participants may be seen as vulnerable or disadvantaged. Issues to be aware of when doing research with these groups are the reinforcement of stereotypes, exploitation of vulnerable participants or causing distress. In most cases, before children can participate, consent is usually obtained from a parent or guardian based on information about what is involved and why, usually provided through an accessibly written information sheet, video or pictures. You also need to ensure you gain assent from the child, which means that if the child appears concerned or uncomfortable you need to stop the interview or activity you are doing with them.

Working in partnership with the research community

As you undertake a research project you will be assigned a supervisor who will offer guidance and advice on the design of your study. Once you have been granted ethical approval you should schedule a meeting with your supervisor within four weeks. When you meet together make sure you are well prepared with an agenda of items you would like to discuss. You should email drafts of each chapter to your supervisor, who will give detailed feedback only once, so make sure it is your best work. You should also share the research design with the setting in which you are conducting your research and consider how you will disseminate your findings so that it can have a positive impact and possibly lead to further research.

Managing data

Once you have collected your data you need to decide what to do with them. One approach is *cutting and coding*. Cutting involves writing text segments on note cards, highlighting meaningful chunks in a word processor or marking the chunks in a data analysis software package. Coding is generally done to accomplish one of two things: description or analysis. Descriptive coding is a process of summarising or describing the text. Analytical coding means deriving codes based upon what the researcher believes is going on. Coding provides clues to meaning and these clues and the connections are used as early stage analysis.

Forms of analysis

Once codes and categories have been developed, they are converted into themes. Qualitative data analysis is an ongoing process that involves breaking data down into meaningful parts for the purpose of examining them. These are some of the main ways of analysing data:

Key word analysis

A key word analysis involves searching out words that have some sort of meaning in the larger context of the data. The idea is that, in order to understand what the participants say, it is important to look at the words with which they communicate. For example, you could look for frequent repetition of terms and unusual use of terms.

Constant comparison

Constant comparison is a method that researchers use to develop themes and ultimately generate theory. This method has since been adapted across qualitative research approaches and involves some of the following basic steps:

* identify categories in events and behaviour;

* continually compare codes and passages to those already coded to find consistencies and differences;

* continue the process until the category *saturates* and no new codes related to it are identified;

* determine which categories are the central focus;

* undertake content analysis, which is an analysis of the frequency and patterns of use of terms or phrases.

Thematic analysis

Thematic analysis is a method of identifying, analysing and reporting patterns in the data. There is no clear agreement for what thematic analysis is or how to do it. The idea is to get a feel for the whole text by living with it prior to any cutting or coding. Braun and Clarke (2006) recommend doing the following when conducting thematic analysis:

*   familiarise yourself with your data;
*   generate initial codes;
*   search for themes;
*   review themes;
*   define and name themes;
*   produce the report.

Having chosen a means of analysing data you then need to move to interpretation.

Data interpretation

Data interpretation can be a confusing part of the research process, largely because it is difficult to identify a precise set of steps to achieve it. Many researchers, for example, use the phrase *the findings emerged* to describe interpretation, a phrase that seems to intimate an almost magical process, almost as if by leaving data lying around for a few days it will all make sense. Moving from analysis to interpretation is one of the greatest challenges a qualitative researcher faces (Savin-Baden, 2004). This process involves exploring the subtext of the data (what is going on underneath); think about the example *'I am no sexist but...'*

Once you have made sense of your themes and gained an interpretation of them, you need to put them together. Ways of putting the description and data together include:

1.   mixing quotations with your own descriptions;
2.   making a statement and illustrating it with several examples;
3.   incorporating the data directly into the text.

An example is provided in Figure 14.2.

Writing up

The final challenge of your research project is the discussion chapter. This is often rushed as time is short and has not been planned very well. However, this is a very important chapter as it is where you discuss the findings and show how important your work is. It is a *place to stand* and say what you think about your research.

There are guidelines for writing up your research project that will be provided on your course. Yet it is still important to put a plan in place: Writing a plan is a vital stage, not an easy one, but one which in the long run will make life easier:

Stage 1 – A broad overview of the planning including times, dates, structure

Stage 2 – A provisional work plan with major headings, sub-headings and content

Stage 3 – A re-writing of various parts, expansion of some sections

Stage 4 – A final tidying up: What's missing? Is this nice quote really needed?

Sarah's experience of being visited for the first time by a health visitor is presented interpretatively below:

My description of Sarah

Sarah was a graduate who had her first child at 39. She was a lecturer at a local university and had become pregnant soon after moving to a new job there. During her pregnancy she was active, relaxed and continued to work just beyond her due date. Despite wanting a home birth her labour was long and troublesome, resulting in an emergency caesarean section and difficulty feeding the baby afterwards. Having had a good relationship with her community midwife, Sarah expected the same care and respect from her health visitor. However, Sarah experienced a credibility gap between her perception of the health visitor as a professional and the role played by her health visitor when she visited her home. Sarah believed that even though the health visitor spoke of wanting to devolve power to her as a mother, in practice the health visitor just wanted her to behave in a particular way:

Quotation that I believe represents her perspective

'To my mind it feels there is an element of hanging on to power because to devolve it to the parents is like "Who are you to know?". The health visitors have certain things they need to say and messages they need to pass over as well as things they ensure happen, but it felt to me as if she assumed I did not know anything and I had not done any reading. She stayed for over 2 hours and I was just so tired already I couldn't believe it. She also said it would be "nice for me to come to the clinic to get baby weighed". I nearly hit the roof. This was not just because of the lack of a personal pronoun for my child but also because when I asked why it would be nice she didn't reply but implied it would give me something to do. I felt voiceless and patronised.'

My reflection and interpretation

Not being heard by a professional and feeling patronised by someone she expected to be a support and guide resulted in Sarah feeling angry and frustrated. Sarah believed a health visitor should be someone who would guide her learning as a mother and not tell her what she was supposed to do in a prescribed way. Sarah wanted to use her ability as a lecturer and learn to think through her role as a mother rather than being told what to do and how to be. Being patronised was disabling and unhelpful.

Here we see how my values about Sarah and her position resulted in this particular interpretation. In this example as a researcher you see me siding with Sarah because I felt mothers needed to have their voices heard.

Figure 14.2 An example of interpreting data

Once you have a plan in place you not only need to put it into action, but also remember the following.

- Remember you are never 'ready' to write; it is something which involves a conscious decision.

- Starting to write often produces a high degree of anxiety.

- Your structure should have an introduction, a core and a conclusion.

- Don't necessarily start at the beginning.

- Aim to write 300 words a day – 'your quota'.

Frequently asked questions

How long should my research project be?

Usually about 8,000 words, but your course document will guide you. This might seem like a lot of words but it is not when you break it down into chapters.

What happens if I do not get through the ethics board?

You will need to talk this through with your research supervisor and resubmit the project proposal.

How long does it take to collect data?

It depends what you are collecting but in general it is useful to give yourself two to three months to do this.

What happens if some of my participants drop out?

This is not usually a problem as long as you recruit enough in the first place; it is therefore better to over-recruit initially.

How long does it take to transcribe and interview?

For every hour of recording it takes five to eight hours to transcribe verbatim.

What are the most common reasons for failing a research project?

Not following the guidelines

Poor data collection

Unclear analyses and interpretation

Omitting a discussion section

Failing to reference anything.

Chapter reflections

»   *Your research project should focus on something you are really interested in, as well as filling a gap in the literature.*

»   *It is vital to plan the project from beginning to end.*

»   *Make sure you check everything with your research supervisor and ask lots of questions.*

»   *Enjoy your research!*

Further reading

Creswell, J W (1994) *Research Design: Qualitative and Quantitative Approaches*. Thousand Oaks, CA: Sage.

Savin-Baden, M and Major, C (2013) *Qualitative Research: The Essential Guide to Theory and Practice*. London: Routledge.

References

Bogdan, R C and Biklen, S K (1992) *Qualitative Research for Education: An Introduction to Theory and Methods*. Boston: Allyn and Bacon.

Braun, V and Clarke, V (2006) Using Thematic Analysis in Psychology. *Qualitative Research in Psychology*, 3(2): 77–101.

Carr, W and Kemmis, S (1986) *Becoming Critical: Education, Knowledge and Action Research*. London: Falmer.

Hine, C (2000) *Virtual Ethnography*. London: Sage.

Patton, M Q (1990) *Qualitative Evaluation and Research Methods*. 2nd ed. Newbury Park, CA: Sage.

Savin-Baden, M (2004) Achieving Reflexivity: Moving Researchers from Analysis to Interpretation in Collaborative Inquiry. *Journal of Social Work Practice* 18(3): 365–78.

Shakespeare, W (1597, 2008) *Love's Labour's Lost*. Oxford: Oxford University Press, p 237.

15 What next?

MICHELLE MALOMO AND SAMANTHA SUTTON-TSANG

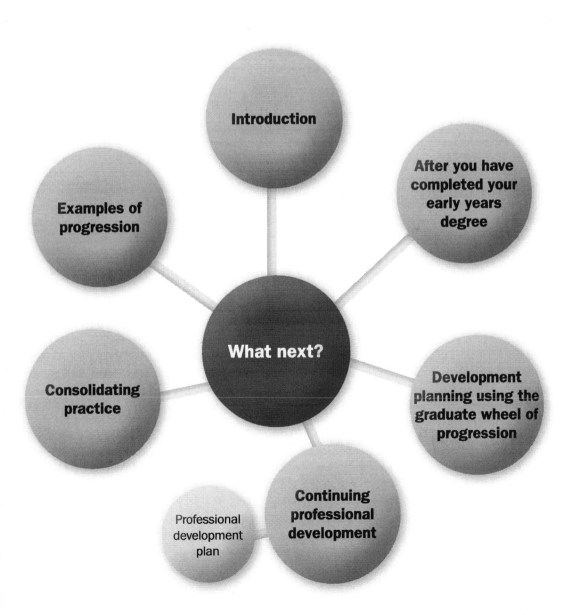

Introduction

After you have completed your early years degree

Examples of progression

What next?

Consolidating practice

Development planning using the graduate wheel of progression

Professional development plan

Continuing professional development

Choose a job you love, and you will never have to work a day in your life.

Attributed to Confucius

Introduction

This chapter aims to support you in considering the path that you will take following your graduation. It will examine the importance of continuing to develop both your practice and your academic progression routes. It is also intended to enable you to continue the process 'of becoming' an early years practitioner. The chapter will consider case studies, reflection points and suggest practical tasks to support you in your next steps. The content will also support you in the creation of a professional development plan which will enable you to remain focused as you continue your progression as a graduate early years practitioner.

After you have completed your early years degree

Upon achieving your degree often there is a sense of relief that you have arrived at the end of your programme of study. You have achieved the goal that has been a focus for the past three years. Graduating is a time of celebration and rightly so as the demands of study and placement have been achieved and you are now a graduate practitioner. However, although this is the end of one pathway, your career as a graduate practitioner has only just commenced. Initially, once you have graduated you will need to seek employment. This can be an exciting and challenging process. Moreover, there can be a sense of isolation as you step into more challenging roles and leave university life.

In a report by Kandiko and Mawer (2013), it was recommended that more guidance and support on the process of employability and development opportunities should be made available to assist students in higher education. Having a plan for your next steps can support you in being confident in securing employment or returning to education to complete a postgraduate award. It may even be that you will be considering achieving both. Planning your progression path as a graduate practitioner enables you to ensure that any future improvement reflects your needs for development and supports you to be organised in a new phase of your working life. Having a planned approach enables you to think in a manner that also reflects your professional development needs at a given time but also should be framed to reflect the needs of the early years sector (Kennedy, 2015). This approach when shared with potential employers highlights your reflective, organisational and developmental skills.

Development planning using the Graduate Wheel of Progression

When considering developing a plan for continuing professional development (CPD) progression we created the Graduate Practitioner Wheel of Progression model (see Figure 15.1). Graduate practitioner progression can take on many forms, but for the purpose of this chapter we have identified two forms, academic and practice related. It is important to understand that progression is a continuous process. This can change and adapt to you as an individual graduate and as you are influenced by extrinsic and intrinsic factors, including the motivating factors that spur you on towards achieving your aspirations.

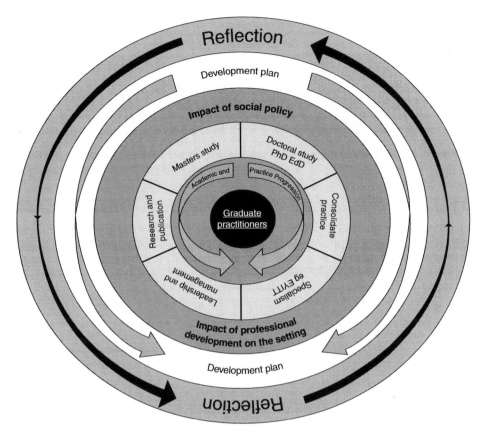

Figure 15.1 *Graduate Practitioner Wheel of Progression*

The principles of Early Childhood Education and Care (ECEC), stated in the statutory frame-work for the Early Years Foundation Stage (DfE, 2014), guided the process of developing the model and plan. Graduates should consider the following when identifying their progression routes and development in the ECEC sector.

Practitioners:

- are unique and will continue to learn, be resilient, capable, confident and self-assured in their practice and development;

- should learn to be strong and independent through positive relationships with their colleagues and learning groups;

- will continue to learn and develop in enabling environments, in which their experiences respond to their individual needs;

- will develop and progress in different ways and at different rates.

(Adapted from DfE, 2014, pp 4–5)

When you were studying your degree, you grew and developed as a practitioner and as an academic. In a similar way, professional practice and academic progression requires there to be an ongoing process which is planned and supported. This process should continue even after graduation, reflecting the principles of practice with children's learning and development as you progress through your education. Your progression after graduation will be determined by your individual circumstances (including employment/practice setting, interests, personal situation) and aspirations; therefore, your pathway will be inevitably different from a fellow graduate's. A key message is that progression is a continuous process that is required to maintain a level of practice and quality of work.

Professional development should be more personalised as it relates to your individual practice and connects to the areas of interest that you may wish to explore or improve upon. A professional development plan (PDP) (see Table 15.1 further along in the chapter) may be a useful tool to aid you in identifying the outcomes that you wish to achieve on a personal and professional level and with your setting of practice. It should also impact and develop your practice with children. Blandford and Knowles (2009, p 326) state that:

> *Improving outcomes for children is dependent on practitioners having good knowledge, skills and understanding not only in relation to children's developmental needs and subject knowledge but also in relation to new or recognised good pedagogic practice.*

In addition to this, Stewart and Pugh (2007, cited in Allen and Whalley, 2010, p 10) suggest that an early years pedagogy is:

> *... the understanding of how children learn and develop, and the practices through which we can enhance that process. It is rooted in values and beliefs about what we want for children, and supported by knowledge, theory and experience.*

Once you begin to practise as a graduate practitioner there needs to be a realisation that your practice and development is not without the influences of, and to some degree will be controlled by, the social policy and political agendas of government. This in turn is usually linked to the outcomes and requirements of regulatory frameworks. Within the Graduate Practitioner Wheel of Progression, academic and professional progression are bound and contained by the impact of social policy and also the requirements of the setting to ensure that they reflect this and adhere to the requirements this may place on the CPD of the early years team. For example, recent social policy and legislative changes have developed and further defined the need to have a lead practitioner in the areas of both safeguarding and special educational needs within the setting. The EYFS (DfE, 2014) and the Special Educational Needs and Disability Code of Practice (SENDA, 2014) both outlined new requirements and expectations for practice within these areas. Legislation and regulatory requirements of this nature drive and impact the practice within a setting. Often these roles are undertaken by senior and experienced practitioners. Graduate practitioners as leaders within the setting often have been best placed to lead the team in these areas. Both roles are a reflection of best practice for children and those that work with them. Kennedy (2015) supports this notion and suggests that often CPD is given more value when it has usefulness for practice rather than having a personal usefulness for the practitioner. This contrasts with and at times may restrict the focus of the graduate practitioner's development plan as it may not reflect their desires and dreams for the future.

Throughout this book the importance of reflection has been highlighted and where there is a requirement for CPD that has been generated as a result of social policy or legislation, reflection must inform the usefulness and purpose of this type of CPD. It is important to consider who this type of CPD might have value for and whether development of other members of the team could benefit from this.

Continuing professional development

At this point it is important to consider what continuing professional development means for the graduate early years practitioner; this will help in developing your plan and determining the relevance of the progression wheel within this process. Moreover, defining the need for CPD has been the focus of recommendations for the workforce and has been considered as crucial in the professionalisation of the early years workforce (Nutbrown, 2012; Teather, 2013; DfE, 2014). For the purpose of this the chapter, we have developed the following definition:

> Continuing professional development for an early years graduate involves the continual and ongoing process that enables the continued development of a highly skilled workforce, who are dedicated to improving outcomes for children in all aspects of their lives. It supports the continual process 'of becoming' an Early Years Practitioner and supports this as a process of lifelong development. Graduates develop their own knowledge and skills to improve not only their own knowledge and skills but also through this process to improve and develop the skills of others while becoming leaders and managers of best practice within the sector.

The expectation of this definition is vast; it highlights the reasoning and expectation for constantly improving practice.

Returning to the Graduate Practitioner Wheel of Progression (Figure 15.1), reflection is a key component that encompasses the wheel. It is fundamental for graduate early years practitioners to continue their reflections on a personal and practical level. In Chapter 3, you will have examined the practice of reflection and will by now understand the need for continuous reflection, which is why reflection is indicated on the Wheel of Progression as a process that drives the different elements of the progression.

According to Bubb and Early (2007, cited in Hallet, 2013, p 138), reflective practitioners must continue to learn, even as they progress throughout their career and demonstrate a commitment to self-improvement. This is a hallmark of an emerging professional who is part of a profession where it is vital to maintain high levels of quality and experiences for children within practice.

Having considered the reasoning behind the need for progression and the type of progression you wish to embark on, using Figure 15.1, you can begin to formulate a plan. Through the creation of a PDP, a focus for your progression and professionalism in ECEC can be developed. The plan should be treated as an emerging and responsive document by the developing practitioner, even after graduation. This can then support you in your career path and future aspirations.

Table 15.1 outlines an example of what a development plan could look like for you as a new graduate practitioner. It is linked to the critical questions asked within this chapter and the reflections at the end of it. The critical questions will support your development as a reflective practitioner and guide you in your own thoughts for CPD using the examples of progression and case studies. The template below includes critical questions as well as functional questions to aid you in organising your development.

Professional development plan

Table 15.1   Template for professional development plan

Current context (Where am I now?): *Reflect on your current situation. Where does this fit in with current social policy/the professional development of your setting?*					
My goal (academic/practice progression):					
Timeline (dates)	What activities will I complete as part of the process?	How will I achieve and complete each activity?	Resources required to achieve and complete each activity.	When am I going to complete each activity by?	Review and reflect upon the activity.
Review and reflect on my achievements:					
My next steps:					
Review in 6 months. *Do I need to rethink my plan? Has my situation changed?*					
Review in 12 months. *Do I need to rethink my plan? Has my situation changed?*					

You may wish to use Table 15.1 to develop your thoughts about your own progression path and how you intend to reach your goals. It is a useful tool to review after 6 and 12 months and to update as a working document to correspond with your current situation. You may find that employment opportunities that you hadn't foreseen arise or changes occur in your existing job role. It may be that you have a change of personal circumstances or find that the targets that you had originally set are not compatible and that you may have over- or underestimated your time frame, the processes required and even financial situation.

Task: Using the development plan template, identify a set of activities that will support you in your academic/practice progression in the short, medium or long term following graduation.

Consolidating practice

Even before graduation and in the midst of final deadlines you may also be considering seeking and gaining employment. When applying to work in the early years sector the expectation of wanting the best possible candidate is central to the application process. It is therefore really important to develop a curriculum vitae (CV) and an approach to completing applications that enables you to articulate the experience that you have gained. At the end of the chapter within the *Further reading* section, you will find web links to support you in developing your written CV. It's a challenge juggling so many thought processes and pressures. However, it can also be an exciting and daunting prospect, often a thought-provoking and time-consuming process, to seek a role within the early years sector. For some students this may be when they decide to consider a wider and broader scope of employment. This may for instance involve a slight change of direction – for example, some students in our experience have moved on to social work, child-health-related roles and some move into family support roles. However, initially it is important that you recognise where your passions are and how you have developed throughout your degree programme. Often students struggle with this; for others there is such clarity and direction. The important point here is to embrace this change using the disposition, attributes and skills that you have developed as an undergraduate and embrace this next step in a reflective process. Nutbrown (2012) highlighted this aspiration for the sector by stating that:

> As a country we need to raise our expectations of what it means to work with young children, and attract the best people into the workforce.
>
> (Nutbrown, 2012, p 6)

In the development of degree courses we have consulted with a range of managers within the sector and there are some clear messages about what they are looking for in the graduate practitioner. Primarily, managers wanted graduates who were confident to lead practice, could lead and work within a team and families and finally be able to show initiative. The dispositions, attributes and skills that are required were highlighted further within the Nutbrown Review (2012). These included practitioners that could improve the quality of provision through 'excellent pedagogical leadership' (2012, p 7), which in turn enables the narrowing of the attainment gap for children from differing economic backgrounds. Further attributes and skills that are highlighted within the review include: a clear understanding of child development (all aspects including emotional well-being), the importance of play, safeguarding and child protection, health and safety, nutrition, basic first aid, an understanding of legal frameworks and obligations, inclusion and diversity.

Critical questions

Take a few moments to consider what would be your dream role following graduation. It is often helpful to consider the following within this reflective process, critically asking yourself:

» *What am I passionate about when thinking about working with children and their families?*

» *Which modules did I enjoy or maybe challenged me and developed me as a practitioner?*

» *Thinking about my practice experience during my studies, which placement(s) enabled me to have an insight into the work that I would like to pursue following graduation?*

Examples of progression

There are many areas of progression which support or require a practical and/or academic application. Typical areas of academic progression include further study towards Level 7 Masters and Level 8 Doctorate studies, either an EdD (Doctorate in Education) or a PhD (Doctorate of Philosophy). An EdD is more practically oriented towards individuals who wish to pursue leadership roles, whereas a PhD is theoretically oriented towards researchers and individuals who wish to pursue a career in academia.

When deciding on your progression pathway, you should bear in mind that further study may not necessarily mean an upwards step towards higher-level qualifications. For example, the upskilling of specific skills and refresher courses on safeguarding and first aid encompasses continuing professional development. Therefore, it is important to value all types of further study and not just the ones that have a degree or publication outcome.

Examples of practice progression may include the consolidation of practice, putting into practice what you have gained from your university studies, progressing into leadership and management roles or determining a specialism within your field. Research has suggested that for professional development to have an impact, it must be related to a person's practice. They must be actively participating in a continuous and interactive method of engagement rather than having episodic moments of participation, where information is transferred in a non-engaging format that does not relate to the individual's experiences or practice (Webster-Wright, 2009). The following case studies are examples of progression, all of which have an overlap between academic and practice progression.

CASE STUDY

Afia

Afia completed her BA (Hons) in early childhood professional practice at university, during which she secured employment at a nursery on a part-time basis which led to a full-time position during her last semester at university. Following graduation, 18 months later, Afia applied for a position as deputy manager at a nursery attached to a school and was successful. After a couple of years, the school developed a partnership link with a local children's centre. The manager of the nursery requested that Afia take a lead role in developing the partnership and encouraged her to apply to complete the Early Years Initial Teacher Training (EYITT) qualification through the graduate-entry employment-based route which was being funded by the National College for Teaching and Leadership (NCTL). Before commencing her studies in the EYITT, Afia completed her professional skills test to enrol onto the graduate-entry employment-based route where she studied part time alongside her existing job role to achieve Early Years Teacher Status (EYTS).

Up-to-date information and further details of the different training routes can be found from the National College for Teaching and Leadership or www.gov.uk/guidance/early-years-initial-teacher-training-a-guide-for-providers#training-routes.

Table 15.2 EYITT training routes

	Graduate entry (mainstream)	Graduate entry – employment based	Undergraduate entry	Assessment only
Description of typical trainee	Graduate, not employed within the sector, undertaking ITT (EYTS) through mainstream academic route.	1. Graduate in an early years setting who requires training and further experience to demonstrate the Teachers' Standards (Early Years). 2. Graduate newly recruited to an early years setting to undertake ITT (EYTS) through an employment-based route.	Undergraduate completing a degree in early childhood related subject including EYTS.	Graduate with experience of working with children from birth to five and able to demonstrate the Teachers' Standards (Early Years) without further training. Eg overseas early years teachers.
Normal duration	12 months Full time	12 months Part time	3 years Full time	3 months

Critical question

»   How did further study, following on from her degree, enhance Afia's practice role?

During Afia's EYITT studies, she developed expertise in working with babies and parents in partnership and multi-agency working. She now uses this knowledge to support her practice and her role in managing the partnership between the nursery and children's centre, confidently liaising with other agencies and developing her job role.

CASE STUDY

Julia

Julia is a vocationally trained lecturer in a further education college. Prior to this, she trained as a social worker after studying a BA (Hons) in social work at university, working as part of integrated services in a children's centre. After having her own children, Julia decided to study for a Masters in early childhood studies. During this time, Julia left her job working at the children's centre and began lecturing part time at a further education college. After her Masters qualification, Julia decided to combine her knowledge of early childhood studies with integrated working experience to develop her PhD thesis. Using her PhD thesis, Julia has published and advised exam boards on integrated services, undertaking consultancy work with the local authority alongside her lecturing role.

Critical question

»　*While studying or working in further and higher education there are often links made between theory and practice. Why is it important to stay up to date with current practice?*

Julia has benefitted from undertaking practice experience in social work and early years to support her academic progression. Her academic progression will also have an impact on the professional development within a setting through her published work. The early years sector is a rapidly changing sector that is greatly influenced by new research and government policy. It is important to stay in touch with current practice and this can be done through reading and research, but most importantly through visiting settings to gain first-hand experiences of any changes to the sector.

CASE STUDY

Arun

Arun is a male manager of a nursery which is part of a chain across the West Midlands. Before securing employment as a nursery manager, Arun studied AS levels, but after his first year, he decided to change to a vocational route and transferred to a BTEC National Diploma in Children's Care, Learning and Development course at college. Following completion of his Level 3 childcare qualification, Arun decided to continue his studies to fit in alongside with employment that he had secured following a successful placement on his Level 3 course. Arun chose to study a foundation degree in early years at a local college near to the nursery setting so that he could attend lectures. During his studies on the foundation degree, Arun was promoted to room leader at the nursery.

After graduation, Arun decided to continue studying and applied for the top-up degree (BA (Hons) Integrated Working with Children and Families) through a flexible and distributed route so that he could study online. He also applied for a deputy manager position at the nursery, which he was successful in. During the top-up degree, Arun completed his dissertation on leadership and management and the role of males in early years. This led to him applying for a position as manager at the nursery, which had expanded into a chain over the years. With his knowledge and experience, Arun now manages one of the nurseries within the chain and a recent Ofsted inspection praised his mentoring of other members of staff, with a focus on CPD, safeguarding and SENCo practice.

Critical questions

» *How does working in the setting support Arun's studies?*

» *How do Arun's studies support his work in the setting?*

Through academic study, Arun has been able to progress in his career choice and also develop the professional practice within the nursery setting. The daily involvement within the nursery ensures that Arun is consolidating practice, reflecting upon it and developing it further. Using his experiences during his studies, Arun is able to confidently lead and manage his staff team, using current practice guidelines.

In this chapter, the examples of progression described above explain the different routes and illustrate how practice and academic progression can interweave over the course of one's career. As part of your professional development plan, you must take into account your current context, reflecting on your situation as well as identifying your future aspirations or goals. Review points are encouraged at 6 months and 12 months to ensure that the development plan is current to your situation, social policy and/or practice setting.

Chapter reflections

This chapter has provided a starting point to your progression after your undergraduate studies. Whatever route you decide to embark on following your studies, be mindful that there could always be a change in your career direction as you grow and develop as an early years practitioner, including deciding on your specialism and building upon your knowledge in the workplace. Through the process of reflection, and critical thinking, you can begin to establish your progression route, reviewing it over time.

It is important that your approach to CPD is an essential part of your development as a graduate early years practitioner. Over the past 20 years there have been many developments within our sector and it is hoped that these will continue in a desire to improve outcomes for children and their families. Social policy agendas will come and go as governments bring their own political stance to the sector. However, at the heart of your own development the shared ethos of improving outcomes for children and being an advocate for children's rights with this remain across the sector. Your own development should focus on your passions but you should be mindful of the impact of social policy and how this can affect your own development needs as you develop as a practitioner.

Critical questions

» *Using a model of reflection (Chapters 3 and 11), reflect on your own professional development. What are the implications of this for your practice?*

» *How has formal learning from your course contributed to your professional development?*

» *How might you enhance and develop the learning opportunities open to you?*

Further reading

Abrahamson, L (2015) *The Early Years Teacher's Book*. London: Learning Matters.

Biggam, J (2015) *Succeeding with your Master's Dissertation: A Step-by-Step Handbook*. Maidenhead, Berkshire: Open University Press.

Campbell-Barr, V and Leeson, C (2015) *Quality and Leadership in the Early Years: Research, Theory and Practice*. London: Sage.

Foley, P and Rixon, A (eds) (2014) *Changing Children's Services: Working and Learning Together*. 2nd ed. Bristol: Policy Press.

Hayes, C, Daly, J, Duncan, M, Gill, R and Whitehouse, A (2014) *Developing as a Reflective Early Years Professional: A Thematic Approach*. Northwich: Critical Publishing.

Job Centre Plus (2016) *Writing a CV*. [online] Available at: www.job-centre-vacancies.co.uk/career-advice/writing-a-cv.html (accessed November 2016).

Johnson, J (ed) (2014) *Becoming an Early Years Teacher*. Maidenhead, Berkshire: Open University Press.

Lindon, J, Beckley, P and Lindon, L (2016) *Leadership in Early Years: Linking Theory and Practice*. 2nd ed. London: Hodder Education.

Prospects (2016) *CVs and covering letters*. [online] Available at: www.prospects.ac.uk/careers-advice/cvs-and-cover-letters (accessed November 2016).

References

Allen, S and Whalley, M (2010) *Supporting Pedagogy and Practice in Early Years Settings*. Exeter: Learning Matters.

Blandford, S and Knowles, C (2009) *Developing Professional Practice 0–7*. Abingdon: Routledge.

Department for Education (DfE) (2014) *Statutory Framework for the Early Years Foundation Stage: Setting the Standards for Learning, Development and Care for Children from Birth to Five*. [online] Available at: www.gov.uk/government/uploads/system/uploads/attachment_data/file/335504/EYFS_framework_from_1_September_2014_with_clarification_note.pdf (accessed November 2016).

Hallett, E (2013) *The Reflective Early Years Practitioner*. London: Sage.

Kandiko, C B and Mawer, M (2013) *Student Expectations and Perceptions of Higher Education: Executive Summary*. London: King's Learning Institute.

Kennedy, A (2015) 'Useful' Professional Learning… Useful for Whom? *Professional Development in Education*, 41(1): 1–4. [online] Available at: http://dx.doi.org/10.1080/19415257.2014.983787 (accessed November 2016).

Nutbrown, C (2012) *Foundations for Quality: The Independent Review of Early Education and Childcare Qualifications. Final Report*. [online] Available at: www.gov.uk/government/publications/nutbrown-review-foundations-for-quality (accessed November 2016).

Special Educational Needs and Disability Code of Practice: 0 to 25 Years (2015) FdE, DfH. [online] Available at: www.gov.uk/government/uploads/system/uploads/attachment_data/file/398815/SEND_Code_of_Practice_January_2015.pdf (accessed January 2017).

Teather, S (2013) Sarah Teather in 'Nursery World' on graduate funding for Early Years workforce. [online] Available at: www.gov.uk/government/speeches/sarah-teather-in-nursery-world-on-graduate-funding-for-early-years-workforce (accessed November 2016).

Webster-Wright, A (2009) Reframing Professional Development through Understanding Authentic Professional Learning. *Review of Educational Research*, 79(2): 702–39.

Woolfolk, A (1982) Toshiko Takaezu, *Princeton Alumni Weekly* 83(5), p 32.

Appendix

Handy reckoner for key contact details

Finance queries

Name:
Email:
Room no:
Telephone:

Personal tutor

Name:
Email:
Room no:
Telephone no:

Doctor

Name:
Email:
Room no:
Telephone:

IT issues

Name:
Email:
Room no:
Telephone no:

Course leader

Name:
Email:
Room no:
Telephone:

Student services

Name:
Email:
Room no:
Telephone no:

Index